Images in Language,
Media, and Mind

Images in Language, Media, and Mind

Edited by

Roy F. Fox
University of Missouri–Columbia

National Council of Teachers of English
1111 W. Kenyon Road, Urbana, Illinois 61801-1096

Manuscript Editor: Michael Himick

Staff Editors: Michelle Sanden Johlas and Marlo Welshons

Cover Designer: Carlton Bruett

Cover Art: *The Webs of Fancy Are Spun into the Sky* by Margaret Sutton. Mary Washington College Galleries, Gift of Alfred Levitt. Reproduced by permission. (For more information, see p. 246.)

Interior Book Designer: Doug Burnett

NCTE Stock Number 22817-3050

Library of Congress Cataloging-in-Publication Data

Images in language, media, and mind / edited by Roy F. Fox.
    p. cm.
  Includes bibliographical references (p.) and index.
  ISBN 0-8141-2281-7 : $25.95
  1. Visual communication. 2. Psycholinguistics. 3. Imagery (Psychology). 4. Mass media—Psychological aspects. I. Fox, Roy F.
P93.5.I47 1994
302.2'22—dc20
                                       94-21522
                                         CIP

Contents

Acknowledgments   vii

Introduction   ix

I. Images in Language

1. Image Studies: An Interdisciplinary View
   Roy F. Fox   3

2. People Prose
   Alan C. Purves   21

3. Imaging, Literacy, and Sylvia Ashton-Warner
   Nancy S. Thompson   29

4. Photographs, Writing, and Critical Thinking
   Carol P. Hovanec and David Freund   42

5. Child Talk: Re-presenting Pictures in the Mind
   Stevie Hoffman   58

II. Images in Media

6. Where We Live
   Roy F. Fox   69

7. From War Propaganda to Sound Bites: The Poster
   Mentality of Politics in the Age of Television
   Linda R. Robertson   92

8. Reading Ollie North
   William V. Costanzo   108

9. Instant History, Image History: Lessons from the
   Persian Gulf War
   George Gerbner   123

10. Authorship of Metaphoric Imagery in "Live"
    Television Sportscasts
    Barbra S. Morris   141

11. Ad Images and the Stunting of Sexuality
    Carol Moog   152

12. "Don't Hate Me Because I'm Beautiful": A Commercial
 in Context
     Gerald O. Grow   170

III. Images in Mind

13. Beyond "The Empty Eye": A Conversation with
 S. I. Hayakawa and Alan R. Hayakawa
     Roy F. Fox   183

14. The Image Is Not the Thing
     Herb Karl   193

15. Analyzing Visual Persuasion: The Art of Duck Hunting
     Kay Ellen Rutledge   204

16. The Riddle of Visual Experience
     Vito Signorile   219

Index   233

Editor   241

Contributors   243

About the Cover   246

Acknowledgments

I am grateful to the University of Missouri–Columbia Research Council for providing the Summer Research Fellowship that enabled me to complete part of this book. I am also indebted to William Lutz, Walker Gibson, and other members of the NCTE Committee on Public Doublespeak for their early encouragement. For their support and confidence, I wish to thank Joe and Jeri Peterson, as well as former colleagues in the English Department of Boise State University. And I am grateful to Susan Baruffi and David Lineberry for their skilled editorial assistance. Beverly Fox, as usual, supplied solid judgment and sanity; this book could not have been done without her. I thank Emmy Fox and Joel Fox as well, not only for tolerating my being locked away in an office, but also for never letting me forget what images are for. Finally, I thank Norine V. Fox. Even in the chaos of running a large family, she kept an endless stream of blank paper and gentle words flowing my way. This book is dedicated to her.

Introduction

Roy F. Fox
University of Missouri–Columbia

Like many first-grade classrooms, mine was equipped with Gilbert Stuart's famous portrait of George Washington. Each day of the 1955 school year, we looked up at this framed print affixed to the front wall, high above the blackboard. Washington—regal, paternal, silvery—watched over us.

Like many images, this one was surrounded by words. Mrs. Pearl Snavely, our teacher, told us that Washington was the "father of our country." I had heard of Washington and Eisenhower on television and radio. I was aware that they were great people. At Sunday School, I had also heard about "our Father in heaven." Since this portrait of Washington showed unmistakable white clouds billowing under him, I figured that the General was gazing down from heaven, or wherever it was that God lived. So, in my mind, during that year, the father of our country and our Father in heaven became the same person. Washington was God, God was Washington, and He was in charge.

I don't remember how this matter ironed itself out. The biggest disappointment, though, came when I learned that Stuart didn't intentionally place Washington amidst fluffy clouds. In fact, he didn't place the General in heaven at all; Stuart simply never finished the painting. What I had taken to be the white, downy vapors of celestial perfection turned out to be blank canvas. Although I continue to make excursions into the bowels of verbal and visual illiteracy, I now know that presidents are human and that artists run out of time, energy, and even money to buy paint.

Such misconceptions, of course, are a natural part of childhood. Yet my learning was also part of the discourse community of Mrs. Snavely's first-grade class, nestled within the larger community of Linden East Elementary School, north of Kansas City, Missouri—all of which lay smack in the middle of Cold War America. Specific people took part in this learning: my teacher, my family, my classmates. The words they spoke and messages from television and radio were equally influential. But most important, then and now, was what I saw.

Today our inner and outer worlds are dominated by images—whether we receive them, send them, or think them; whether they happen inside our heads or outside our skin; whether we find them in proposals or poems, in casual conversations or environmental impact statements, in dreams or in ads for Dodge trucks or on computer screens, in films or scientific reports or Pepsi commercials. In this book, *image* (and imaging) refers to any form of mental, pictorial representation, however generic or fleeting. Images can be sensory experiences that exist only for us, with or without the actual stimuli present, or images can refer to actual pictures, from the simplest scrawl on a piece of paper to the ceiling of the Sistine Chapel. Images and imaging may involve the possible as much as the actual.

Of course, had I attended first grade in Caracas and looked up at a portrait of Simon Bolívar, my response could have taken different routes. But one thing would have stayed the same: images are integral components of thinking, speaking, listening, writing, and reading. Regardless of gender, age, race, medium, discipline, issue, genre, theme, or author, images are common, useful tools. Imaging is something we do every day. The image, in whatever form, is the primary underlying structure in language, media, and mind—our most basic element in communicating and creating.

What Are the Purposes of This Book?

The contributors to this book, representing such disciplines as composition, photography, education, rhetoric, journalism, clinical psychology, communication, and sociology, are old enough to remember what life was like before the image/information explosion and young enough to be sensitive to its potential. Because they have one foot in each world, this book first of all bridges gaps between old and new, verbal and visual. For example, Herb Karl links the Sapir-Whorf hypothesis about language to images, and S. I. Hayakawa and Alan R. Hayakawa discuss how language principles from general semantics operate in television. Second, this book describes important ways that images function, in turn underscoring what language, media, and mind have most in common. Third, this book demonstrates that language and images are inextricably linked—in how we generate them, how we make meaning from them, how we use them, and how we remember them. After all, every writer and reader of this book must use one image system—language—to unravel other image systems. Finally, this volume describes some of the roles that images play in shaping such important social issues as materialism, learning and literacy, war, entertainment, politics, and sexuality. Within these specific contexts, I hope you will find that images-as-products cannot be separated from imaging-as-process.

What Does This Book Assume?

This book makes several assumptions about the development of literacy and the making of meaning. First, this book assumes that *the most important kind of meaning is constructed from personal interactions with images; we use images, often mediated by language, to make sense of our world, and this activity resides at the core of thinking and literacy development.* This assumption encompasses another: that cognition and perception are not separate processes, each going its own way. Instead, this book views thinking and feeling as the same thing. One without the other never works. For example, Stevie Hoffman shows how young children "re-present" their very personalized encounters with images and then use language to build meaning. My own chapter ("Where We Live") defines "symbolspeak" and explains how visual messages transform us through emotion. Elsewhere, Vito Signorile untangles the riddles we face in trying to comprehend images.

Second, this book assumes that *images and imaging can be viewed through the prism of language and out of their original contexts if you keep these facts in mind throughout your reading.* It is important to remember that you will not experience the images in question, but instead, print-encaptured images of them. For example, Barbra Morris presents five minutes of "sportstext" from a televised basketball game to show how a skilled director selects camera shots and then weaves them into a narrative for an at-home audience watching what it believes is "live" action. While Morris directly addresses the issue of context, she must do so in considerable isolation, since you cannot view for yourself the game video or even clips of it. Instead, you must rely upon Morris's verbal images of what happened.

Experiencing reproduced images out of their original contexts not only alters their nature, but also our resulting perceptions. The reproduced advertisements in Carol Moog's chapter, for instance, appear to be complete. But when such ads are bound within the pages of, say, *Harper's Bazaar,* and held in the hands of a specific person, someone processing them in unique ways in a specific time and place, then they can represent something quite different from what you may interpret when reading Moog's discussion. Both of these limitations, the prism of language and the removal from context, are unavoidable. Yet they are manageable if you keep them in mind throughout your reading.

Third, this book assumes that *images are natural parts of any discourse community and thereby highly intertextual.* Although several chapters detail the snares of images, the whole book celebrates them. Images are natural, life-giving, and life-sustaining. They are woven into any discourse community, from the shared experiences of only two people, to a small group of students in your classroom, to an entire community, culture, or era of history. Any phenomenon so natural and widespread must also be highly intertextual, capable of "flagging" meanings in other symbol systems across time and space. Hence, several chapters develop "case studies" that detail the intertextuality of the images surrounding specific people and situations: William Costanzo on Ollie North, Nancy Thompson on Sylvia Ashton-Warner, Alan Purves on today's students, Gerald Grow on an anonymous fashion model.

Fourth, this book assumes that *images are rhetorical in nature.* Pictures—whether they glimmer in our own minds, flicker upon a screen, rise to meet us as we read a text, or slowly evolve from a culture—shape how we think about our world. Whatever their form, images often persuade us. George Gerbner's analysis of imagery and the Persian Gulf War and Linda Robertson's inquiry into World War II propaganda posters reveal how images were manipulated for entire populations, in turn affecting future attitudes and behaviors. And in her chapter, Kay Ellen Rutledge describes classroom methods for analyzing such visual persuasion.

Finally, this book assumes that *image products and processes are just as important as language products and processes in the making of meaning.* Most discussions about "creativity," "critical thinking," "insight," "cognition," "invention," and a gaggle of other terms and concepts involve images and imaging in some form, mediated through language. In photographer David Freund's and English teacher Carol Hovanec's chapter, this symbiotic relationship between images and language is practiced in the classroom, as students read, write, and discuss images to become better critical thinkers. Indeed, in all disciplines, thinking requires us to summon forth and manipulate that which is not present (see my chapter on the sources of "image studies"). If we cannot visualize, we are said to be "lacking in imagination," a condition mainly caused by little practice in exploring *possibilities*—in generating, inspecting, combining, transforming, and manipulating images, in viewing them from a distance or entering into them, in using language to evaluate and revise them.

Overall, we tend to regard images as artifacts that have been preserved within literary texts—exquisite porcelain to dust off, admire, and place back on the shelf. Or, we treat images and imaging as dessert—as some kind of filler for students who do not like (or cannot digest) the main course. These approaches, as I hope this book demonstrates, are scarcely appropriate for phenomena as basic as DNA, as common as dirt. We should tend not only to images, to those things that look alive to us, but also to the aliveness of looking.

I Images in Language

1 Image Studies: An Interdisciplinary View

Roy F. Fox
University of Missouri–Columbia

This chapter briefly reviews selected sources, influences, and undercurrents of images and especially imaging, the act of thinking visually. A topic so broadly conceived—I'll call it "image studies"—runs deep and wide, swirling out in all directions. Hence, I can provide only a glimpse of how this magical river flows through the sciences, social sciences, and arts and humanities. Along the way, though, I promise a few sidetrips.

From Earrings to O-Rings: Influences from the Sciences and Engineering

Because we usually think of scientists and engineers as practical people who work with "real things," their accounts of visual thinking have intrigued us for some time. Miller (1978), for instance, details how imaging aided physicist Niels Bohr's development of quantum theory, while Gruber (1978) traces Darwin's irregularly branching tree, an image central to his evolution theory. After studying da Vinci's notebooks, Hughes (1985) states that "Leonardo thought visually or verbally according to the circumstances and subject" (30).

Einstein said that imagery was even more central to his thinking—that his thoughts were dominated by "certain signs and more or less clear images which can be 'voluntarily' reproduced and combined" (Hadamard 1945). In fact, Patten (1973) connects Einstein's violence as a child to his frustration at not being proficient in verbal thinking and communication. According to Einstein's sister, as a preschooler, Albert heaved a bowling ball at her and attacked her with a trowel. Only after Einstein began studying at a school founded by Johann Pestalozzi, which operated on the principle that all understanding is rooted in visual thinking, did Einstein's talents begin to unfold. Einstein, of course, continued to engage in playful, fluid visual thinking. He called such thinking "thought experiments." For example, he would imagine a man in a falling elevator and then try to see what would happen to the keys in the man's pocket (Rico 1983, 71).

Such imagistic nimbleness helped Einstein to generate and revise his abstract theories, as well as to clarify his writing.

According to O'Neil (1944), Tesla, the inventor of fluorescent lights and the AC generator, claimed that he could generate detailed images of his machines and conduct "dry runs" mentally, setting his imaginary devices into operation for weeks at a time and then later inspecting parts for wear. After reviewing such accounts, Gowan (1978) states that "in the case of every historic scientific discovery which was researched carefully enough, we find that it was imagery . . . which produced the breakthrough" (26). Similarly, Galton's 1874 study concluded that many English scientists and engineers relied on visual thinking, fueling a debate that continues today.

Bruner (1973) claims that more sophisticated thinkers abandon visual imagery in favor of verbal reasoning, while Arnheim (1986) refers to this distinction between thinking and seeing as "absurd" (139). To illustrate, Arnheim recounts the Piagetian "conservation" experiment in which a child examines two identical containers, each filled with the same amount of water. The contents of one container are then emptied into a third container that is taller and thinner than the first two. When asked to identify the vessel that contains more liquid, a young child will often choose the tall, thin one, even though the child watched the water being poured. Older children will usually know that the quantity did not change.

People who believe that verbal, abstract reasoning is superior claim that older children are no longer duped by the shape of the container and therefore cannot be misled into thinking that tall means more. They believe that more mature thinkers are not "fooled" by perception because they use pure verbal reasoning. Bruner agrees, concluding that to succeed, the child "must have some internalized verbal formula that shields him from the overpowering appearance of the visual displays" (5).

Arnheim, though, offers an alternative explanation. Arnheim believes that older children do not abandon visual thinking; they simply use it more effectively. Instead of evaluating just one quality, older children consider the "interplay between two, namely height and breadth"—an operation accomplished not by abandoning perception, but by "going more deeply into it" (137). Arnheim believes that thinking occurs in a visual medium and that language, while helping us think, plays only a secondary role. According to Arnheim, we think "by means of the things to which language refers—referents that in themselves are not verbal, but perceptual" (138).

Sidetrip to Scoptophilia and Ancient Nippur

By the turn of the century, Galton's 1874 study of scientists and engineers may have fueled more than a scholarly debate. Abraham's 1913 study documents individuals obsessed by their desire to visualize, a condition he called "scoptophilia." Abraham described a young man who

> *was not content with brooding and with abstract forms of thinking alone, but used to endeavor to get a visual image of how thoughts arose in the brain and how they "come out" of it. He desired actually to see this process. (211)*

About the same time, another person, anthropologist H. V. Hilprecht, assembled pieces of ancient artifacts in a museum and, in a monograph, described them as rings that their owners wore on their fingers. In a dream, however, Hilprecht was informed by a priest from ancient Nippur that the fragments were really earrings cut from a cylinder. The priest then explained the artifacts' history and how and when they were cut. After the dream, Hilprecht investigated further, concluded that the information he had received in his dream was correct, and noted this change in the introduction to his paper (Newbold 1897). Of course, we'll never know whether Hilprecht ever met the obsessed patient mentioned earlier, who tried to watch his thoughts arise in his own brain, but if so, their collaboration could have been mutually rewarding.

The eccentricity of scoptophilia and the dreaming anthropologist raise three points: (1) self-reports about people's visual thinking must be treated cautiously; (2) such incidents nonetheless serve a purpose; and (3) such incidents tend to polarize our attitudes about image studies. First, self-reports by scientists—or anyone else—should not be taken wholesale. When dealing with the past, too many things can go wrong. Samuel Taylor Coleridge often presented himself as a mystic, reporting shimmering images in flashes of intuitive reverie. The most well-known example is how the poem "Kubla Khan" appeared as a dream, which Coleridge then wrote down. There is no doubt that Coleridge probably experienced images. But in *The Road to Xanadu: A Study in the Ways of the Imagination* (1927), Lowes argues that Coleridge freely borrowed images and wording from what he had been reading. And Perkins (1981) summarizes how accounts by Coleridge and others are prone to misrepresentations, memory lapses, and concerns for public image.

As misguided or as hokey as the scoptophiliac and the dreaming anthropologist may seem today, they still deserve credit for fearlessly, if indirectly, contributing to useful applications. Who knows, for example, how scoptophilia may have contributed to the development of what we now call "scientific visualization," a computerized method for seeing the unseeable? The turn-of-the-century man who wanted to watch how thoughts "come out" of the brain does not reside far from the scientists and engineers who determined why the Challenger space shuttle exploded in 1986. They converted numerical data about the shuttle's O-rings into computer images to help them "see" how the O-rings failed in cold weather (Ward 1989).

Finally, accounts such as those about the obsessed visualizer and the dreaming anthropologist, like the notion of Coleridge's dream-fix, tend to polarize our overall perceptions of image studies: if we're not mystical about images, we're cynical. And if we're neither of these, we're probably just bamboozled by images. None of these stances help our students become more literate, thoughtful, or humane.

From Stream of Consciousness to Stream of Lights: Influences from the Social Sciences

Because the social sciences have contributed so much to image studies, their influences are better communicated if we divide them into two groups. First is the "image-before-word" group, which comprises disciplines that have focused more on images than on language. This group includes humanistic, cognitive, and Gestalt psychology, as well as semiotics. Second is the "word-before-image" group, which includes general semantics and literacy education and has focused more on language than on images.

The Image-before-Word Group

Influences from Psychology

Although wedded to healing through words, Sigmund Freud and Carl Jung helped us see the previously unseen unconscious, establishing the legitimacy of internal images. Much of Freud's work—his use of "constructions," free associations, and analyses of dreams and childhood memories—heavily depends on visual processes. Freud himself is said to have possessed "strongly developed" visual abilities (Eissler 1965, 396).

Jung's work is a more direct source for image studies. "On the Relation of Analytical Psychology to Poetry" focuses on all artists' absorption in the creative process and their relationships to it (Adams 1971). Jung's concept of "archetypal" images—the most sweeping application of images, as well as the most personal—places them at the center of culture and the human spirit. Most of all, Jung insisted that our communicating with dream images is nothing more than what any healthy and whole person should naturally do—that it is neither mysticism nor voodoo in the dark.

In 1890, William James's discussion of the "stream of consciousness" and his notion that "the personal self rather than the thought" should be the focus of psychology changed our notions of visual thinking (James 1974). According to James, "thought is constant change. . . . There is no proof that the same bodily sensation is ever got by us twice" (155). Here, James explains that we come to know one thing by what precedes it, underscoring sequence and contrast, elements basic to visual thinking and even film. He also says that thought is "without breach, crack, or division" and that this stream is consistently characterized by feelings of "warmth," "intimacy," and "immediacy" (160)—all of which essentially describe imaging. Our language, James adds, cannot keep up with this fast-running stream (159), which forces us to "ignore most of the things before us" (163).

Aldous Huxley (1954) would agree with James's notion that we "ignore" stimuli. Huxley believed that the brain and nervous system—and language, as a part of them—work as "reducing valves" that shield us from the avalanche of stimuli that we face every day as we struggle to survive like all the other animals. But Huxley thought that we devote too much energy to surviving: "Most people, most of the time, know only what comes through the reducing valve and is consecrated as genuinely real by the local language" (22). Huxley further suggested that mescaline, because it reduces sugar in brain cells, helps us forget about those little niggling things—"spatial and temporal relationships"—that preoccupy us as we work at surviving. When taking mescaline, our ego weakens, and "Mind at Large seeps past the no longer watertight valve" (170), opening the doors of perception. Eventually, we reach the final stage of egolessness and an ultimate understanding that "All is in all—that All is actually each" (170).

Koestler (1964), too, viewed language as somewhat limiting to the creative process. Koestler contrasted verbal thinking—the "snares of language"—with visual thinking. He concluded that an overdependence on verbal thinking can make us see concepts as rigid and fixed. On the other hand, the quicksilver, ever-changing nature of images makes them easier to combine, manipulate, and play with—essential activities for discovering ideas. In the spirit of James, Huxley, and Koestler, many other psychologists, including Polanyi (1958), Luria (1968), Kepes (1951), Gardner (1982), and Sacks (1990), have made unique contributions to image studies.

Influences from Cognitive Psychology

From the fifties to the present, as interest drifted away from behaviorism and toward cognition, psychologists have pursued "mental imagery." Some of this renewed interest is due to other events, such as the brainwashing of POWs during the Korean War, the drug culture of the sixties, and the serious hallucinations suffered by solo fighter pilots. Mental imagery is now a major field of study, with researchers studying imagery in memory, thinking, perception, emotion, sports, and advertising. The list of journals and national associations devoted to mental imagery keeps growing.

Allan Paivio (1986), mental imagery's most influential voice, proposes a "dual coding" theory to explain how we think. Paivio contends that we store experience and information in two kinds of codes: imaginal and verbal. Any experience we have is classified as being either a linguistic event or a nonlinguistic event, depending on whether a logogen or an imagen is activated. *Logogens* are small bits, such as morphemes, syllables, or words, arranged sequentially. An *imagen* is a pictorial representation. Whether a logogen or an imagen is activated first, further processing may occur either in the alternate system or within the originating system. In this model, stimulation can cause either system to act on its own. For example, the word *dog* is associated with other words it has occurred with, including categorical and inclusive terms. Here a logogen can activate other logogens—a verbal association that can result in a chain of words. In the same way, an image of a dog may elicit other images, specific or generic. That is, an imagen can activate other imagens. Both kinds of association allow activity to spread in either system separately. Yet action within one system can also cause activity in the other: words may arouse other words, or they may arouse images; likewise, images may arouse other images, or they may arouse words.

After reviewing empirical support for Paivio's theory, Begg (1983) notes that "any verbal activity in response to things must be imaginally mediated" and, conversely, that "any nonverbal activity in response to linguistic events must be verbally mediated" (293). Begg concludes that "imagery and language are intimately . . . related at many levels" (291). Other major sources of image studies, such as Kosslyn (1983), Neisser (1976), and Salomon (1979), share Paivio's notion that more than just language accounts for how we think—that perception and imagery are at least as fundamental as language.

Influences from Gestalt Psychology

The "moving" stream of lights on the movie marquee illustrates the "phi-phenomenon," an early principle of Gestalt psychology—an illusion of movement created when stationary lights flash in sequence. This illusion of a single moving light represents our *whole* perception, and this whole differs considerably from its parts, such as each separate bulb and the frame for the sign. What's important, according to Gestaltists, is that we should view all phenomena first as a whole structure—"from above"—before we analyze its parts or view it "from below" (Arnheim 1992). Of course, as the movie marquee reveals, also important is the interaction between the whole and its parts. This notion that a whole is greater than or different from its parts was investigated around 1910 by German psychologists who later immigrated to America: Max Wertheimer, Wolfgang Kohler, Kurt Koffka, and Kurt Lewin. The most influential Gestaltists of the last forty years have been Rudolf Arnheim, E. H. Gombrich (1982), and Erving Goffmann (1979).

The notion that the whole interacts with its components leads to another Gestalt principle often overlooked: that such interactions and forces naturally drive toward simplicity—toward the "simplest, most regular, most symmetrical organization available" (Arnheim 1992, 207). Wertheimer's laws of grouping show how this works; for example, several dots placed close to each other tend to be perceived as a single structure. This tendency toward simplicity reduces tension and commonly occurs in nature. A complex interaction of gases and temperatures, for example, will lose tension and move toward simplicity by raining. Arnheim believes, however, that this tendency toward simplicity does not explain how perception works. Instead, he argues for a "counter-tendency" to simplicity—one that forms and articulates shapes, segregating and differentiating structures. Unlike the movement toward simplicity, this tendency increases tension. It also occurs in nature—gravity and electricity, for instance. Perception, Arnheim concludes, is the interaction between these two simultaneously opposing forces: one that *simplifies* perceptions and one that *forms* perceptions. Arnheim's ultimate Gestalten force is balance.

Influences from Semiotics

Semiotics is the study of signs—things that stand for something else. It focuses on how we make signs, what they mean, and how we use them. Semiotics has been applied to objects, music, gestures, film, advertising, food, language, clothes, and to many disciplines as a fundamental principle of relations. According to C. S. Peirce (1839–1914), who founded American semiotics, "the entire world is perfused with signs, if it is not composed exclusively of signs" (Sebeok 1977).

This principle is hard to deny. Just about everything stands for something other than what it actually is: a red rose *stands for* love, a cat *stands for* companionship, and a bank check *stands for* money (and money *stands for* work, and work *stands for* education and training, and on and on). Signs quickly multiply into intricate networks and systems. This stands-for relationship involves more than just replacing one thing with another. Rather, signs bear meaning, in the way that a teacher, for example, might interpret a student's unusually somber tone of voice.

Semioticians study three elements of this stands-for relationship: (1) the object or referent, (2) whatever the object stands for, and (3) the person using the object to stand for something. These elements form a triadic relationship. According to Peirce, the sign and the interpretation fuse into one relationship that is partly controlled by another sign (Sebeok 1977). As Siegel and Carey (1989) phrase it, "one thing stands for another in terms of a third (the interpretant)" (18). Also, a change in one element changes the other elements.

Semiotics owns a long history, from the ancient Greeks to Poinsot's *A Treatise on Signs* in 1632 to Eco (1976). An excellent starting place is Sless's *In Search of Semiotics* (1986). Suhor (1992) offers an accessible introduction for English teachers, while Siegel and Carey (1989) explain how semiotics relates to critical thinking. Costanzo (1992) provides a clear account of semiotics and film study. These sources and germinal ones such as Barthes (1977), Metz (1974), Jakobson (1985), and Scholes (1982) illuminate a fascinating discipline.

The Word-before-Image Group

Influences from General Semantics

General semantics, founded by Alfred Korzybski in the 1920s, is a system for examining the relationships between language, behavior, and reality. General semantics grew in part from the practice and study of propaganda or manipulative communication. Korzybski's principles, popularized and extended by Hayakawa (1990), Lee (1941), Johnson (1946), and others, reject the Aristotelian system of language that, according to Korzybski, has been "inflicted" on each generation, "training them in the primitive magic of words" (Pula 1991–92). According to Korzybski, Aristotle and his followers blindly accepted the structure of their language and developed a philosophical grammar from it that they called logic, a grammar that eventually became defined as the "laws of thought." Korzybski believed that over time we absorbed this faulty system unconsciously and that, in turn, we project this irrationality onto the world around us.

The result is that we often react to events in irrational ways ("semantic reactions"). General semantics tells us that verbal reports are not the same as actual experience—that the word is not the thing, that the symbol is not the thing symbolized. In short, the map is not the territory. Overall, Korzybski and others believe that the Aristotelian system of language "enslaves" us. These principles, many of which apply to images, are important if you believe that language shapes thought and reality.

Because general semantics applies such principles as time-binding, the process of abstracting, and the allness orientation to everyday life, it has raised mass consciousness about how symbols can distort our perceptions of reality. General semantics is important to image studies because it reminds us that "first-order reality," or actual experience, must always take precedence over mere symbols *about* that experience.

––––––––––

Sidetrip to Propaganda Pictures Past

Propagandists have always used images, such as the Liberty Tree symbol of the eighteenth century and, of course, the flag. According to Nelson (1981), brief propaganda films helped fuel the Spanish-American War. In 1898, the film "Tearing Down the Spanish Flag" showed American soldiers doing just that, before running up Old Glory. Theater audiences cheered wildly. Another

popular film that same year, "The Campaign in Cuba," also showed American
troops in action. Never mind, though, that these movies were filmed in New
York City and rural New Jersey (325).

As these propaganda films from the Spanish-American War suggest, we need to keep our responses to images rational too, for they are also symbols. Like words, images are "abstractions" of reality, selected and crafted by someone else. Indeed, general semantics is important not only for communicating about and understanding such symbols. It also reminds us of the conditions necessary for simple mental health: much of the time, reality, language, and images of reality should roughly correspond.

Influences from Literacy Education

Just as image studies have begun to alter our conception of what it means to be literate, literacy education—that is, literary criticism, the development of reading and writing abilities, and analyses of our information environment—has influenced image studies. I. A. Richards's emphasis (1929) on the *reader's* response to literature, and not just on the text itself, suggests a more central role for imaging, especially given his emphasis on "feeling," "tone," and conscious or unconscious "intention" as representing meaning in poetry. Literacy scholars heavily influenced by Richards, such as Rosenblatt (1978) and Berthoff (1984), have marked the roles that imaging plays as we construct personal meaning with texts:

> The capacity of the human being to evoke images of things or events not present, and even never experienced, or which may never have existed, is undoubtedly an important element in art. It is especially important in . . . speech and verbal text [and] . . . is basic to any kind of verbal communication (Rosenblatt 1978, 32).

Paradigmatic shifts of the last twenty years are just beginning to acknowledge the importance of images in developing students' literacy. Emig (1971) redirected research on writing when she focused on composing process rather than on product. Emig emphasizes the similarities between writing and creative processes in general, thus suggesting that students employ nonlinguistic modes of thinking while composing. Emig's study also revealed that writing and thinking do not lend themselves to being taught as isolated subskills. This trading of our obsessions about product and form for a focus on writing process forced us to consider thinking processes as well, which in turn allowed us to see for ourselves the considerable degree to which our students think visually.

Research by Britton and his colleagues (1975) made us aware of the incubation stage, where writers must not only "get right" with the facts, but also get right with themselves—a polarity that Britton connects to "the foundations of language itself involved in [Susanne Langer's] presentational and discursive symbolism" (27), processes in which imaging plays a central role. Britton further validates imaging by placing expressive language at the center from which other forms of discourse evolve. According to Britton, expressive language is close to the self—the kind of informal, probing, immediate, metaphoric, reflexive, abbreviated, malleable, speculative language akin to Vygotsky's inner speech. This stream of language that we use to communicate with ourselves and with well-trusted others flows just above a more purely imagistic thinking. Hence, expressive language is often our best vehicle for accessing and interacting with images.

More directly than Britton, Flower and Hayes (1989) acknowledge that writers represent meaning to themselves in a variety of ways, including metaphor and imagery, even conceding that linguistic representations such as propositions and verbalized schemas differ in the amount of linguistic information they contain. Other research in literacy education, such as Perl's discussion (1983) of "felt sense" in writing and Brand's study (1989) of emotion in writing, which takes images to be a form of "pure meaning" arrived at after one fully internalizes inner speech (28), is shedding even more light on images and imaging.

Allender's study (1991) of imagery in teaching and learning tries to harness both expressive language and the direct teaching of imagery. After using imagery techniques to teach spelling and arithmetic to elementary students—which did improve their learning—Allender's graduate seminar looked at how imaging has been used in education and in mental health situations. Course reading included *Psychosynthesis: A Manual of Principles and Techniques* (Assagioli 1965), *The Metaphoric Mind: A Celebration of Creative Consciousness* (Samples 1976), and *Seeing with the Mind's Eye: The History, Techniques, and Uses of Visualization* (Samuels and Samuels 1975). Students kept journals describing class discussions and responses to readings. The course featured a series of "experience experiments" in which students applied course concepts—ones they thought would improve their imaging skills—to their daily lives. According to Allender, the students

> used dreams and wishes to alter the everyday facts of their lives. They kept their definitions of reality open.... They believed that just as reality knocks down dreams, dreams can knock apart reality. (137)

Allender rightfully doubts the teacher's role as "great maker of curriculum." In his experimental classes, he let each student's ever-changing thinking and feeling become the curriculum:

> We began with ourselves and involved our imagination in significant ways, and quested after deep personal meaning.... We didn't meditate, fast, undertake vision quests and outward bound experiences, or emphasize the spiritual nature of our learning, but there was a similar spirit. (215)

What happens when images become the focus of a classroom, especially when the emphasis is not on mere imagery techniques, but on imagery as a way of thinking? The search for connections dominated Allender's class. Quality, Allender reminds us, is not a thing, but an event. These classes had goals and structures, but they took a back seat to what was happening in class. Most prized was "trying to respond dynamically to what was learned by ourselves and the students every day," rather than "searching for static information about what works" (212). What some people may call "irresponsible" teaching, Allender calls "change-oriented" and "dynamic," qualities common to all unusual learning environments.

The most crucial concern raised by Allender's study is the perceived "loss of control," due of course, to the nature of imagery. Allender wonders how applicable imagery work really is to education:

> No one would disagree that imagination, a main component of imagery, is an important source of creativity, but it is different when one truly believes that fantasy and reality are inextricably interconnected. (136)

If Allender and his students truly accepted images as having a "magical quality that challenges ordinary logic" (136), if we really believe that images can affect reality in the same way that reality can affect images, in effect choosing to believe rather than to doubt, then there is indeed a loss of control. As we have already seen, concern for such "losses of control" is a steady undercurrent throughout image studies. But where does this loss of control occur? It is mainly the external elements that lose power, not the individual. On the contrary, because of imagery work, individuals—including the students and teachers in Allender's classes—increase their internal control. Making image studies the heart of a class says that power resides inside of us, not in authority imposed from the outside.

Finally, McLuhan (1964), Paglia and Postman (1991), Sontag (1977), and others provide a sociocultural perspective on literacy development and images. Postman believes that we do not have any tools to help us combat the "seductions" of imagery, as opposed to language, where we wield logic and rhetoric to help us combat the seductions of words. Paglia states that watching television has nothing at all to do with thinking and analyzing—that television watching is more like interstate driving or quarterbacking, in which we do not analyze, but instead, scan and read the field, work by instinct, and store information for later use (49).

Regarding the *kinds* of meanings that images elicit, Postman worries that our culture's images hold only secular meanings for people because our icons grow out of commercialism, which drains traditional religious symbols of meaning (50). Equally important is the notion that an image-soaked environment can alter our concept of what is real and what is not. Sontag (1977) suggests that we expect our lives to be like images of it, not the other way around, and Cross (1983) details how children choose to watch a film of an event over the actual event itself (230). As Boorstin (1962) states, we run the risk of being "the first people in history to make their illusions so vivid, so persuasive, so 'realistic' that we can live in them" (240).

From Huck to Leonardo: Influences from the Arts and Humanities

Most of the people, theories, and movements discussed so far have one thing in common: their quest for wholeness or balance. From Jung's work in making us whole by recognizing our other self, the unconscious, through James's "unbroken" stream of consciousness, to the Gestalt notions of achieving balance through both simplifying and forming shapes—all have tried, through their concerns with images, to unify, to balance, to make whole. This same struggle applies to the arts and humanities, where philosophers, artists, composers, and writers have long waged this battle closer to home.

Most of us can point to people who affected our lives through powerful, artistic images—special teachers like Van Gogh, Kandinsky, or Thomas Hart Benton who have helped us to see some whole meanings in fragmentation, some complete or sensible shapes in the mist. Or, we may identify with literary magicians of imagery, such as Keats, Twain, or William Carlos Williams, authors who lead us through their pattern of images into knowing and realizing something whole—a truth.

In the sciences and social sciences, but especially in the arts and humanities, most struggles for wholeness and balance can be traced back to that ultimate conflict we all live with: Yes-rejoice-in-life or No-we're-going-to-die. These are the ultimate parts to make whole; this is the final rift to heal. Although this healing can never really occur, images and imaging are stronger forces for wholeness than anything else.

What image might we point to and say, yes, there is an image that, across the centuries, has made infinite fragmentations whole, has united infinite dualities? Da Vinci's capacity for "dualism" or flexibility qualifies him for this honor. Da Vinci's ability to move back and forth between the verbal and visual is even more true of Leonardo, the artist. After observing that all artists "labor in, with and through light, always light," Eliot (1959) suggests that changes in how artists handle light can also reflect shifts in culture. Eliot places Leonardo's struggles with light and shadow into a larger context so that we can better understand all dualistic forces:

> Leonardo . . . saw the powers of light and darkness as twins, equally matched and locked in an eternal struggle. Thus he looked back to . . . pagan thought and forward to . . . scientific thought. In his own day such dualism smacked of witchcraft; it was considered evil. Yet by inventing chiaroscuro to express it, Leonardo bent the path of art, and thought as well, his way.
> Chiaroscuro figures are shaped of light and shadow only. Contours blur like smoke upon the air. (11–12)

What better way to remind ourselves of the image's power to create wholeness than to recall Leonardo's own struggles embodied in the Mona Lisa's revolutionary gradations of light and dark, in her all-knowing glance? What better way to remind ourselves of imagery's power to unify than to recall that half-smile, which reconciles all dualities and conflicts—light and dark, pagan and Christian, right and wrong, male and female, objective and subjective, romantic and realistic, Apollonian and Dionysian, logical and intuitive, verbal and visual? Imagine that quiet, grandly encompassing smile and find refuge there.

Works Cited

Abraham, Karl. 1949. "Restrictions and Transformations of Scoptophilia in Psycho-Neurotics." In *Selected Papers on Psycho-Analysis,* 169–234. London: Hogarth Press and the Institute of Psycho-Analysis.

Adams, Hazard, ed. 1971. *Critical Theory since Plato.* San Diego: Harcourt Brace Jovanovich.

Allender, Jerome. 1991. *Imagery in Teaching and Learning: An Autobiography of Research in Four World Views.* New York: Praeger.

Arnheim, Rudolf. 1986. *New Essays on the Psychology of Art.* Berkeley: University of California Press.

———. 1992. *To the Rescue of Art.* Berkeley: University of California Press.

Assagioli, Roberto. 1965. *Psychosynthesis: A Manual of Principles and Techniques.* New York: Penguin.

Barthes, Roland. 1977. *Image, Music, Text.* Translated by Stephen Heath. New York: Hill and Wang.

Begg, Ian. 1983. "Imagery and Language." In *Imagery: Current Theory, Research, and Application,* edited by Anees Sheikh, 288–309. New York: John Wiley and Sons.

Berthoff, Ann, ed. 1984. *Reclaiming the Imagination: Philosophical Perspectives for Writers.* Upper Montclair, NJ: Boynton/Cook.

Boorstin, Daniel. 1962. *The Image; or, What Happened to the American Dream.* New York: Atheneum.

Brand, Alice. 1989. *The Psychology of Writing: The Affective Experience.* New York: Greenwood Press.

Britton, James, Tony Burgess, Nancy Martin, Alex McLeod, and Harold Rosen. 1975. *The Development of Writing Abilities (11–18).* London: Macmillan.

Bruner, Jerome. 1973. "The Course of Cognitive Growth." In *Beyond the Information Given: Studies in the Psychology of Knowing,* edited by Jeremy Anglin, 325–51. New York: Norton.

Costanzo, William. 1992. *Reading the Movies.* Urbana, IL: National Council of Teachers of English.

Cross, Donna W. 1983. *Mediaspeak: How Television Makes Up Your Mind.* New York: Coward-McCann.

Eco, Umberto. 1976. *A Theory of Semiotics.* Bloomington: Indiana University Press.

Einstein, Albert. 1961. *Relativity, the Special and the General Theory.* 16th ed. New York: Crown.

Eissler, K. R. 1965. *Medical Orthodoxy and the Future of Psychoanalysis.* New York: International Universities Press.

Eliot, Alexander. 1959. *Sight and Insight.* New York: McDowell, Obolensky.

Emig, Janet. 1971. *The Composing Processes of Twelfth Graders.* Urbana, IL: National Council of Teachers of English.

Flower, Linda, and John Hayes. 1989. "Taking Thought: The Role of Conscious Processing in the Making of Meaning." In *Thinking, Reasoning, and Writing,* edited by Elaine P. Maimon, Barbara F. Nodine, and Finbarr W. O'Connor. New York: Longman.

Galton, Frederick. 1874. *English Men of Science: Their Nature and Nurture.* London: Macmillan.

Gardner, Howard. 1982. *Art, Mind, and Brain: A Cognitive Approach to Creativity.* New York: Basic Books.

Goffman, Erving. 1979. *Gender Advertisements.* Cambridge: Harvard University Press.

Gombrich, E. H. 1982. *The Sense of Order: A Study in the Psychology of Decorative Art.* 2d ed. Ithaca, NY: Cornell University Press.

Gowan, J. C. 1978. "Incubation, Imagery, and Creativity." *Journal of Mental Imagery* 2 (Spring): 23–31.

Gruber, Howard. 1978. "Darwin's 'Tree of Nature' and Other Images of Wide Scope." In *On Aesthetics in Science,* edited by Judith Wechsler, 121–40. Cambridge: MIT Press.

Hadamard, Jacques. 1945. *The Psychology of Invention in the Mathematical Field.* Princeton, NJ: Dover Publishers.

Hayakawa, S. I., and Alan Hayakawa. 1990. *Language in Thought and Action.* 5th ed. San Diego: Harcourt Brace Jovanovich.

Hughes, T. 1985. "The Graphic Truth." *American Heritage of Invention and Technology* 1.1: 28–30.

Huxley, Aldous. 1954. *The Doors of Perception.* New York: Harper and Row.

Jakobson, Roman. 1985. *Roman Jakobson: Selected Writings.* Edited by Stephen Rudy. Berlin: Mouton.

James, William. 1974. "The Stream of Consciousness." In *The Nature of Human Consciousness,* edited by Robert Ornstein, 153–66. New York: Viking.

Johnson, Wendell. 1946. *People in Quandaries: The Semantics of Personal Adjustment.* New York: Harper and Row.

Kepes, Gyorgy. 1951. *Language of Vision.* Chicago: Paul Theobald.

Koestler, Arthur. 1964. *The Act of Creation.* New York: Macmillan.

Kosslyn, Stephen. 1983. *Ghosts in the Mind's Machine: Creating and Using Images in the Brain.* New York: Norton.

Lee, Irving. 1941. *Language Habits in Human Affairs: An Introduction to General Semantics.* New York: Harper and Brothers.

Lowes, John. 1927. *The Road to Xanadu: A Study in the Ways of the Imagination.* Boston: Houghton Mifflin.

Luria, A. R. 1968. *The Mind of a Mnemonist.* New York: Basic Books.

McLuhan, Marshall. 1964. *Understanding Media.* New York: McGraw-Hill.

Metz, Christian. 1974. *Film Language: A Semiotics of the Cinema.* Translated by Michael Taylor. New York: Oxford University Press.

Miller, Arthur. 1978. "Visualization Lost and Regained: The Genesis of the Quantum Theory in the Period 1913–27." In *On Aesthetics in Science,* edited by Judith Wechsler. Cambridge: MIT Press.

Neisser, Ulric. 1976. *Cognition and Reality: Principles and Implications of Cognitive Psychology.* San Francisco: W. H. Freeman.

Nelson, Richard. 1981. "Propaganda." In *Handbook of American Popular Culture,* edited by M. Thomas Inge, 3: 321–83. Westport, CT: Greenwood Press.

Newbold, William. 1897. "Sub-conscious Reasoning." *Proceedings of the Society for Psychical Research* 12: 11–20.

O'Neil, J. 1944. *Prodigal Genius: The Life of Nikola Tesla.* New York: Washburn.

Paglia, Camille, and Neil Postman. 1991. "She Wants Her TV! He Wants His Book!" *Harpers,* March, 44–55.

Paivio, Allan. 1986. *Mental Representations: A Dual Coding Approach.* New York: Oxford University Press.

Patten, Bernard. 1973. "Visually Mediated Thinking: A Report of the Case of Albert Einstein." *Journal of Learning Disabilities* 6 (August-September): 415–20.

Perkins, David N. 1981. *The Mind's Best Work.* Cambridge: Harvard University Press.

Perl, Sondra. 1983. "Understanding Composing." In *The Writer's Mind: Writing as a Mode of Thinking,* edited by Janice Hays, Phyllis Roth, Jon Ramsey, and Robert Foulke. Urbana, IL: National Council of Teachers of English.

Polanyi, Michael. 1958. *Personal Knowledge: Towards a Post-Critical Philosophy.* Chicago: University of Chicago Press.

Pula, Robert. 1991–92. "Alfred Korzybski, *Collected Writings: 1920–1950*: An Appreciation and a Review." *Etc.: A Review of General Semantics* 48 (Winter): 424–33.

Richards, I. A. 1929. *Practical Criticism: A Study of Literary Judgment.* New York: Harcourt Brace Jovanovich.

Rico, Gabriele. 1983. *Writing the Natural Way: Using Right-Brain Techniques to Release Your Expressive Powers.* Los Angeles: J. P. Tarcher.

Rosenblatt, Louise. 1978. *The Reader, the Text, the Poem: The Transactional Theory of the Literary Work.* Carbondale: Southern Illinois University Press.

Sacks, Oliver. 1990. *The Man Who Mistook His Wife for a Hat and Other Clinical Tales.* New York: HarperCollins.

Salomon, Gavriel. 1979. *Interaction of Media, Cognition, and Learning.* San Francisco: Jossey-Bass.

Samples, Bob. 1976. *The Metaphoric Mind: A Celebration of Creative Consciousness.* Reading, MA: Addison-Wesley.

Samuels, Mike, and Nancy Samuels. 1975. *Seeing with the Mind's Eye: The History, Techniques, and Uses of Visualization.* New York: Random House.

Scholes, Robert. 1982. *Semiotics and Interpretation.* New Haven, CT: Yale University Press.

Sebeok, Thomas, ed. 1977. *A Perfusion of Signs.* Bloomington: Indiana University Press.

Siegel, Marjorie, and Robert Carey. 1989. *Critical Thinking: A Semiotic Perspective.* Bloomington, IN: ERIC Clearinghouse.

Sless, David. 1986. *In Search of Semiotics.* Totowa, NJ: Barnes and Noble Books.

Sontag, Susan. 1977. *On Photography.* New York: Farrar, Straus and Giroux.

Suhor, Charles. 1992. "Semiotics and the English Language Arts." *Language Arts* 69 (March): 228–30.

Ward, Fred. 1989. "Images for the Computer Age." *National Geographic* 175 (June): 718–51.

2 People Prose

Alan C. Purves
University at Albany, State University of New York

i

In *Counterblast* (1969), Marshall McLuhan argues (1) that by putting things in writing, particularly by putting them in print using a printing press, people could analyze their world in new ways and (2) that with the coming of television and the new acoustic media could come an awareness of the world that is synthetic rather than analytic.

According to McLuhan, the newspaper was the first print medium to challenge the linear movement of print and its resulting "if-then" logic. Perhaps it also challenged the linearity of our rationalist approach to the world. Acoustic space has no dimensions; visual space has three; normally, print depends on two. But the newspaper uses three dimensions: pages have two, and sections add a third.

McLuhan argues that the media that surround us inevitably affect our perception, particularly the ways in which we organize our ideas. Such arguments help us to understand something about the nature of the sea-change in our rhetoric, our approach to text, our pedagogy, our curriculum, our view of the classroom, even our strategy for investigating these phenomena.

Many of us grew up in a print-dominated culture, and we tend to think in terms of print. We have learned to value the rationalist ideal and language. That sort of language rules the academy and our academic view of our subject. We value the approach to the world that is encapsulated in texts and tables and ordered lists with classes and subclasses, the world that can be mapped and put on paper. Our culture hero is Peter Roget.

Look back to the 1960s and see the culmination of the print approach to the teaching of the language arts. Note the jargon: *the tripod of language, literature, and composition; structuralist criticism and grammar (with its transformational modulation); reading comprehension; text-based rhetoric; structure and sequence; Socratic or inductive teaching; the acquisition of skills; comprehensive norm-referenced; and experimental design and linear regression models in research.*

In the 1990s, different jargon dominates our view: *whole language, reader response, student empowerment, language experience, commu-*

nicative competence, recursive processes, composing, discussion-centered or student-centered classrooms, portfolio assessment, and ethnographic research. All of these terms betoken a multidimensional space, perhaps a hyperspace. It is a space dominated by images that emerge from television and the computer.

Our students—brought up in a world of television and educated through "Captain Kangaroo," cartoons, and "Sesame Street" before eventually graduating to MTV—come to our classes having read magazines and newspapers more than textbooks and complex linear arguments. And when they fail, they are castigated for being nearly beyond redemption.

ii

In "Utterance and Text in Freshman English" (1989), Edward Lotto suggests that one of the major problems faced by teachers of incoming college students is the students' persistent use of a language that is oral in nature. (He also suggests that they prefer *Friday the 13th* to *Hannah and Her Sisters.*) Like several others who discuss the differences between the "normal" practices of neophyte and expert academic writers, Lotto argues that these differences, like the supposed differences between those who inhabit preliterate and literate cultures, are differences in thought rather than differences in style.

Maybe they are, but I'm not so sure. I will concentrate on Lotto's essay, which has both strengths and weaknesses. I do so simply because he reflects many of the attitudes and beliefs of those who teach academic prose (or prose in the academy).

Oral societies are capable of producing grammars, taxonomies, novelties, and other evidences of what we consider "rational" thought. At the same time, it seems naive to think that today's college students, no matter how "remedial" or "basic," come from an oral culture and are entering into a literate one. Inevitably, they inhabit and are well aware of the nature of a literate society and literate behavior. But they also inhabit a media society, which is greatly different from the academic world and which has changed prose from its rationalist print form to other forms.

There's the rub. Unaware of the particular norms of academic literacy, students inhabit and are impressed by the literate structures that dominate their environment. The academic structures are but minor figures in a literate world grounded in multiple messages, intense images, and discourse that brings together graphics and graphemes in ways far different from the pages of *PMLA* or *The Bulletin of Atomic Physicists.*

The two prose passages that Lotto uses to press his point and depress his students differ in many respects but perhaps not in the terms he uses to describe them. One is "detailed and carefully proves a thesis," while the other is "full of nice-sounding clichés that appeal to the students' self-images." The second is also referred to as "general." Here are his samples:

> (1) Atop a hill overlooking the Housatonic River Valley in Midwestern Connecticut is a backwoods grass airfield, housing in its two 50 × 50 foot four plane hangars, and the burned-out concrete pit of what used to be a third, a dozen planes and the workshops of their owners, builders, or pilots. This is where my father spends most of his spare time, in his corner of a roof-sagging Ansonia Airfield hangar. Here there is little but the sliding 10-foot high aluminum doors, which often fall off their tracks when being pushed open, the concrete floor, cracked badly, with crabgrass growing through in the northeast corner, and the old oak door on sawhorses—the workbench—and a shiny yellow and black Pitts S-1 aerobatic biplane, its wingspan no greater than the length of a Volkswagen. My father is usually crouched within the open single cockpit, or lying beneath the cowl, or ducking into the fuselage, meticulously checking and refurbishing the many parts of the plane. The decayed hangar doesn't bother him, but for the airplane itself he spares no pains.

> (2) Sailing is a free spirit's dream. Just imagine floating upon the wild untamed seas, hair whisked back and the sun beaming upon beautiful brown-skinned bodies in shiny sailing crafts daring Poseidon to stop them with his mighty waves and winds. Then moments later these small crafts disappear into the sunset. Interesting, don't you think? All that excitement with no motor, no fumes and no noise, except for nature's own language. Sailing provides the most natural adventure upon the seas.

Which one do you think teachers and other academics would prefer? Looking at the samples that Lotto gives, I would argue that the differences are less those between "text" and "utterance" than between an "academic prose" (general "American prose") and *People* prose." Both passages are clearly written products, and both make their points well. But the former is that preferred by certain types of American academic writers, particularly by a group of those who teach academic prose.

The differences are cultural; societies other than ours tend to value the more image-rich and elliptical style of the second passage.

So do the writers of much of the prose that our students see. The specificity in phrasing, literalness, and periodicity in sentence structure of the first passage are the peculiar properties of "English department prose." The metaphor, sentence fragments, and rhythmic connections of the second passage are the qualities of advertising copy and magazine writing. That Lotto's students prefer the second simply shows the type of prose to which they have become inured, in which they have been immersed—the type of prose they see as successful. It is the style of *USA Today, People,* and other journals of that ilk:

> Gurdon admits, officially, that she is indeed Lloyd Webber's "friend," but is otherwise keeping mum, if not altogether out of the public eye. Her principal statement so far: "My solicitor has told me not to say anything." One day after Lloyd Webber's announcement, the couple made a conspicuous appearance outside his office in London's Palace Theatre—which he partially owns—where *Les Miserables* is playing. Luckily, Lloyd Webber didn't write *Les Miz*, because there would be no parallels between the downtrodden of that epic and "Gurtie" Gurdon. The convent-educated daughter of a retired brigadier, she has been a high-profile three-day event rider for almost a decade. Some bad news: She lost her favorite horse, Midnight Monarch, last year in the trials at Badminton, when he broke his leg at the water jump. Some good news: She is as chic as she is swift, designing an exclusive line of leather-and-suede clothes. Princess Anne, reportedly, is a customer. (*People,* 23 July 1990, 58)

This passage is devoid of the typical logical connectives of academic prose. The writer connects ideas with repetition, allusion, and opposition. (The allusions demand cultural literacy, but it is not what we would expect from a quick read of E. D. Hirsch, Jr.) Such prose is not difficult to follow, but for someone trained in the rhetoric of academe it seems difficult, if not barbaric.

Bill Moyers's PBS television series on United States culture included a detailed discussion of images and the fact that the new media, particularly television, have changed the way in which people perceive and take in information. In the series, Neil Postman suggests that the old logical structures do not hold up in this world of images and pictures that tell stories and give messages succinctly and tellingly. That is why Reagan was successful and why people wear names on their clothes to be part of an image they see on television or in magazines. That sense of imagery explains what Lotto's "utterance" example is. It is not oral discourse. It is a "new media discourse," for want of a better term. Students like it because it is what they are used to in the pages of magazines and in television messages, particularly those on MTV.

In distinguishing utterance from text, David Olson (1977) suggests that American (and perhaps European) essayist prose has slowly developed a set of structures to enable readers to get meaning from the text without having to make great inferences concerning intention. These structures are limited in the same way that the "kernel sentences" of transformational grammar are limited (in the same way that any set of building blocks is limited), but they may be combined in an almost infinite number of ways to form a complex essay or book.

The structures determine conventional sequences of events, objects, or ideas into paragraphs or larger units, and each structure has its set of appropriate markers—usually connecting or signaling intersentential words. As ways of sequencing events or ideas in text, these structures become associated with logic or thinking, although they may have little to do with the way ideas are generated, only with the way they are to be arrayed in texts of a particular sort. There may be other structures of presentation—lists, tables, charts, rhymes, image or feeling clusters, and the like—that serve to transmit information effectively, but these are not associated specifically with essayist prose and do not have the academic cachet. Essayist structures inform the models of good writing that currently exist in the heads of trained academics.

The major essayist structures are temporal, spatial, and classificatory. These structures can be subdivided as follows:

1. temporal
    a. narrative
    b. process
    c. cause-effect
2. spatial
    a. physical display
    b. anatomy
3. classificatory
    a. classification
    b. definition
    c. analogy
    d. comparison-contrast

The major forms of written argument—the deductive and the inductive—tend to be composites of these. Such forms of argument and connectives simply do not mark the prose of *People* or the prose that many students write.

iii

When people think of the effect of media on prose, they often refer to the content and not sufficiently to the style. John Powers's article (1990) on language in *The Boston Globe Magazine* begins by comparing the inaugural addresses of Lincoln and Bush:

> With malice toward none, with charity for all, with firmness in the right as God gives us to see the right, let us strive on to finish the work we are in, to bind up the nation's wounds, to care for him who shall have borne the battle, and for his widow and orphan—to do all which may achieve and cherish a just and lasting peace among ourselves and with all nations.

> A new breeze is blowing and a nation refreshed by freedom is ready to push on. There's new ground to be broken and new action to be taken. There are times when the future seems thick as a fog. You see and wait, hoping the mist will lift and reveal the right path. But this is a time when the future seems a door you can walk right through into a room called tomorrow.

It is obvious that Powers prefers Lincoln to Bush; so would most teachers of composition. Powers goes on to say that "the English that Americans use today is a language that has become vague, pretentious, mushy, dishonest, and filled with jargon. It has been shaped by advertisers (the Average American has seen more than a million commercials by age forty) and by politicians, both of whom deal in illusion and euphemism" (17). He cites Orwell, Barzun, and many others as examples and proponents of the "better" essayist way.

It is not simply the advertising copywriter and the politician, though. After all, Lincoln was no mean politician, and his second inaugural address was indeed a political speech. It is a matter of style, and the style lies primarily in the connectives.

iv

Does this suggest that when we teach writing, we have to resurrect an older and perhaps outmoded propositional discourse? Or do we start teaching the academic uses of the new discourse?

Lotto endorses exercises in combining kernel sentences into complex ones. This practice would serve to establish patterns of expression and style rather than patterns of organizing discourse. He suggests that it may influence the way students think. I have found little evidence that types of prose have anything to do with styles of thinking or with thought in any way. And I am not sure that one can work backward.

While I agree with Lotto that instruction in writing should reinforce the conventions, I would stop there and not add the bare word *text*. The conventions that many of us yearn for in our students are the conventions of American academic prose. These form a subset of specialized and culture-bound conventions rather than a set that is inherent in the very fact of written language and text.

I frankly admire academic prose with its order and appearance of reasonableness. I realize that academic prose will help students succeed. They need it to pass their courses in history and business administration (if indeed they have to write at all). But I also realize that the most powerful prose stylists of the nineteenth and twentieth centuries broke away from that kind of style and moved toward a prose of images and metaphors. Consider Arnold, Ruskin, Lawrence, Gould, Dillard, Berry, and Baldwin. Take a look at Ad Reinhardt and M. F. K. Fisher. All of these writers have a command of written discourse, but their writing is not academic in the sense that most of our teachers would want.

I believe that we need to explain to our students how form follows function in writing as it does in so many other things. What is the function of academic prose? It is to present one or two ideas clearly and succinctly, giving the reader a sense of a detached, rational mind that is part of a community of detached, rational minds. Given that function, the most succinct form is the five-paragraph theme using one of the expository structures that I have listed above.

Academic prose is meant to do more than inform readers. It also serves to make you a member of the detached, objective community. Don't tell students to be too interesting or imaginative; watch out for images and metaphors; keep personality out of it. Don't make the reader work. Save that for creative writing, ad writing, or after class. Of course, the academic community is changing. Textbooks are nice examples of new designs and styles meeting new functions. Desktop publishing may change the scholarly article.

So what does all this add up to? Just because students follow models of writing that surround them does not mean they are dumb. We should try to find out why they write texts that look the way they do. We should encourage them to try the academic way if they want to make it in our world. And we should try to write the imagistic way if we want to make it in theirs.

Works Cited

Lotto, Edward. 1989. "Utterance and Text in Freshman English." *College English* 51: 677–87.

McLuhan, Marshall. 1969. *Counterblast.* New York: Harcourt, Brace and World.

Olson, David. 1977. "From Utterance to Text: The Bias of Language in Speech and Writing." *Harvard Educational Review* 47: 257–81.

Powers, John. 1990. "Bitespeak." *The Boston Globe Magazine,* 15 July, 16ff.

3 Imaging, Literacy, and Sylvia Ashton-Warner

Nancy S. Thompson
University of South Carolina

Whatever our child is, that's what his education is when you use his own imagery as working material.

Sylvia Ashton-Warner

New Zealand's famous teacher Sylvia Ashton-Warner (1908–1984) has fired the imaginations of teachers around the world. Ashton-Warner wielded words to make vivid images arise in her readers' minds. But more important, she understood imagery as an important mental process, an organic biological function, universal among humans:

> The pictures in his mind are part of his mind as the heart to the body, as the kidneys, stomach and lungs. His feeling, combusting in imagery, is a functioning organ. (Ashton-Warner 1972)

Considering her life and work from the vantage point of my own study of imagery, I began to see that Ashton-Warner's contributions to literacy education originate in her recognition of imagery in her personal life.

From Imagery to Imaging (and Literacy Learning)

In order to place imagery and imaging as literacy learning activities, let me first define them. When I began using visuals as a stimulus for writing, I explored the relationship between imagery and language (Thompson 1988). Paivio (1971) helped me understand that the brain processes both visual and verbal information.

We usually consider imagery to be a visual phenomenon, while language is usually defined as a verbal one. Thus, they are not parallel: *visual* is a sensory term, while *verbal language* refers to a cultural symbol system. This symbol system, however, is sensory in that it is aural when we hear language spoken and visual when we see language written. Thus, as with imagery, the pathways for verbal language are sensory—visual or aural. The common element is the sensory nature of both verbal language and imagery.

Further, though we often assume that imagery is visual, it should not be limited to that sense. Using sight as a model—since it is so important in our mentality—we can understand that the other senses can be re-presented in the mind in just the same way as the visual sense. Just as we experience an image in the mind's eye when we read a poem, we can experience hearing words and other sounds in the "mind's ear." Who has not heard a song replay in their mind off and on all day? We imagine movement too, such as the feeling of falling in a dream.

Imaging, then, the act of experiencing mental images, is a broader phenomenon than visual imagery; it is connected to all the senses. Just as we have the ability to re-present information processed visually, we can also re-present aural information (hearing words in the mind) or kinesthetic information (practicing movements in preparation for a sport). In fact, imaging defined to include all sensory information suggests an internal representation system: sensory information re-presented in our consciousness can be seen as the medium through which we experience mental activity in general.

Thus, imaging is an internal representation system that mediates our conscious mental experience. Embodying all kinds of sensory thinking, it underlies both visual imagery and verbal language. Spoken language is re-presented through the aural and motor systems, while visual imagery is re-presented through the visual and motor systems. These and other systems such as kinesthetic, olfactory, taste, and all the other senses form our sensory internal representation system, which underlies all thinking.

As Ashton-Warner's work demonstrates, visual imagery is the most legitimate entry for studying mental processes. Her published and unpublished work exemplifies how imaging functions in thinking and literacy learning.

A Pilgrimage

I traveled to New Zealand to gather material and to examine imagery in Ashton-Warner's thinking and writing, because as an artist, musician, writer, and teacher, she relied upon visual imaging. I found that imagery, important in many ways to her life and work, was the foundation of her literacy learning theory. Her published and unpublished work provides concrete examples and vivid accounts of the thought process of imaging.

Ashton-Warner is best known for her work in *Teacher* (1963) on the "Key Vocabulary": those words that teachers help children to identify as captions of their vivid images. At the Maori infant school where she taught, Ashton-Warner talked to children so that they could describe the vivid images of their inner lives, usually basic, highly emotional ones, like fear or love. She recognized words such as *kiss, ghost, mommy,* and *daddy* as captions of children's inner images, and when such a word arose, she would write the caption-word on a large card and give it to the child. She tested a word's viability as a true Key Vocabulary word by checking to see if the learner recognized it the next day. If not, that word was abandoned and others tried. True Key Vocabulary words are emotionally charged and thus more likely to be understood and retained. Hence, Ashton-Warner viewed these words—and the images that generate them—as crucial to literacy development.

After a series of articles about her teaching methods were published in New Zealand journals in the mid-1950s, Ashton-Warner published her first novel, *Spinster* (1958), a fictional account of her teaching. Biographer Lynley Hood (1988) writes that "the book was hailed as the best [novel] ever written in New Zealand, and was more discussed and praised in the media than any previous New Zealand novel." In 1963, Ashton-Warner published *Teacher,* which she considered her "thesis." After a string of novels, she produced another book on the Key Vocabulary idea, *Spearpoint* (1972), applying the idea to teacher education in an early-1970s alternative school in Aspen, Colorado. Her last book, her autobiography *I Passed This Way* (1979), won the 1980 New Zealand Book Award. She died in New Zealand in 1984, shortly after agreeing to cooperate with Hood on her biography, *Sylvia!* (1988), a work that was followed by Hood's diary (1990) of the process of writing the biography. All of these publications, in addition to other unpublished fiction, personal letters, diaries, video interviews (Shallcrass 1975; D'Audney 1980), Michael Firth's film (1985), and interviews with former colleagues, students, and other acquaintances, reveal the commanding role that imagery and imaging played in Ashton-Warner's life and work. I begin with an influential event in her personal life, a crisis that forced her to look closely at herself.

Images of the Crisis

In the late 1930s, when Ashton-Warner was in her early thirties, she persuaded her husband to apply for service with the Maori schools so that she could join him in teaching (Ashton-Warner 1979). After a year on the rugged east coast of New Zealand, however, she became very weak, unable to teach or care for their three small children. The imagery that had always been important in her mental life raged out of control.

In unpublished letters to Dr. Ivan Allen, her neurologist-therapist, Ashton-Warner states, "It was when I was lying for those eleven weeks too tired and ill to read that the dreaming got hold of me." She later recounted that she could not even sit up in bed because her dreams were "too heavy" (1979, 276). Later, while being treated by Dr. Allen, Ashton-Warner told her sister, "I can't read and big black clouds keep rolling towards me. . . . When I get to the next word I've forgotten what the first word was" (1979, 280). To Dr. Allen, Ashton-Warner wrote:

> I'm going to pull the bedclothes over my shoulders now and dream and dream and dream. Not just sleep dreams but special even beautiful ones. . . . If it was not for my babies and husband and the ones that love me I'd like to go mad and just lie and dream somewhere.

More than any of her other autobiographical writings, these letters to Dr. Allen reveal just how rampant the imaging that she experienced was:

> Dreaming went on regardless, trying to explode in reality. Unexpectedly the dreams would peer out from their undermind confinement at a line of poetry or the flash of a tune, [or] at a moment in my nightgown on the veranda . . . dreams of what I had meant to be.

Growing up, Ashton-Warner had always had high hopes for herself: "Sylvie" was an artist, her mother had always insisted. She took a commercial art class and tried freelance art work. After becoming ill, however, she returned to her mother's home and abandoned dreams of being an artist. Shortly thereafter, she took teaching jobs and married Keith Henderson, whom she met at college. For the next five years they built their marriage and family. In the isolated Maori coastal community where they taught, she wrote:

> As I lay in the darkness at night hearing the thud of the breaking waves my dreams had a chance to surface, trying to surge

over my mind, but at least I had the sense to counter them, for I was coming to fear them, as I feared almost everything. (1979, 275–76)

It was the fear—the awareness of which surfaces in her own life and in her later work with the Key Vocabulary—that ultimately drove Ashton-Warner to seek the help of Dr. Allen. He encouraged her to write, initially as a means of treatment. Ashton-Warner's relationship with Dr. Allen produced a revealing set of letters, many of which were never mailed. The writing itself seemed to serve as therapy. The letters to Dr. Allen reveal her strong fears and inner struggles. They also contain the seeds of ideas that grew into much of her professional work, such as the fear words she identified as the basis for children's Key Vocabulary:

> What is it? What frightens me? . . . The ogre, doctor: reality. This immediate reality of the river Awatere who runs sullen between us and village: who has washed three men out to sea in the spring flood; of the threat to my babies of being left without a mother. . . . The reality of K[eith] crossing the Awatere for stores twice each Saturday; of the possibility of his being left to live alone. . . . And all the stored fears of the past: of falling: of anger: of the dark: of madness: of choking: of flooded rivers, of deep waters.

Though she appears suicidal in the passage above, no other material gives that impression. Ashton-Warner reports how Dr. Allen helped her control the dreaming/imagery:

> "Reading," he said, "is taking into the mind new images, but your mind is too packed with native imagery to allow room for anything else in. You've got to harness those dreams of yours." (1979, 283)

From then on, she consciously struggled to discipline—but not to overpower—the imagery. Though the imagery caused her difficulty in some ways, it was an important mental strength that fueled much of her productive life as artist, musician, actress, writer, and teacher.

The Imaged Selves

The imaging continued, but it was channeled into her various roles, first into the artist that had emerged in childhood. Her father's vivid storytelling helped to train the imagery ability that the young Sylvia put to work drawing horses. Later, these horses show up with beautifully expressive faces in a series of paintings completed for a children's book (Special Exhibit of the Auckland College of Education). The subjects of Ashton-Warner's artwork were often drawn from her personal life. For example, a sculpture of her friend Joy Alley (whom she refers to as Opal in her autobiography) embodies their passionate friendship, and an elaborate drawing of "The Pied Piper" was inspired by a notable event in her infant school classroom. The unpublished "Essays on Artist" that she wrote late in life expresses her image of the artist as a male part of herself who had emerged to have his way with her in demanding expression.

Throughout her life, Ashton-Warner also studied the piano. Her mother insisted that young Sylvie and her brothers and sisters should not be disturbed to do chores if they were practicing their music. This art shows up in *Teacher* (1963) as the first eight notes of Beethoven's Fifth Symphony played on the classroom piano to get the children's attention. Though she never became an accomplished musician, her piano playing accompanied her private flow of imaging. Late in life, she stated that her calling was really to be a concert pianist: "It's my language [that] . . . comes from the great masters. . . . They speak in magic" (Shallcrass 1975).

Acting, also discovered in childhood, helped her escape reality. Taking cues from Daphne, an older sister who entertained the family with her childhood acting, Ashton-Warner often disguised her real feelings by acting out the persona that she wanted others to see. Two incidents illustrate Ashton-Warner's theatrical tendencies. First, in a letter to Dr. Allen, she reveals her self-understanding:

> Finally to protect myself from further injuries I covered my whole body with a coating of Affective Indifference. Then I recut the cloak in a bright scarlet openwork material of acting. I cut it in a slim yet voluptuous line, trimming it with the bright yellow buttons of showmanship and setting the whole thing off over a black underslip of drama. . . . The next time Fear drove me into Fantasy it was more wonderful than ever before. . . . I slipped naked out of the stiffened covering and sent not myself, but my shell, out to face reality.

And in Hood's biography (1988), an anonymous former colleague of Ashton-Warner's recalls how she could be a "seemingly blatant poseur":

> The occasion was a gathering of East Coast primary teachers on a Saturday at my school. While the families played in the school grounds . . . we were deep in debate on some aspect of teacher grading for our Educational Institute remits. Suddenly our eyes were riveted on the doorway. There appeared Sylvia: wide-brim-hatted, and wearing a pencil-slim skirt accentuated by a

> bright yellow cummerbund. She held aloft a huge bunch of
> buttercups just wrenched muddy and dripping from the stream
> bed and declaimed, "I am filled with the pregnancy of Spring!"
> For a moment there was utter dumbfounded silence—then she
> disappeared. (114–15)

Hood goes on to observe that the choice of a yellow cummerbund to
match the yellow buttercups at a time in her life when she dressed
almost exclusively in black, white, and red "reveals the planning that
must have preceded this apparently spontaneous drama" (115).

Writing, a skill developed long before her encounter with Dr.
Allen, allowed Ashton-Warner to live out whatever persona the imaging artist-actress-self wanted to take on. In an early novel (never published in original form), she shapes her childhood as she might have
imagined it to be. According to Hood, even the autobiography, her last
book, is laced with fiction. One notable example of living through
fiction is her novel *Three* (1970), which explores the relationships
among a mother, her married son, and his wife, written during
Ashton-Warner's stay in London with her son Elliot and his wife
Jacquemine, who were trying to resolve some marital problems. The
novel is so unabashedly autobiographical that it is impossible to tell
what is real and what is fiction.

All of these roles culminated in the teacher, for which Ashton-
Warner is best known, even though she maintained a love-hate relationship with teaching, alternately loving it and then despising it
because it robbed her of the time and energy needed for other arts.
Although all these other roles generated imagery, teaching best illumi-
nates the role of imaging in her professional life and work.

Teacher

Strong imagery is the basis for the Key Vocabulary concept that
catches the imagination of so many readers. Like the images of fear
that bubbled up through her "undermind," Ashton-Warner identified
emotionally loaded images of fear and other intense emotions as the
native imagery of the Key Vocabulary in her young students. In *Spinster* (1958), Anna, the main character, discovers the Key Vocabulary
concept:

> "What's this word?"
> "Kiss."
> A strange excitement comes over him. He smirks, then
> laughs outright, says it again, then tugs at Patchy nearby and
> shows him. "That's 'kiss,'" he says emotionally. "K-I-S-S."

Patchy lights up too in an extraordinary way. They both spell it. The reading is held up while others are called and told and I feel something has happened although I don't know what. . . .

Why this sudden impetus in the reading, I wonder, putting up the words from the imported books on the blackboard for the day? What's this power in a word like "kiss"?

. . . I see that this word is related to some feeling within them; some feeling that I have so far not touched. . . .

"It's got some relation," I say [to the headmaster], "to a big feeling. I can't put my finger on it."

"Do you mean it's a caption?"

Caption! . . . caption. . . .

The whole question is floodlit. This word is the caption of a very big inner picture . . . a huge emotional picture. . . . There must be many more words like this, analogous to these two; captions of other instincts, desires, resentments, horrors and passions. What are they? How do you get hold of them? How do your hands plunge into their heads and wrench them out? (178–81)

The fragile thought becomes more visible a few days later, when Ashton-Warner imagines a "tower of thought," on top of which was the shape of a key (189). This discovery of Key Vocabulary fueled Ashton-Warner's teaching for the rest of her career. Like her own imagery, which was so overpowering that she could not read, the children's images got in the way of taking new images into their minds. Her discovery of "native imagery" from Dr. Allen's treatment was an epiphany arising from the life crisis that had made her take stock of her "heavy dreams." This "key" she discovered—captions of children's inner pictures, of their native imagery—clarified what Ashton-Warner thought was most important: the mind of the learner.

Later, at Simon Fraser University, she began her seminars with young teachers by putting a chart on the wall entitled "The Mind of the Child" that would be filled in during the course. Her earlier work with imagery and the Key Vocabulary had led her to believe that the key to initial learning was to match the classroom material with the structure of imagery in the child's mind. She called this an "organic" approach to initial literacy learning because the "working material" was taken from the images that arose instinctively in each child's mind. In this way, the vocabulary for teaching literacy could be native to each child.

There would, of course, be an overlap among a given group of children. In *Spinster* (1958), for example, several children said they were afraid of the ghost. Still, the words had to be taken daily from the individual child. Each day, the child's interaction with family and community events would create a unique mindset and therefore produce corresponding imagery to be captioned in Key Vocabulary words. Hence, every morning Ashton-Warner found out what was on each child's mind and then picked a word from that child's talk to see if it fit. This process is highly individualized. In the source of this native imagery, the "undermind," emotion prevails over the conscious mind, arriving in the images the child experiences. These images can be translated into spoken and then written language. The child learns the concept of reading by connecting written visual marks with the spoken sounds of words that stand for mental images—a process fueled by using the child's native imagery.

Ashton-Warner's writing is itself replete with strong images. She illustrates her notion of the "undermind" by comparing it to a volcano, a natural, archetypal image for New Zealanders. Her image is that the child, using language, expresses imagery through the "creative vent" rather than through the "destructive vent." Creative expressions of the "undermind" should erupt in language or some other symbol system, such as music, art, or dance, rather than through the destructive vent of violent actions. Language in its expanded (semiotic) sense of symbol systems is the key to directing energy constructively rather than destructively. In her ideal, unlocking the creative vent of the mind with the key of language dries up the destructive vent, causing it to atrophy.

Another image that Ashton-Warner mines is the concept of *Spearpoint*, the title of her 1972 book about teaching in America. *Spearpoint* signifies the young North American children that she saw as the spearpoint of civilization; she later referred to her Canadian student-teachers as "spears." She viewed these North American children and teachers as the vanguard of change. While teaching in the early seventies in the alternative-school movement in Aspen, Colorado, however, Ashton-Warner discovered that the native imagery for Key Vocabulary of these reared-on-television children was difficult to uncover for use in initial literacy instruction:

> As our child sits hour after hour before the man-made screen, as the radio intrudes on the background of his mind or as the rabble-rousing beat of the latest hit booms through the trembling house, it is not that the channel outward is blocked to his imagery; it is that his defenseless mind, the frail, unique human marvel of his living feeling, is bombarded into sedation by over-stimulation or even into extinction. . . .

> The native imagery is being replaced by outside imagery concocted by man. It might be very good imagery too, but you can get too much of it. In all of it there is one thing wanting: it doesn't happen to be alive. It could fuse with the native imagery and become alive . . . if there were any native imagery left. (1972, 85–86)

This stream of artificial images coming from television, she believed, filled the mind of the child, but at the expense of the child's own active mental process of generating the images out of life experience. Hence, this creative vent atrophies.

Spearpoint, her autobiography *I Passed This Way,* and Hood's biography all record the culture shock, poor health, and stress under which Ashton-Warner worked while in this country, which she felt was at the head of the march into the future. Though these media children were different from those she had encountered in her native New Zealand, she said:

> The professional formula—"Release the native imagery of our child and use it for working material"—remains timeless, changeless and axiomatic, but the application of it needs constant variation. (1972, 40)

Though Ashton-Warner was a controversial figure, people who knew her say that her power as a teacher came from a special rapport she had with her pupils, often created when "taking the Key Vocabulary" of the children and adults she came in contact with. Selma Wassermann, who worked with her at Simon Fraser University, reports how a grown man was transported mentally to another place and time far in the past as Ashton-Warner conversed with him about important events in his childhood to identify his Key Vocabulary (Thompson 1991). This kind of conversation made people feel as if they were the most important person in the world. She elicited their most private, emotionally loaded images, cutting through to a deep level of intimacy with them. She was fascinated with the images in the human mind, including her own:

> In my non-stop novel, unruly native imagery found a channel through which to surface, clearing out on its way the delirium of both music and paint to enrich the main stream. Writing siphoned off the effervescence of dreaming, the constant opposition party, and there was discipline required for that. (1979, 347)

In fact, Ashton-Warner said that she didn't really do the writing. Instead, she went to her table and looked up. Then she just watched the images playing out in her inner vision and typed them.

Ashton-Warner's imaging was so strong that the line between fiction and her own life is not clear. For instance, Anna Verontosov in *Spinster* (1958) is in many ways Ashton-Warner herself, as we learn from her teaching diary. Though not a spinster herself, Ashton-Warner's lifelong admiration of single women emerges in the life that Anna leads. Later, characters in *Bell Call* (1964) are patterned after a couple that she knew, and the quest for personal freedom that she explores in the female character Tarl is a quality that she identified in herself. Through the character of Germaine in *Incense to Idols* (1960), Ashton-Warner examined her own love-hate relationship with God. Even in her autobiography, *I Passed This Way* (1979), it is sometimes hard to know what is fact and what is fiction. In it, Ashton-Warner recalls that she and her sister stole no less than 144 dolls from a local department store. Biographer Hood, however, discovered that the sister reported only two dolls, while a brother said there were none. In the unpublished preface to the Hindi edition of *Teacher*, Ashton-Warner's son, Elliot Henderson, states that his mother "invented her life, as much as she invented her work."

When imaging—the medium of consciousness—stops, then life, too, stops. Near the end of Ashton-Warner's life, illness had taken the imagery of her own working material. During the last few months of her life, she enrolled in a correspondence course on playwriting. With no imagery of her own, Hood (1988) tells us that she turned to an old Brazilian novel, *Epitaph of a Small Winner* by Machado de Assis, and used its imagery as the working material to adapt into a play (246). If she could not produce her own imagery, she would borrow someone else's as raw material for the writing.

Like almost everything else about Ashton-Warner, her New Zealand reputation is controversial. Those who knew her consider her with either adulation or disdain. Her detractors say she didn't do anything new, that she was responding to New Zealand's educational climate of the times, led by a progressive minister of education, Walter Beeby. They say that infant teachers all over New Zealand were doing the things she writes about: using Maori language for teaching these other-culture youngsters, having children write their own books for learning to read, integrating the arts into infant education.

The special thing she did do was to respond creatively to her environment by writing about it and thus communicating her insights, eloquently, to a broad audience. Through five articles in New Zealand's *National Education* in 1955 and 1956 that formed the core of *Teacher,* Ashton-Warner can be seen as the spark that ignited the whole-language movement, transforming early childhood education in the United States. A teacher who worked with her in Aspen prophesied that she would go down in history as "one of the seminal thinkers of our time" (Hood 1990, 200). No one else from her time and place focused on the importance of children's imagery as the raw working material for education. Her ultimate contribution may be her naming of this phenomenon the "Key Vocabulary," as she describes in *Spinster,* the book she considered her masterpiece. This and her other writings allow us to peer into the mind of an artist who struggled to apply her own native imagery toward creating her life as the ultimate art.

Works Cited

Ashton-Warner, Sylvia. 1958. *Spinster.* London: Secker and Warburg.

———. 1960. *Incense to Idols.* London: Secker and Warburg.

———. 1963. *Teacher.* New York: Simon and Schuster.

———. 1964. *Bell Call.* New York: Simon and Schuster.

———. 1966. *Greenstone.* New York: Simon and Schuster.

———. 1967. *Myself.* New York: Simon and Schuster.

———. 1970. *Three.* New York: Knopf.

———. 1972. *Spearpoint.* New York: Knopf.

———. 1979. *I Passed This Way.* New York: Knopf.

———. "Essays on Artist." Typescript. MS-Papers-4425-083, The Papers of Sylvia Ashton-Warner, Alexander Turnbull Library, National Library of New Zealand, Wellington.

———. Letters to Dr. Ivan Allen. Mugar Library, Boston University.

D'Audney, Angela. 1980. Transcript of Kaleidoscope interview with Sylvia Ashton-Warner, 24 March, TVNZ, Auckland, New Zealand.

Firth, Michael, director. 1985. *Sylvia.* Feature film. Los Angeles: Metro-Goldwyn-Mayer.

Hood, Lynley. 1988. *Sylvia!* New York: Viking.

———. 1990. *Who Is Sylvia?* Dunedin, New Zealand: John McIndoe.

Paivio, Allan. 1971. *Imagery and Verbal Processes.* New York: Holt, Rinehart and Winston.

Shallcrass, J. 1975. *Sylvia Ashton-Warner.* Television documentary. Wellington, New Zealand: Endeavor TV, National Film Library.

Thompson, Nancy S. 1988. "Effects of Verbal Ability, Audio-Pictorial Stimuli and Print-Verbal Stimuli on Reading and Writing Abilities of Early Adolescent Students." ED289162.

———. 1991. Personal interview with Selma Wassermann, 27 April, Vancouver, Canada.

4 Photographs, Writing, and Critical Thinking

Carol P. Hovanec and David Freund
Ramapo College of New Jersey

Although such terms as "visual literacy" and "visual culture" have enjoyed currency for years, their precise meaning is elusive. They imply that because we encounter numerous pictures—usually photographs—every day, we can or should be able to read them. Yet while most people find images in books and magazines interesting, they tend to glance at them, satisfied by a momentary stimulation—not the serious attention or careful analysis we allot to words or numbers. Fostered by our culture and our educational system, the result of these indifferent habits of seeing is that most students are not trained to be observant, either of their physical surroundings or of visual images structured to convey messages about those surroundings.

In most cases, students cannot decipher the inferences of the written page any better than they can see meaning beyond their feelings about pictured subjects. Because we feel so strongly that visual literacy is closely linked to verbal literacy, we developed a teaching approach over a decade ago that we use in our writing across the curriculum program and in composition classes at various levels.

The key element in all rhetoric is persuasion, and photographers, authors, and other artists order pictured situations to suggest meanings to the viewer, even though current theory indicates that these meanings may go far beyond those intended. These meanings can emerge from the objects themselves. In our culture, for example, there are certain obvious implications to depicting formal or sports clothing, even in similar settings. Subtler distinctions are conveyed by showing, say, a sweatshirt instead of a sweater, which in turn may be either a standard gray sweatshirt or a brightly colored one with a designer label, which may be further distinguished by being clean or soiled. The social meanings we may infer are those we would get whether the wearer were pictured or present, for the rhetoric belongs to the clothing.

The rhetoric of photography, however, emerges from *how* the garments are shown: Is the wearer near or far? In or out of focus? Contrasted with or blending into the background? Does the vantage point of the camera connect the wearer and other significant objects or people present? Is the vantage point low or high? Is the light delicate or harsh? The photograph can alter the meanings that various objects, people, and places would tend to have by adjusting their emphasis, tone, and context.

In addition, there are functional and psychological elements of design to be considered. Photographs tend to be read from left to right, and the viewer's eye must be led to points of emphasis by, for instance, the arrangement of the lines or colors, to ensure that certain objects will be looked at more closely than others. In addition, lines and colors have subtle connotations that must be considered.

In our society, one of the most pervasive and easily accessible examples of these theories is advertising, where illustrations will usually admit to several layers of deconstruction. For example, in a recent vodka ad, the names SUEBILLANNJOE are painted on the stern of a boat elevated in dry dock (figure 4.1). The text begins with the phrase "sharing the work," yet the only work seen is suggested by a stained glove with which the sign painter indicates her handiwork. The real message of vodka-enhanced sociability is emphasized by the foursome's unlikely pose, which is as close as their abutted names. The names themselves are about as straightforward and unaffected as the primary colors of the group's clothes.

Although the more genteel tradition of sailing is suggested by a fragment of mast and canvas, we are deflected from thoughts of this sport by the low camera angle, which eliminates any nautical details, as well as by the airbrushed masking and text, which divert the eye from the disorder under the boat. Other details leave many unanswered questions: Why are the other people looking at the painter and not the sign she points to? Why is her paint brush so small and clean? Why, in the original ad, is the paint on the glove a different color than the paint on the sign?

In this advertisement, the overt message is that vodka is consumed by young, wealthy, popular people and that the viewer can share in this lifestyle by obtaining a bottle of liquor. The fact that such a premise is illogical—as are many of the details depicted—becomes obvious under close scrutiny. In classroom discussion, as students visually excavate images, details are often discovered that the teacher has overlooked. For example, one student observed that "Ann" in

Figure 4.1. "SUEBILLANNJOE."

SUEBILLANNJOE sounds like "and," suggesting the erotic possibility of a *ménage à trois.* Some in the class found this a convincing inference, while for others it was "reaching." From a teacher's point of view, its validity is ultimately undeterminable, but the observation does have some rhetorical plausibility and was encouraged as a result of employing the methods central to the exercise.

In documentary photography, the aim might be regarded as more serious, for a picture may argue for social change or for increased awareness of a social problem. Of course, it is crucial for the photographer to communicate his or her meaning; however, the viewer soon learns that the intentions can become clear only when he or she can read the rhetorical codes.

For instance, in a photograph by Walker Evans taken in Alabama in 1936 (figure 4.2), we see a long row of white shoes followed by a dark pair at the end, lined up on a board under the word "SHINE," which has been carefully painted on the wall of a building. Many white shoes appear next to a single black pair. These shoes rest directly below the key term "shine," which functions both as a title and a

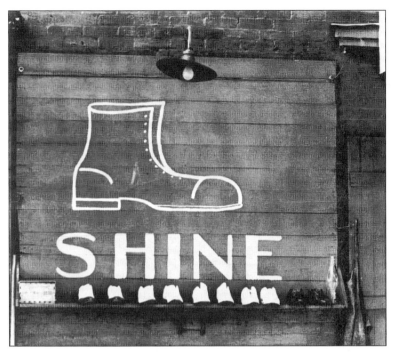

Figure 4.2. *Shoeshine Sign in a Southern Town*, Walker Evans, 1936.
© Estate of Walker Evans.

reminder of the likely race of the one who cleaned these objects. This creates a powerfully ironic allusion to racism.

Elsewhere, the Cherokee Chief Standing Deer, another member of a minority group, appears pictured in a mid-century postcard in bogus tribal regalia, bow in hand, standing beside a commercial archery target peppered by holes, none of which are close to the bull's eye. Every detail of the picture—from the inept archery, to the substitution of the target for game, to the inappropriate costume—functions to demean him. In this case, the rhetoric revealed is due to the viewer's skill, not the photographer's.

Communication also depends on audience. In the Evans photograph, for instance, the word "shine" has lost its derogatory intent for many viewers, who do not realize that the word was once a denigrating label for African Americans. But many in Evans's audience in the 1930s would have been familiar with this usage and would have understood how the picture merges the diction of racism with an example of its practice.

Similarly, in Jacob Riis's famous 1890s work *How the Other Half Lives,* the photographs and text were planned to raise the consciousness of middle- and upper-class New Yorkers who were ignorant of or indifferent to conditions in the tenements of the Lower East Side. Riis intended to shock these readers with indisputable statistics, brutal anecdotes, and graphic illustrations. Though the immigrants themselves did not read of babies suffocating or men living in coal bins, their descendants see and study this inhumanity in our classes today. Riis was striving to sensitize the wealthier people of his time, who were ignorant of the slum-dwellers' squalor, or who were indifferent because their visual experience of "the other half" included only the romanticized images that were often used to portray them.

In the carefully titled photograph *Ready for Sabbath Eve in a Coal Cellar, A Cobbler on Ludlow Street* (figure 4.3), Riis shocks us with the cobbler's degrading living conditions. The power and economy of the details that communicate this degradation, as well as a subtler, contrasting idea, are the photograph's main strengths. First we are struck by the grime of the place and the incongruity of household furnishings in such a setting. Our attention is quickly drawn to the man because his bright face emerges vividly from the darker background and because several linear elements lead to him. A few objects similar in size and shape to his face help to emphasize him and to pull our eye through the rest of the photograph: the hat over his head, the shiny metal container in the upper left, the objects on the table, the hanging coat, and the hands holding a shovel to the right.

As we begin to make inferences, constructing meaning from these details, students might protest that we are just "making it up" and that everyone's opinion will be different. We do not have to arrive at a certain truth, but we must arrive at a plausible tale, carefully based on what we see. More than one narrative may be convincing, but it is unlikely that many will. And one narrative—taking into account all of the elements seen and employing convincing inferences—will prevail.

In Riis's photograph, there is a common, household table, its turned legs in need of dusting. The scrap of oilcloth on the table is so filthy that many would hesitate to eat the glistening challah sitting on it. But a tablecloth hints at civility, as does the cobbler's coat, which is cleaner than his pants (similar in condition to the hanging jacket). Perhaps he put on his better garment for his Sabbath meal, or perhaps he wished to look his best in the photograph. In any case, the jacket, his good hat hanging overhead, and the relatively expensive challah suggest that hope and pride survive in this bleak situation. On the

Figure 4.3. *Ready for Sabbath Eve in a Coal Cellar, A Cobbler on Ludlow Street*, Jacob A. Riis, undated. The Jacob A. Riis Collection, #286, Museum of the City of New York.

table, another hat rests on a book, possibly a Siddur, both perhaps deposited as he returned from Shul. The function of the hanging container is unclear, but it brings our eye to the left side of the photo, where we see his shop sign. The sign is in; the work day is over. We see only one chair—perhaps he will eat alone. It is unclear if he will be joined by the person whose hands are on the shovel, who may be the janitor arrived to stoke the furnace. In any case, the tool shown as a fragment disrupts the scene's domesticity.

An interesting tension exists between the visual sophistication of the photograph and the gritty truth it portrays to the viewer. It seems as if Riis did nothing but record the facts as he encountered them. Even the moment of exposure seems to record a conversation taking place between the cobbler and someone off-camera. Only after students build a narrative based on careful observation does the rhetoric of the photograph seem obvious.

Point of view, or stance, is another central act of photography because it involves the careful selection of a viewpoint. In *Cartier-Bresson's France,* one of the scenes of Paris (figure 4.4) shows two lovers

Figure 4.4. *The Quays, Paris*, Henri Cartier-Bresson, 1970. Copyright Henri Cartier-Bresson/Magnum Photos; used by permission.

in the lower right-hand corner under an arch, which is part of a bridge over the Seine. The couple is a small part of the whole, but they are the center of interest, positioned so that the viewer's eye is led continually to them by the diagonals, the framing arch, and the contrasts in black and white.

In this photograph, Cartier-Bresson's vantage point allows him to simultaneously show the lovers as hidden and public. The couple is no larger than the more prosaic strollers who approach them unaware, but the photographer's (and viewer's) point of view invests the lovers with more meaning. The rhetorical complexity of this photograph becomes clear as we recall more conventional close-ups of lovers.

In two photographs of New York City, point of view creates completely different interpretations of the city. In one, *The Flatiron*, taken by Edward Steichen in 1904 (figure 4.5), the camera is placed at the exact point a person might enter the scene if he or she were walking toward the Flatiron Building. The soft focus is a rhetorical

Figure 4.5. *The Flatiron*, Edward J. Steichen, 1904. The Metropolitan Museum of Art, The Alfred Stieglitz Collection, 1933 (33.43.43). All rights reserved, The Metropolitan Museum of Art.

device that suggests reverie. Thus, Steichen seems to be inviting the observer in an appreciative, romantic stroll to join the other walkers.

On the other hand, in a photograph taken by Alfred Stieglitz from higher up (figure 4.6), there is no sense of being able to participate in the scene; rather, the city becomes an object for study. The sharp focus of the photograph and its high contrast, which eliminates visual information in the shadows, emphasize its more objective nature. Rather than suggesting subjectivity, the photograph becomes a design.

Point of view also determines the details shown: what is included or not included creates the viewer's impression of the subject, consciously or not. In his portrait of Georgia O'Keeffe (figure 4.7), Alfred Stieglitz emphasizes her face in the left half of the photograph against a plain, weathered door frame, which fills the right half. Our eye is first occupied with her calm expression, her slightly knit brow suggesting some preoccupation. Yet Stieglitz has structured the picture so that our eye is drawn to the texture of the wood. Given this structure, a student response that these elements were "just there" seems

Figure 4.6. *From an American Place, North,* Alfred Stieglitz, 1935. Alfred Stieglitz Collection, © 1994 Board of Trustees, National Gallery of Art, Washington, D.C.

Figure 4.7. *Georgia O'Keeffe,* Alfred Stieglitz, 1922. The Metropolitan Museum of Art, Gift of David A. Schulte, 1928 (28.127.3). All rights reserved, The Metropolitan Museum of Art.

inadequate. The objects in the photograph and the viewer's eye movement link O'Keeffe's makeup-free skin and expression to the enduring, unpainted wood.

This point becomes clearer when the Stieglitz photograph is compared to Bruce Davidson's photograph of Flossie Arlington (figure 4.8). Davidson's view of this elderly inhabitant of Georgia's coastal islands eliminates all background detail, letting the woman's grim expression and suffering eyes indicate his intention to convey misery. Any other viewpoint could include such details as the tropical beauty of the island or the minutiae of her home and possessions, detracting from our intense concentration on her face.

To the student's question of whether Stieglitz or Davidson intended this meaning, there are two answers. The first one states that a photograph may embody more complex ideas than positive or negative tropism on the part of the artist. Although one cannot tell from a single photograph, an analysis of several works by the same person will reveal a consistency that cannot be explained by chance.

Figure 4.8. *Flossie Arlington*, Bruce Davidson, 1973. Copyright Bruce Davidson/Magnum Photos; used by permission.

The second answer is that even if the inferred meaning was not intended, a photograph, like other cultural objects, can and should be examined. If the analysis takes into account all that can be seen, then what we have said, as far as we have been able to go, is what the photograph means. This also applies to implications that we may feel certain the photographer did not intend. In the earlier vodka ad (figure 4.1), we would not think that the photographer or art director would say directly that women, impetuous and lacking in skill, could not neatly paint the boat's name. Nonetheless, in our culture, many viewers would have thought it incongruous if Bill or Joe had been pictured as the inept painter.

Adopting a specific point of view is a technique. Usually, however, the term *technique* applies to the use of mechanical devices such as lighting and focus. Sometimes, light can be described as revealing, even democratic, in that it suggests that we are not being fooled, that our inferences are as direct and inevitable as the facts of a truthful scene before our eyes. In the first of the New York examples (figure 4.5), for instance, the light romanticizes and makes the street more attractive than in the other one (figure 4.6), which seems harsh by comparison.

But light has other uses. In a picture by Edward Weston (figure 4.9), a cabbage leaf emerging from darkness appears to possess a dramatic intensity heretofore hidden from us, more beautiful and worthy of our attention than we had thought.

We should stress that the interpretations suggested in these brief readings of photographs in no way exhaust the possibilities. We mean only to point out certain meanings that may be inferred from visual conventions of fairly well-established pedigree. As with literature, readers may debate subtler meanings.

We first began to use the rhetoric of photography in a college-wide writing across the curriculum project fifteen years ago. Required core courses were linked to classes in reading, writing, and the freshman seminar. Without knowing each other's disciplines or even each other very well, we designed our syllabi for "Introduction to Photography" and "Structures of Writing," a first-semester English class, to provide students with a complementary experience. We did so at first by including traditional expository types of writing—comparison/contrast, analysis, and argument—while using a textbook called *Here and Now II* (Morgan 1972), which pairs fiction and poetry with paintings and photographs. We included a number of parallel exercises, such as asking students to construct camera obscuras in photography

Figure 4.9. *Cabbage Leaf,* Edward Weston, 1931. © 1993 Center for Creative Photography, Arizona Board of Regents.

class and then to describe the process in their English class, asking students to compare and contrast photographs during a museum visit and then to analyze a poem and a film on the same subject as a composition assignment, and asking students to research a photographer for one teacher while learning how to prepare that research from the other.

As we became more experienced, we decided to use a work of photojournalism as the text in the writing class. We tried three different books in subsequent semesters: *Subsistence U.S.A.* (Hill and Davidson 1973), *Let Us Now Praise Famous Men* (Agee and Evans 1966), and *How the Other Half Lives* (Riis 1971). The last was the most successful and relevant because Riis appeals to students in many disciplines.

With *How the Other Half Lives* as our rhetoric, we developed a syllabus using photographs for prewriting exercises, for grammatical and mechanical review, and as subject matter for compositions. We used portions of the text to illustrate expository or grammatical principles and to provide subject matter for argument and research. Since Riis's book does not have a single narrative but is a collection of studies of different areas and ethnic groups, it can be used in segments, in any order. We organized the course in units, each consisting of a slide lecture where we introduce students to the concepts we want them to learn, a follow-up workshop to which class members bring their own photographs or pictures from magazines or elsewhere (to analyze orally or in groups according to guidelines we set), and a subsequent writing assignment and collaborative evaluation.

For example, in our unit on describing places, we analyze some of Riis's chapters that detail the Lower East Side. We then ask students to bring in photographs that show contrast, that have a vantage point that brings the viewer into the scene, that use one small detail to suggest the larger perspective of the place, or that indicate an important choice of detail. Groups are then asked to choose the picture they find most effective, to list everything they see in it, and to then write a brief, focused analysis of the picture. The following is an example of one student's photo (figure 4.10) and an excerpt from her analysis:

Excerpt from a Student's Analysis

The young man is relaxed, with his arm resting comfortably on his raised knee. He is viewing the far mountain range and valley from his vantage point "on top of the world". . . . The softness of the distant mountains implies that although this fearless young man drives a tough car, he is a lover of beauty and possibly a dreamer too, who is totally comfortable and at home in this atmosphere. Although his angled perch looks somewhat precarious, he is solidly in control, as reflected by his relaxed pose. The line of rocks that break through the top of the hill represents not only the Jeep's strength and solidity, but also that of the young driver.

Because oral work is also important for these prewriting sessions, in a later assignment, we have students present oral reports and receive feedback from others, comparing and contrasting the photographs and essay in a chapter of their choice before they complete their writing assignment or take photos themselves.

One of the most effective units is on logical fallacies. Riis often stereotyped immigrant groups, and some of his language can be studied to see how he uses vocabulary or includes certain information to sway the audience to his point of view. In this case, we draw a comparison with contemporary advertising and ask students to bring in ads that they feel illustrate familiar logical fallacies. In a collaborative workshop, groups of students are then asked to choose one ad from

Figure 4.10. Jeep ad selected for a student's analysis.

the group that best fulfills the assignment and to describe it in detail. Finally, they write letters to the ad's sponsor critiquing it.

In this unit, students move from personal response to critical thinking to composing. After each group's spokesperson presents the group's findings to the rest of the class, students write letters at home for the next class meeting. In an evaluation session, each group picks the letter that they decide is the most effective in describing the advertisement in detail and in arguing why they are offended by it. To help the groups respond with more candor, students are allowed to use fictitious names or preassigned numbers.

The assignments in the course progress from analyzing single objects to critiquing fiction, the latter tied in to the visual material by its thematic similarity. For example, Stephen Crane's *Maggie: A Girl of the Streets* (1896) and Willa Cather's "Neighbor Rosicky" (1930) complement *How the Other Half Lives* (Riis 1971), showing how observers can communicate the plight of immigrants through the mediums of fiction and journalism.

The advantage of these and other exercises is that by the end of the semester, students feel less intimidated by photographs than by other visual art because they know they can make or find photographs easily and can share experiences with their groups. This security helps students take the often difficult first step of finding a subject that has meaning and relevance for them.

Almost without exception, students bring in pictures that they have chosen thoughtfully. They quickly become better at finding unintended or overlooked meanings in snapshots or advertisements and are willing to give the attention necessary to discover the careful organization of information in the work of Riis and other skilled photographers. And as they begin to see better, they begin to think and write better.

Works Cited

Agee, James, and Walker Evans. 1966. *Let Us Now Praise Famous Men.* New York: Ballantine.

Hill, Carol, and Bruce Davidson. 1973. *Subsistence U.S.A.* New York: Holt, Rinehart and Winston.

Morgan, Fred. 1972. *Here and Now II: An Approach to Writing through Perception.* New York: Harcourt Brace Jovanovich.

Riis, Jacob. 1971. *How the Other Half Lives.* New York: Dover.

Additional Sources on Writing and Photography

Alinder, James, ed. 1980. *9 Critics, 9 Photographs.* Carmel, CA: Friends of Photography.

Barrow, Thomas F., Shelley Armitage, and William E. Tydenan, eds. 1982. *Reading into Photography: Selected Essays, 1959–1980.* Albuquerque: University of New Mexico Press.

Barthes, Roland. 1977. *Image, Music, Text.* New York: Hill and Wang.

Becker, Howard S. 1981. *Exploring Society Photographically.* Evanston, IL: Mary and Leigh Block Gallery, Northwestern University.

Berger, John. 1972. *Ways of Seeing.* London: BBC; Penguin.

Berger, Paul, Leroy Searle, and Douglas Wadden. 1983. *Idea Networks in Photography.* Seattle: Henry Art Gallery Association, University of Washington.

Burgin, Victor, ed. 1982. *Thinking Photography.* London: Macmillan.

Earle, Ed. 1979. *Points of View: The Stereograph in America—A Cultural History.* Rochester, NY: Visual Studies Workshop.

Goffman, Erving. 1979. *Gender Advertisements.* Cambridge: Harvard University Press.

Hicks, Wilson. 1973. *Words and Pictures.* New York: Arno Press.

Liebling, Jerome, ed. 1978. *Photography: Current Perspectives.* Boston: The Massachusetts Review; Rochester, NY: Light Impressions Corp.

5 Child Talk: Re-presenting Pictures in the Mind

Stevie Hoffman
University of Missouri–Columbia

What is a "grandmommy" to an eighteen-month-old child whose only connections to her grandmother for nearly a year have been those associated with the words "It's from Grandmommy" when telephone calls, cards, letters, or packages arrive from far away? What image has she created in her mind that gives meaning to the word?

We ascribe meaning to each thing around us: things have no meaning until we give them meaning, and then they are only what we mean them to be. So it was with my granddaughter, Emily. It was not until she and her parents returned home to the United States that we had opportunities to be together often enough for her to discover just who this "grandmommy" person really was.

In overhearing conversations between her mother and me, Emily came to know her mother as Amy and me as Mom. When Emily joined us, though, Amy became "Mommy." It was not long before two words merged, seeming to express a newly formulated image for Emily: this grandmother person was "Mom-mommy," a name created from personal and meaningful associations with two mothers—one her own "mommy" and the other her mother's "mom." Some months later, Emily's "Mom-mommy" became "Grandmommy," but the revision was of her own construction—her own image.

Michael Halliday (1978) might speak of this happening as a child "learning how to mean" through and with language. His belief is that in an exchange of meanings with more proficient language users, children try to make sense out of their world of people, places, things, and events—a process Frank Smith (1983) describes as building a theory of the world.

These notions parallel the constructivist's view of cognitive growth. According to Piaget (1964), children's development of knowledge is evidenced most clearly when they begin to substitute mental images for things and people not actually present and for events that have occurred or may occur and can translate these symbolic representations through and with language. Discovering what these images are and how they have developed reveals how children wrestle with their ideas and find words to represent them.

For years I have collected children's language stories—child-talk—that offer insights into the connections children make between previously constructed meanings and less familiar or new notions. Language stories like Emily's compel us to appreciate those pictures in children's minds that are shared with us only if we try to hear—and to see—as they do.

From this ever-enlarging collection of child-talk, I want to share a few of the language stories that, for me, give credence to the images of young meaning makers. Because the context of the situation is important to language-in-use—and, therefore, significant for the verbal expression of a child's image or images—I include each story's setting.

Constructing Knowledge, Building a Theory of the World: Pictures in a Child's Mind

Since moving to Missouri, my family and I spend as much time as possible at my beach condominium in Florida. During one of these sojourns in Florida, my daughter Ann and my three-year-old grandson Brad regularly drove from Gainesville after Ann's classes ended on Friday to spend weekends with me. On the last Friday of my vacation, though, they could not come until very late at night. We thus decided that I would drive to Gainesville on Friday morning and bring Brad to the beach, so that we might have one more day together.

About halfway to Crescent Beach is a McDonald's where we often stop for that quick, on-the-road Happy Meal, and this day was no exception. Brad and I got our hamburgers and milkshakes at the drive-through window and continued on our way, eating and drinking and talking as we drove along.

Upon my return to Missouri, I made my usual "I've-arrived-safely" call to Ann. Brad picked up the extension phone and asked, "Are you coming over to my house, Grandmom?" When I said that I couldn't because I was too far away, his response was, "Only a hamburger away."

It was apparent that he was making a connection with our stop at McDonald's on the way to the beach just a few days earlier, so I told him that I wasn't at my beach home but at my Missouri home. Brad was quiet for a moment, and then he said, "Oh, that's more than a hamburger away. You have to drive all day and night or fly in an airplane, don't you, Grandmom?"

For a young child who had previously experienced long trips to Missouri, as well as the more recent weekend drives to the beach, Brad's words reveal personally meaningful images to re-present distance (or time) from his house to mine. Clearly, "a hamburger away" trip is much closer than an "all day, all night" one.

Chickens, Clowns, and Kangaroos: Images in Child-Talk

The following language story grows out of the reconstruction of "Chicken Little" by one child who began to role-play the story she had just heard her teacher read. Leaving the playhouse area with a dress-up purse in one hand and a string bag in the other, Katie announced that "Chicken Little was going to the mall." Somewhat surprised by this comment, Mrs. Davis asked, "Why is she going to the mall, Katie?" To which the child replied, "To buy grain to make bread."

It was apparent that "going to the mill" had been translated and connected to a familiar experience: going shopping at the mall. A mental image of a mill did not exist for this city child; nor did grinding grain for bread make any meaning. But going to the mall to shop could include buying bread. For Katie, this made sense. For her teacher and me, it was a child making meaning, re-presenting an image.

Associations made by children between familiar ideas and new notions are exemplified by the questions they raise and the comments they make. Recently, I heard this story from another teacher. Five-year-old Chris's father is a marine who, in conversations with his wife, often shares what happened at work. In the course of one such husband-wife dialogue, Chris asked, "When are you going to take me to the marine circus, Daddy?" Puzzled, his father answered, "Marine circus? The marines don't have a circus, Chris. What made you think that?" The child responded, "Well, you just said that you work with a bunch of clowns, Daddy." One word—clowns—implied a very different image to Chris than it did to his father.

Sometimes, information is just too novel and unrelated to what children know for them to make the connections that adults may expect. Such was the case for the youngsters in this next language story, told to me by a Head Start teacher. It was the day to introduce "-er" words to that group of four-year-olds. At least, that was what the programmed "reading readiness" materials said to do. Following the script in the instructional manual, the teacher began: "We call someone who walks a walker. We call someone who sleeps a sleeper. What do we call someone who jumps?"

Tommy quickly provided an answer: "A kangaroo!" The other children nodded their heads in agreement and clapped their hands as Tommy demonstrated a kangaroo's jump all around the room. And why not? It made sense to Tommy, just as it apparently did to his classmates.

Certainly the concept of "-er" words was too novel for new meanings to be constructed by these children. Furthermore, "-er" words do not make pictures in the mind very easily. Television cartoons, Discovery Channel programs, or illustrations in a book may well have provoked an image of "someone who jumps"—a kangaroo! Things are nothing until we make them something.

Electric Oranges and Holy Squirrels: When Images and Words Conflict

Children often rely on their peers to provide that piece of information needed to help them wrestle with a new notion, as one can hear in this next language story. Bill and Jimmy were sitting on pillows in the book area of their pre-kindergarten classroom, browsing through picture book after picture book, until Bill tapped Jim's arm and asked, "What do we get juice from?"

"An orange," Jimmy answered without taking his eyes off his book. After all, it was a pretty easy question with an obvious answer.

"Oh," Bill responded, "that's where electricity comes from!" Jimmy turned to his friend with a perplexed look. Bill explained, "You know, juice—electricity juice."

There's little doubt that both boys knew about orange juice. But Bill wanted help with picturing where one gets a very different kind of juice. Not knowing his friend's agenda, Jim answered with a logical statement of fact. What is interesting is that the concept of an orange producing juice seemed to present no contradiction in imaging for Bill at the time. At least, his willing acceptance of Jim's information gave no hint of image conflict. Bill instantly made the image fit Jim's information, demonstrating that quicksilver ability children have to mediate between the verbal and the visual cues available to them. I still wonder, though, if Bill pictured that electricity juice being squeezed from an orange or zigzagging out from its skin.

Jerome Harste of Indiana University tells a story, "Holy Squirrel," that shows how the context of a situation can cause conflict in the images children have already created. Jerry's nephew, who was studying to become a minister, gave the children's sermon at a small church one Sunday under the scrutiny of an experienced mentor. Gathering all of the children together at the front of the church, he nervously began: "I'm thinking of something that is small and brown and runs up trees. Tell me what you think that might be."

There was complete silence. He elaborated on his description: "This little creature has a bushy tail and carries nuts in his mouth. Now, what do you think it might be?" Still there was silence—that kind of "no response" that makes the fledgling presenter most uncomfortable. "Can't anyone tell me what I'm thinking of?"

One little fellow, Tim, raised his hand tentatively. With prompt and eager encouragement from the speaker, Tim said, "Well, ordinarily I'd say it was a squirrel, but I think you want us to say Jesus."

Here, the context and the questions did not match. The description of a bushy-tailed creature, skittering up a tree with nuts in its mouth, undoubtedly made a match with Tim's image of a squirrel. They were not outside, though; they were in church. And in church, one talks about Jesus, not squirrels.

Jerry's language story seems to illustrate Eleanor Duckworth's notion (1987) that we often make other people's words fit into what we are thinking:

> Words that people hear—and the younger the child is, the stronger the case—are taken into some thoughts that are already in their minds, and those thoughts may not be the ones the speaker has in mind. (22)

One hears this mismatch between the child's expectations and the speaker's intention in Tim's response to the novice minister. And yet, we are aware from the child's own words that he tried to incorporate someone else's ideas into the images he had created for himself from prior experiences. Duckworth explains:

> [A good understander of explanations is] aware that [his or her] first interpretation of what is being said may not be the right one, and keeps making guesses about what other interpretations are possible. (22)

In this story, the words of the adult created an image for the young boy that confused him because of the context in which they were spoken and heard. Images did not change for Tim, although he was uncertain that an appropriate match had been made. Here, the immediate setting and context—the pulpit, the long pews, the stained glass windows, a minister speaking—may have become an "overpowering" image itself, one that rivaled the child's initially logical image of squirrels.

Words from someone else may, of course, help a child make new connections when a way has been suggested. The connections, however, must be a personal extension of the child. In other words, the elaboration revises or creates new imagery the child's way. This seems to be the case in this last language story that I want to share—one more from the grandmother/grandchild file.

New Grandmoms and Snow Juice: When Words Create New Images

When my older daughter entered graduate school, she and Brad joined me in Missouri. Two afternoons each week, I picked Brad up at his child care center because Ann was in class. One day, Brad noticed a small yellow bus as we were driving toward home: "Look, Grandmom, there's my school bus."

Supporting the association he had just made and offering new data to extend his existing idea, I responded, "You're right, Brad. That does look like your school bus. However, it's a special kind of bus that takes old people—you know, grandmas and grandpas who don't drive any more—to the library, or the doctor's office, or the grocery store."

Brad was quiet for awhile. Then he said, "That's nice, isn't it?" I assured him that, indeed, it was a nice way to help others. In the rearview mirror, I saw a thoughtful expression on his face—you know, that furrowed-brow look. Gradually, a smile appeared and I heard him say, "You must be a new grandmom 'cuz you drive a car. Isn't that right, Grandmom?" How could I have disagreed with that interpretation?

Gordon Wells (1986) suggests the importance of this dialogue when he describes children as meaning makers, using language to learn: "We can discover the nature of the knowledge [children] must possess, and from that we can draw conclusions about the workings of [their] minds" when we listen to child-talk. So, too, I believe that children create pictures in their minds from significant personal experiences and use language to construct meaning from those interrelated images, especially when revision appears necessary to them.

Where do these significant experiences come from? We can answer with the obvious: from their world of people, places, events, and things; from the words, songs, poems, books, and pictures of others; from television and videotapes played and replayed. And in re-presenting this experience through their images, we have to remember, simply, the unique perspective of any child, who, as Nelms (1989) writes, "sees the world as no one has ever seen it before—because no one has ever been us, trusting our own vision, clarifying it, valuing it, writing it or telling it or saying it aloud to someone who cares."

Perhaps in going "where no one has ever been" and seeing the world "as no one has ever seen it," children create their own personal images—not reproductions of others. Perhaps they construct and present their own meanings, often quite different from those of adults. Perhaps they re-present these images and meanings with words that, like Humpty Dumpty remarked, "mean just what I choose them to mean."

We hear this in children's use of metaphors: "snow juice" for melted snow, "housecar" for mobile home, "hair getting old" for grey hair. My favorite one comes from a "getting-ready-for-bed" conversation. Going into the bedroom, this young boy reminded his mother, "Put the light on first. I like it because it lights me up in the head." When the mother asked, "What happens when the lights go off?" his response was, "I get dark in my head and then I can't think."

Children do have images to be shared, ideas to be expressed, stories to be told. As I share some of these pictures from the minds of young children, I realize their contribution to my understanding of children's thinking. Because of the powerful images in each one, these stories do not fade with time, nor do they become any less important in their meanings. Perhaps my language stories from children are like so many other stories. As Hughes Moir (1989) reminds us, what really matters is "what is left after the story is over, what I carry away with me."

Works Cited

Duckworth, Eleanor. 1987. *The Having of Wonderful Ideas and Other Essays on Teaching and Learning*. New York: Teachers College Press.

Halliday, Michael K. 1978. *Language as a Social Semiotic: The Social Interpretations of Language and Meaning*. Baltimore: University Park Press.

Moir, Hughes. 1989. "I've Got a Story to Tell!" In *Learning from the Inside Out: The Expressive Arts,* edited by Stevie Hoffman and Linda Leonard Lamme, 86–92. Wheaton, MD: Association for Childhood Education International.

Nelms, Ben. 1989. "Discovering the 'Giftedness' in Us All: Books for Divergent Thinking." In *Learning from the Inside Out: The Expressive Arts,* edited by Stevie Hoffman and Linda Leonard Lamme, 7–21. Wheaton, MD: Association for Childhood Education International.

Piaget, Jean. 1964. "Development and Learning." In *Piaget Rediscovered: A Report on the Conference on Cognitive Studies and Curriculum Development, March 1964,* edited by Richard E. Ripple and Verne N. Rockcastle, 7–20. University of California, Berkeley; Cornell University.

Smith, Frank. 1983. *Essays into Literacy.* Exeter, NH: Heinemann Educational Books.

Wells, Gordon. 1986. *The Meaning Makers: Children Learning Language and Using Language to Learn.* Portsmouth, NH: Heinemann Educational Books.

II Images in Media

6 Where We Live

Roy F. Fox
University of Missouri–Columbia

A plant in Fernald, Ohio, displays red and white checkerboards on its water towers and a sign that reads "Feed Materials Production Center." A television commercial shows a state legislature candidate walking around the statehouse, while the voice-over urges voters to give this man a chance to continue his work.

But something is wrong with these "pictures," these symbols. The plant in Ohio doesn't make dog food or cat chow. It's a uranium processing plant. According to the *New York Times* (8 February 1990, A1, B8), the Department of Energy acknowledged that for years this plant emitted radiation in quantities known to harm people, burying thirteen tons of nuclear waste and poisoning the groundwater. Although no "real" lie is told, the sign's vague phrasing and the Purina-like checkerboard mislead us.

In the televison commercial, the candidate strolling through the legislature had been out of office for two years before the commercial was made (*Idaho Statesman*, 29 September 1990, 4A). Most voters clearly saw an incumbent asking to "continue" his job. Again, no real lies are told: the ad never says that the candidate is an incumbent; it just uses the word "continue" with old film footage.

This is *symbolspeak*—the use of symbols to distort reality *slightly* to mislead *a little bit* (and sometimes, even to lie). Although symbolspeak involves language and other symbols, its main component is the image, for it, too, is a symbol—an abstraction of reality selected and crafted by someone else. Symbolspeak is composed of images that often function in a Jekyll-Hyde way. On the one hand, images are convincing: we look, and what we see is what we believe. On the other hand, images are intrinsically ambiguous. Jung (1971) refers to images as "true symbols" because they are the "best possible expressions for something unknown—bridges thrown out towards an unseen shore" (815). This two-faced nature of images, then, makes symbolspeak a camouflaged beast in a dense jungle.

Although symbolspeak can communicate obvious truths or outright lies, it seldom does. Sontag (1978) notes that photographs—our most common form of imagery—have a flattening effect, making everything appear to be of equal value, which in turn "contributes to an erosion of meaning, to a parcelling out of truths into relative truths" (87). Symbolspeak, then, is the art of suggesting—not directly communicating—these "relative truths." Because symbolspeak is laden with imagery, it is the ultimate tool of nuance and conceptual seed-planting: the intimation, the wispy hint, the soft suggestion, some shade of an idea or truth, some related or comparable truth.

Hence, symbolspeak is more concerned with the overall effect than with specific meanings. Most important, when we experience such overall effects, we feel like we have internally participated in a transaction of sorts. These symbolic transactions, or "internal movements," are central to symbolspeak. Today, internal movements are as common as physical labor was a century ago. We hunger for and seek out these internal experiences with images because they allow us to mentally exercise closer to actual reality, closer to our imaginative stream.

Symbolspeak results from the skillfully manipulated ambiguity of images, for which we are easy prey. Words and phrases such as "insight," "foresight," "hindsight," and "I see what you mean" reveal how language has conditioned us to accept and trust what we see (Bronowski 1978). Second, when we encounter imagery, we feel like we are constructing our own meaning—and we often are, because the diversity of mass audiences requires senders to create messages with many meanings, a surplus of meaning. At the same time, though, the images and context can limit the acceptable range of responses. Our perceptions and experiences shape our visual imagery, which in turn molds our perceptions and experiences. Finally, symbolspeak thrives in a world of information overload, where multiple mediums and channels release endless streams of images. To mentally survive, we have had to depend more and more on a type of thinking that is imagistic, associational, intuitive, quicksilvery. Although cynics would call this type of thinking "fast and easy" (or *McThinking*), it is not a watered-down version of good old-fashioned linear, verbal thinking. Instead, it differs mainly in type. The point, though, is this: in order to penetrate such jaded psyches, messages increasingly demand that we participate in them. Most of all, this participation requires images and emotion.

This chapter describes four levels of symbolspeak: verbal, verbal-with-visual, visual-with-verbal, and visual. Images increasingly dominate each level. The first level, verbal symbolspeak, is primarily composed of imageless language (although images play definite roles). At the opposite end of the spectrum, visual symbolspeak consists entirely of images. At each level, emotion plays a larger role as we become more personally involved with the message. In the verbal levels we tend to be more distanced observers, while in the visual levels we are more emotionally involved participants who actively "enter into" the messages. Here, of course, our sense of right and wrong becomes harder to fathom.

Verbal Symbolspeak

This category, a common form of doublespeak, is relatively free of images, such as metaphors and similes. For example, during the 1980 presidential campaign, Ronald Reagan claimed that General Motors employed 23,000 full-time employees to handle the paperwork required by the government, while General Motors itself stated that only 4,900 of its employees accomplished all of its paperwork (Lutz 1989). Reagan's verbal symbolspeak occurred in single episodes. But verbal symbolspeak can also occur in several episodes over time, as with the language used by the nuclear power industry before, during, and after the accident at Three Mile Island (Lutz 1989, 258).

Messages in this category are not dominated by external or physical images, music, or sound; instead, we usually experience them as "unadulterated" language by reading or hearing about them. If Reagan's "abstract" lines about employees had been delivered on television, with a crowded office in the background, then this message would have been even more imagistically potent (and it would therefore be in a different category).

Just because verbal symbolspeak deals with relatively "imageless" language, though, don't assume that images are not involved. They are. Research in several disciplines shows that thinking depends upon both verbal and visual processes that cannot be separated (Paivio 1986; Kaufmann 1980; Kosslyn 1983; Begg 1983). Verbal symbolspeak, then, employs relatively abstract language; Reagan's statement is propositional (even numerical) and thus easier to track down and verify. But the fact remains that Reagan's language here requires imagistic processes for him (or someone else) to create as well as for us to understand. Indeed, Reagan's "imageless" statement about 23,000 employees may have elicited images in the minds of many people. Therefore, language that *appears* to be devoid of images may in fact rely on them heavily, both in the creation of the message and in our understanding of it.

Verbal-with-Visual Symbolspeak

At this level, words dominate the message, but they are marshalled to suggest a picture. Such verbal images are often referred to as "zingers" or "sound bites." Although they are honed for television, it is the verbal line, laced with carefully selected, supercharged imagery, that catches fire. When these messages succeed, they can galvanize public opinion. (If you don't believe me, just "read my lips.")

Like the other types of symbolspeak, these messages can instantly evoke multiple scenes in the minds of listeners. Imagine the profusion of images and language evoked by then-Senator Lloyd Bentsen's retort to Dan Quayle: "You're no Jack Kennedy!" Because these messages seem to appear so quickly and without warning, we seldom examine their meanings. While mainly visual, they also tap into other senses: Reagan did not want to "*pick* on a cripple" (Dukakis), and Bush's "read my lips" taps our senses of hearing and seeing, while his "thousand points of light" are also there to touch.

Also, employing only the essential persons or ideas, these messages visually depict or suggest one element *in relation to another* in space, time, or value: Bush, as a "lapdog," cuddles up on Reagan's lap; Reagan, who won't "pick on a cripple," is the dominant, vertical person who avoids the wheelchair-bound or horizontal Dukakis, while the elder Bentsen is the father, positioning JFK, the good son, directly above Quayle, the weaker son. Zingers and sound bites, though, are like bees; they sting only once.

Visual-with-Verbal Symbolspeak

This type of message employs both language and external images, although images dominate. Typical examples include magazine covers and advertisements (single episodes), where images usually outweigh the words. Also included here are television programs, debates, and commercials, where verbal and visual text may appear in closer balance. Still, the visual elements often exert the most influence over receivers. Because these genres involve cutting from one view or camera angle to another, they are considered multiple episodes.

Because this level of symbolspeak involves external images and relies less on language, it is less explicit and more suggestive of multiple meanings than the previous types. This ambiguity enables us to feel like we are participating more in the meaning making. Makers of such messages desire some uncertainty: they do not state directly what they want us to believe, but rather suggest it through visual elements and their interplay with verbal elements.

Figures 6.1 and 6.2 illustrate such visual/verbal interplay, though to varying degrees. The May 26, 1975, *Newsweek* cover (figure 6.1) interprets America's rescue of the ship Mayaguez. A single image dramatizes the event. This whole-page image interacts with the verbal text, but only minimally: "The Rescue" tells readers it *is* a real rescue—not an exercise or maneuver or routine mission, but a recovery of something stolen or lost. Also, we are told it is *the* rescue—unquestionably unique in its achievement and glory. The image, however, packs the greatest wallop. Overall, the style and execution of this illustration is much more reminiscent of World War II than it is of the Vietnam War, which was a bad and very fresh memory in 1975. Indeed, those little soldiers could be John Wayne and Lloyd Nolan sailing to the sands of Iwo Jima. We observe this action from a low vantage point; we have to look upward at the huge ships, waving infantrymen, and buzzing planes and helicopters, which even slice into the *Newsweek* nameplate.

Figure 6.1. Cover of *Newsweek*, May 26, 1975. © 1975 Newsweek, Inc. All rights reserved. Reprinted by permission.

Figure 6.2. Atlanta's "most interesting parts."

The dominating reds and oranges traditionally suggest action and violence, as they do here. Also, these colors and shapes "fight" each other: the hard, angular lines of the ship jut into, or oppose, the shapeless, massive orange sky. Overall, this illustration effectively communicates more than what many verbal accounts did: the event was good old-fashioned, heroic, bold action; America was on the move and in control.

Figure 6.2 relies more on the interplay between verbal and visual elements than does the *Newsweek* cover. The lower half of this striking ad is bright red. Spiked heels glisten gold. From the horizon, the pink sky fades to yellow. It is dusk. The black skyline sparkles with lights. For many readers, I'm afraid, the tall, narrow building in the center points to Atlanta's "most interesting parts." The individual elements of this ad—legs, skyline, color, and a simple sentence—are not, by themselves, objectionable. But in combination, they create a subtext that becomes the primary message. Here, the interplay between text and images communicates something that could not be stated directly in language.

When verbal and visual elements occur in more or less equal amounts in film, the interplay occurs more rapidly, affecting us in subtler ways. Visual elements can even overpower the verbal ones, often without our noticing. For instance, Morello (1988) studied the 1984 Mondale-Reagan televised debates, focusing on the interaction between the "visual structuring" of the film and the verbal arguments. His research examined four "points of clash"—those segments when the camera switches back and forth to record actions and reactions, when candidates often employ second or third person ("You said" or "Mr. Reagan stated that"). In many segments, the verbal arguments were inconclusive. In tracing back verbal charges and countercharges, Morello sometimes could not tell who was ultimately most correct. Yet the visual structuring or editing of these segments made it *look* as if one candidate came out clearly on top, even when he appeared, in the analysis of verbal language, to lose or tie with his opponent.

For example, one debate segment involves Mondale accusing Reagan of giving Star Wars technology to the Soviets. The camera shows Reagan's facial expressions as he reacts. When Reagan refutes Mondale's charge, Reagan is in the foreground, as well as the highest image on the screen. Also, when Reagan denies this charge by shaking his head no, he is again the highest image on the screen. Which image is in the foreground, which image is highest on the screen, and which image is on the left determine which image dominates (Wurtzel 1983). Even though Morello could not track down the truth about whether Reagan actually gave away this technology, the images—not the verbal exchanges—clearly gave the impression that Reagan successfully countered Mondale. What's most important, Morello concludes, is that "judgments of winners and losers may rest on factors having little to do with what the candidates said or did and more to do with what television shots occurred" (287).

Visual Symbolspeak

Because this level of symbolspeak employs only images, it contains the most ambiguity, and hence requires the most internal participation by viewers. As with the previous level, though, situations and images can be structured so that, although no direct lies are told, we often interpret the symbols in ways desired by the image makers.

Consider the following example of purely visual symbolspeak. The logo for the National Wetlands Coalition (figure 6.3) depicts one of God's winged creatures flying over a marsh. Drawn with fluid, blue

Figure 6.3. Logo of the National Wetlands Coalition.

lines, the duck silently glides upward. Behind it, marsh grass and cattails waft in the breeze as a huge orange sun unifies marsh with bird, land with life. For most viewers, this image creates an impression of concern, respect, and protection for nature. But a partial (and representative) list of this organization's members suggests otherwise: Exxon Company, U.S.A.; Berry Brothers General Contractors, Inc.; Badger Mining Corporation; International Council of Shopping Centers; Louisiana Land and Exploration Company; the Phillips Petroleum Company. According to the *New York Times* (3 August 1991, A1), the organization represented by this logo urged President Bush to redefine the term *wetland*—a change that would have reduced protected wetlands by one-third. But of course, this is only a picture, so no lies are told.

The power of visual messages resides in five principles. First, as noted earlier, perceiving (largely seeing) and thinking are much the same thing. Second, images are the most effective and efficient vehicle to elicit emotion. Third, heavily visual messages "transform" mundane experiences into something out of the ordinary, mainly through emotion. Fourth, emotional transformations are often achieved by using a sequence of cool-to-warm images. Fifth, a visual message's hyperintertextuality, ambiguity, and incongruity contribute to these emotional transformations.

Emotion: The Main Ingredient of Visual Symbolspeak

Over twenty years ago, the Federal Trade Commission began cracking down on false advertising claims—a trend that drove many advertisers and others toward images and away from verbal claims that could be tested. In doing so, image makers learned a simple truth: that emotion based in physiological arousal is often responsible for motivating and sustaining activity. This embracing of images continues because image makers have learned (and demonstrated) that we mainly think by perceiving and that much of perception is visual in nature. Brand (1989) articulates this link between images and emotion, noting how language and thought become increasingly compressed and abbreviated. As our thinking sheds more of the form and sheer bulk of language, we in turn "gain in substance—that is, images and connotation"—a form of "pure meaning [that] is so richly endowed with images and connotation that it is saturated with emotion" (28). Hence, emotion—not logic, words, or numbers—is the key ingredient of symbolspeak.

Perception, of course, is neutral and innocent: we can usually steer our perceptions in any direction—toward rationality, inquiry, or simple appreciation. This is what good teachers help us do. But professional image makers milk perception for emotion. They care little about logic, proof, or argument and instead focus exclusively on values, attitudes, feelings, sensations, passions, and sentiments. And the golden key that unlocks each of these chambers is emotion. Edell (1990) even states that emotions are "the basis for most decisions," serving as our reason for making judgments in the first place. She further notes that emotions may distract us from attending to logic, thereby limiting the number of rational options we would normally weigh (xiv). And an experienced ad agency practitioner states that "agencies are almost unanimously consistent in their belief that emotions are important—positively important—to the persuasion process" (Agres 1990).

Although "feeling ads" do not yet dominate the media, the trend in advertising research is clearly toward unraveling the syntax of emotion. Instead of testing the effects of an ad's verbal, statistical, or "rational" information, theory-building and empirical studies increasingly focus on emotion. Edell (1990) writes:

> A growing body of mood research suggests that feelings can change the nature of cognitive processing [such as] . . . risk-taking behavior, decision-making strategies, recall speed, and evaluations of many kinds (Isen, Johnson, Mertz, and Robinson, 1985; Isen and Means, 1983; Johnson and Tversky, 1983). . . . The emotional reactions one has in response to an ad may influence what gets activated from memory. (xiv)

Such research has progressed to the point that most investigators no longer study the impact of general emotions, but now focus upon specific emotions and how one interacts with another. Take warmth, for example. Aaker and Stayman (1990) define warmth as a "positive, mild, volatile emotion involving physiological arousal and precipitated by experiencing directly or vicariously a love, family, or friendship relationship" (54). Using a "warmth monitor," these researchers concluded that warmth correlated at .67 with their subjects' galvanic skin responses while watching four warm commercials. In an earlier study, Aaker, Stayman, and Hagerty (1986) found significant changes in "felt warmth" within seven to fifteen seconds, concluding that "feelings can be generated and changed within a single commercial, even a 30-second commercial and probably within a 15-second commercial" (56). Generating and changing feelings in fifteen seconds? No problem. We'll just "undergo transformation."

Emotional Experiences "Transform" Viewers

Visual symbolspeak, epitomized in the transformational ad, tries to give us an experience that differs from what we would normally expect on using a product. After all, swallowing a soft drink is an inherently dull experience. So image makers enhance the activity with images, such as drinking icy Pepsi while sailing with friends on a bright, blue ocean. Consuming a beverage becomes an active, internal journey, entered through the door of images.

Visual symbolspeak partly depends on the unconscious, employing images that work as "bridges" toward something we do not know. Hence, a picture involving few or no words provides the best way to know the unknown, because we believe we are looking right at it. If we can see it, we understand it. Pictures provide us a concrete bridge to step out onto, so that we can view that "unseen shore," or what is inside of us. This little stroll out onto the bridge is the active, internal experience—that participation and transformation so central to visual messages. And it doesn't matter whether we ever find that "unseen shore" which beckons us, because the important thing is the experience of trying. Emotional ads accomplish this work more or less automatically. Puto and Hoyer (1990) note:

> It is not necessary for the consumer consciously to connect the effect with the advertisement or even to be aware of having been exposed to the advertisement. . . . There is ample evidence to suggest that considerable processing occurs below the level of conscious processing (e.g., Hasher and Zacks 1979; Kihlstrom 1990; Lewicki 1986). (71–72)

Rather than depending on ads that require us to recall specific information, the "automatic" nature of transformational ads is tailor-made for an environment so awash in images that we couldn't recall specific brand information if we wanted to. While admitting that transformational ads are a type of persuasion, Puto and Hoyer try to distinguish between persuasion and transformation: "Individuals acquiesce to persuasion; they undergo transformation" (72).

These emotional messages—the transformations that we "undergo"—rely most heavily on images. Because advertisements often occur in a visual medium, researchers follow suit and conduct their research with visual images. And they do so with good reason, since research studies directly link the perception and expression of emotion with images (Bryden and Ley 1983). Supporting elements of sound, language, and music also create images, especially when expertly synthesized with visual imagery—all resulting in a hefty image dose indeed.

Because we undergo so many of these emotional transformations through images, I want to focus on a few elements that allow them to succeed, especially cool-to-warm images and incongruity. Two magazine ads (figures 6.4–6.11) illustrate these principles of visual symbolspeak with multiple episodes. Each ad consists of several full-page images, with little verbal text (only the product's name). These messages are akin to the television commercial, documentary clip, or program segment that employs just film footage and music.

The three photos in figures 6.4, 6.5, and 6.6 appeared in this same sequence in the March 1992 issue of *Vanity Fair* as double-page ads. The burning car, the immigrants climbing aboard the ship, and the dying AIDS patient are three parts of a single ad from Benetton, a company that invested eighty million dollars in this campaign of news photos to promote its spring and summer clothes (*Columbia Daily Tribune,* 14 February 1992, 7A). No language appears with these images, only the company logo, "United Colors of Benetton," and, under that, a statement about the new catalog and a number to call for

Figure 6.4. Benetton ad, first image: flaming car.

Figure 6.5. Benetton ad, second image: refugees.

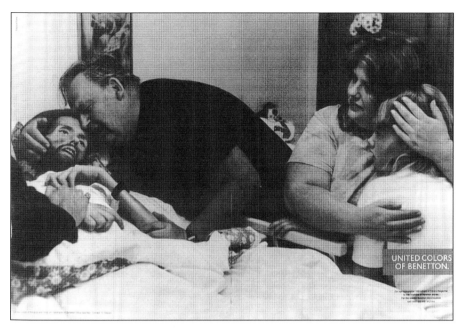

Figure 6.6. Benetton ad, final image: dying AIDS patient.

information. (A spokesperson for this firm states that these are not ads, but "corporate communications.")

The next ad (figures 6.7–6.11) appeared in the same *Vanity Fair* issue (March 1992). These five photos, in this sequence, constitute one message. The first and last photos (figures 6.7 and 6.11) appeared on single pages, while each of the middle photos (figures 6.8, 6.9, and 6.10) consumed a double-page.

Cool-to-Warm Images Transform Our Emotions

A series of images shows the influence of video on print advertising. It is easy to view such multiple images as a film (or as a dream), filling in missing scenes with little effort, providing our own links, actively investing ourselves into the scenario. Because image makers know that meaning is personally constructed, they allow room or ambiguity for each of us to enter into the message and make our own transformation. Also, a series of images often creates a sense of conflict, as images of one kind bump into images of another kind, creating something different in the process.

We can begin to understand a series of images by examining their sequence for warmth—the degree to which each image depicts or

Figure 6.7. Donna Karan ad, first image.

Figure 6.8. Donna Karan ad, second image.

Figure 6.9. Donna Karan ad, third image.

Figure 6.10. Donna Karan ad, fourth image.

Figure 6.11. Donna Karan ad, final image.

evokes responses we normally reserve for family, friends, and other loved ones. For example, we could ask, "Do the images begin with warm ones and proceed to unwarm or cool ones? Or do they begin with cool images and end with warm ones?" Cool to warm is the most common pattern, so that is what I will focus on here. As our culture becomes increasingly visual, single messages formed by a series of images will likely become more common. Hence, whether you consider the sequencing *within* a single message, as I will do here, or the sequencing *between* several messages, the direction of emotions (cool-to-warm, sad-to-happy, etc.) is fundamental.

Across several messages or within just one, contrast—the most basic form of incongruity—is important. Warm commercials are more effective if they occur after a cool commercial or cool segment of a program (Aaker, Stayman, and Hagerty 1986). Conversely, a warm commercial, say, following a warm scene from "The Cosby Show" would be less effective (56). Both messages here (figures 6.4–6.6 and 6.7–6.11) begin with cool images and move to warm ones, allowing us to participate in the warming, to "undergo" the transformation.

The flaming car (figure 6.4) is a non-warm or cool image. It communicates destruction and death—not the love, family, or friendship that characterizes warm images. As the first image in the series, the orange flames contrasting with the dark, urban streets somewhat arouse us. But we see no people, no faces of those who could be family or friends, so we are a little agitated but remain detached, viewing the scene from an emotional and physical distance—like seeing it on the evening news. In this context, the burning car even suggests an act of terrorism, coldly premeditated. Personally uninvolved, we merely begin to inch toward emotion and warmth.

The second image of people clambering aboard a ship (figure 6.5) is also a cool image, but slightly less so than the car. This second image conveys disenfranchisement, poverty, and the struggle to survive—again, not the images of love, family, or friendship found in warm messages. We are still viewing from afar, seeing boat people—foreigners—on the evening news. Also, this image is cool because we do not see individual people, just the faceless, foreign masses.

At the same time, though, this image moves us another step closer to warm emotions: unlike the previous burning car, where we can only imagine, not see, the victim, this image depicts people threatened, however faceless and foreign. While eliciting an essentially cool, detached response, we at least see people—people we *could* more easily associate with the warmth of friends, family, or loved ones. This image, then, brings us nearer to warm emotions but stops.

Compared to the two images preceding it, the final double-page photo of the grieving family huddled around the dying AIDS patient (figure 6.6) is highly emotional and warm, pulling impassioned strings attached to love, family, and friends. The human connections only hinted at in the burning car photo and more strongly suggested in the boat people image now hit us full blast. The angle of the older man's back and of the other people's hands and arms—including the patient's, as well as those in the religious painting on the wall—lead our eyes to the dying man's face and the person embracing him. These people, obviously close to each other, could easily be us. With a close-up shot, we are made to see this image *not* as a detached viewer of the evening news, but as another member of the family, closing around the hospital bed. The hand extending from the foreground, grasping the patient's hand, could be our own.

In three images, we undergo a transformation: from far-away to up-close; from impersonal to personal; from relative equilibrium to disequilibrium; from an absence of people, to faceless foreigners, to a family like ours. We move from observers to members of a family, silenced and encased in a private moment of grief. In only three images, we move from cool to warm emotions.

However exploitative this ad may be, it effectively illustrates transformational advertising because it provides us with an experience that differs from the ordinary, everyday experience of buying and wearing a Benetton sweater. And this internal experience is the kind that hits closest to home, closest to the heart of our emotional lives.

The five black-and-white images in figures 6.7–6.11 also proceed from cool to warm. In the first four images (figures 6.7–6.10), we see an attractive, poised, successful political candidate, probably running for president. We see her confidently making a speech, riding in an open car during a confetti-strewn parade, networking on the telephones, and taking the oath of office. The first three illustrations are cool images: we feel no reason to associate her with friends, family, or other loved ones because she is eminently independent, successful, ambitious, maybe even hard-edged.

By the fourth illustration (figure 6.10), the high-voltage action stops because she has accomplished her goal. And we pause with her as she contemplates the serious responsibilities ahead, solemnized in taking the oath of office. This is the first time we really empathize with her, but we are only a little warmer. As in the Benetton ad, the final illustration (figure 6.11) is the warmest. Here we realize that she is not a mover and shaker after all, but like many of us, only a moist-eyed dreamer. She is not the commander-in-chief at all, but maybe a secretary or a clerk. In this interpretation, the image maker wants us to see a "little woman with big dreams" so that we can identify with her or sympathize with her.

In these five images, we undergo a transformation, moving from observers to participants, from haves to have-nots, from cool to warm emotions. Here again, we are made to view the first four illustrations as uninvolved watchers of a television documentary. The first four illustrations are stock campaign images—the victory sign, the parade, the wheeling and dealing, the oath taking. These can be considered cool images solely because they are visual clichés (except that the candidate is a woman). The first four images are also cool because we never see people's eyes; they are diverted, downcast, or hidden behind dark glasses on hardened faces. This stops us from seeing and knowing them, like we do in warm situations with family, friends, and loved ones.

By the final image (figure 6.11), though, we see the candidate's moist eyes wide open, dreaming into the distance. Directly above her and across the portrait of Washington is the message "In Women We Trust." In this final image, we feel warmly toward the woman because she is not really wielding power, but only dreaming of it. We are transformed from coolly viewing her as an icy winner to feeling sorry for her because she is a loser (or at least has not won yet). We do not usually associate presidents with the warm feelings we harbor for family, friends, or other loved ones; but we *do* feel warmly toward wives, mothers, sisters, daughters, aunts, and friends who *dream* for something they do not yet have. Also, the final image puts us deeper into the participant role because we realize that we had a sneak look at the woman's daydreams. And experiencing someone else's daydreams provides us with a sense of internal action and participation. Seeing the woman's innermost thoughts enables us to feel more like her close ally, if not very much like her.

But this is only one interpretation. Visual symbolspeak is ambiguous enough to elicit a range of possible responses that are acceptable to the message maker. Others will surely interpret these images quite differently, such as in this scenario. Perhaps the woman in the ad works hard and wins the election. In the final image, then, she is not a clerical peon dreaming of the White House; she really is the president. As in the initial interpretation, the first four images remain cool in nature. This independent woman of action elicits little warmth. In the final image, alone and away from the gaggle of men who helped her achieve victory, the new commander-in-chief is finally allowed to be herself. Here, in isolation, she contemplates the major issues in uniquely humane ways—from a woman's viewpoint. In either of these interpretations (and there are more), as the ad states, it is in women we trust—to dream of glory or to achieve glory.

The emphasis and values in this second interpretation differ from those of the first reading, but the direction of emotion, cool to warm, remains the same. But what if a viewer experienced both of these interpretations or transformations at the same time? The likely result would be more complex, simultaneously conflicting emotions—in short, a more active, intense, richer internal experience for the viewer. And the more intense the emotional experience, the more effective the message, for it provides us with an experience that differs from what we would normally expect to have when buying a cotton T-shirt.

Of course, neither of these interpretations make any difference to the message maker. Donna Karan executives do not care whether you believe that women are currently powerful or only capable of dreaming about it. Instead, this image maker is concerned that you experience some sort of internal, emotional journey by "undergoing" a change, in this case, from a cool to warm emotion.

Although the Benetton and Donna Karan ads differ in many ways, they both try to transform us through cool to warm images. Of course, other viewers might create different scenarios, including ones that move in the opposite direction. The interpretation depends, in part, upon us, upon what Gombrich (1982) calls "the beholder's share" of the meaning. Again, visual symbolspeak's ambiguity allows for a surplus of meaning. Placing images on a continuum such as cool-to-warm can help us begin to understand the basic structure of the transformation. We need to understand how we transform images and how they transform us.

Hyperintertextuality, Ambiguity, and Incongruity Aid Emotional Transformation

In order for such emotional transformations to occur, we have to be aroused by initial images. Next, we have to enter into or become submerged or engrossed in them. The most important elements necessary for achieving initial arousal and involvement in images are hyperintertextuality, ambiguity, and incongruity. Here, intertextuality means associating one thing with another, identifying things within each context that strike familiar chords, things that overlap with our previous knowledge and experiences. The "hyper-" prefix indicates the volume and intensity of visual associations. As we have already discussed, ambiguity means sufficient space or room for us to construct one or more personal meanings. Incongruity here means juxtaposition or divergence within an image or series of images. It sometimes means seeing things placed together that we have previously not associated together, such as the liquor ad that depicts an elegantly dressed man and woman standing at a bar, the man's head that of a Great Dane. Of course, none of these principles obey laws of time, space, or logic, but they can nonetheless link images and function as a kind of irrational syntax.

Let's take a brief look just at incongruity in the Benetton and Donna Karan ads. Incongruous elements can link images in a kind of subtle, illogical syntax. Especially in the first ad, the images of the burning car, the boat people, and the dying patient appear quite unrelated. In addition to being connected via the cool-to-warm continuum (an incongruity itself), however, the images are loosely connected by other incongruities or visual "binary oppositions." The image of the burning hot car, in dark tones and flaming oranges, is incongruous with the cool green and white text "United Colors of Benetton"—a minor dissonance repeated in each image. Also, the orange heat of the fire clashes with the cool colors and water of the second photo of boat people. The outdoors fire and water of these first two images are incongruous with the hushed hospital interior in the final one. The Donna Karan ad also contains a consistent, unifying incongruous element: the contrast of a woman surrounded by male subordinates. The final image sets up the starkest incongruity of the entire sequence (according to the second interpretation), juxtaposing the powerful woman—this time alone—with the woman in the previous images, surrounded by male subordinates.

Cool and warm emotions, fed by hyperintertextuality, ambiguity, and incongruity, are the logic of dreams, but they now constitute the syntax of the transformations we undergo through images. As such, they usually evade critical evaluation. In other words, they are the stuff of emotion, the landscape of where we live.

The forms of symbolspeak we have examined share this common thread: they propel us into our imaginal, internal, and hence emotional lives, compelling us to be active there. In the near future, we will increasingly dwell in the purely symbolic environment of "virtual reality," a 3-D, computerized simulation that will enable us to be "participants in abstract spaces where the physical machine and the physical viewer do not exist" (Helsel and Roth 1991). The word, the image, and virtual reality will provide us with unlimited joy and learning. There is no doubt about this.

But words, images, and simulated environments are abstractions of reality, layers of representation that remove us ever further from actual, real life. They remove us from nature, which has always been our best model for any type of representation—indeed, our best model for how we should live. Nature is where humans belong, because it is the only place where humanness can survive whole and remain untainted and undiluted. It also seems natural to immerse ourselves in images, creating, exploring, and living, with mind and body, in new symbolic spaces—even if we are carried further away from actuality and nature. But we will prosper there only as long as we never lose sight of where we really live.

Works Cited

Aaker, David, and D. Stayman. 1990. "A Micro Approach to Studying Feeling Responses to Advertising: The Case of Warmth." In *Emotion in Advertising: Theoretical and Practical Explorations,* edited by Stuart Agres, Tony Dubitsky, and Julie A. Edell, 53–68. New York: Quorum Books.

Aaker, David, D. M. Stayman, and M. R. Hagerty. 1986. "Warmth in Advertising: Measurement, Impact, and Sequence Effects." *Journal of Consumer Research* 12.4: 365–81.

Agres, Stuart. 1990. "Emotion in Advertising: An Agency Point of View." In *Emotion in Advertising: Theoretical and Practical Explorations,* edited by Stuart Agres, Tony Dubitsky, and Julie A. Edell, 3–18. New York: Quorum Books.

Begg, Ian. 1983. "Imagery and Language." In *Imagery: Current Theory, Research, and Application,* edited by Anees Sheikh, 288–309. New York: John Wiley and Sons.

Brand, Alice. 1989. *The Psychology of Writing: The Affective Experience.* New York: Greenwood Press.

Bronowski, Jacob. 1978. *The Origins of Knowledge and Imagination.* New Haven, CT: Yale University Press.

Bryden, M. P., and R. Ley. 1983. "Right Hemispheric Involvement in the Perception and Expression of Emotion in Normal Humans." In *Neuropsychology of Human Emotion,* edited by Kenneth Heilman and Paul Satz. New York: Guilford Press.

Bugelski, Richard. 1983. "Imagery and the Thought Processes." In *Imagery: Current Theory, Research, and Application,* edited by Anees Sheikh, 72–95. New York: John Wiley and Sons.

Edell, Julie A. 1990. "Emotion and Advertising: A Timely Union." In *Emotion in Advertising: Theoretical and Practical Explorations,* edited by Stuart Agres, Tony Dubitsky, and Julie A. Edell, xiii–xviii. New York: Quorum Books.

Fry, Donald L., and Virginia H. Fry. 1987. "Some Structural Characteristics of Music Television Videos." *Southern Speech Communication Journal* 52: 151–64.

Gombrich, E. H. 1982. *The Sense of Order: A Study in the Psychology of Decorative Art.* 2d ed. Ithaca, NY: Cornell University Press.

Helsel, Sandra, and Judith Roth, eds. 1991. *Virtual Reality: Theory, Practice, and Promise.* Westport, CT: Meckler Publishing.

Jung, Carl G. 1971. "On the Relation of Analytical Psychology to Poetry." In *Critical Theory since Plato,* edited by Hazard Adams, 809–18. New York: Harcourt Brace Jovanovich.

Kaufmann, Geir. 1980. *Imagery, Language, and Cognition: Toward a Theory of Symbolic Activity in Human Problem-solving.* Bergen, Germany: Universitetsforlaget.

Kosslyn, Stephen. 1983. *Ghosts in the Mind's Machine: Creating and Using Images in the Brain.* New York: Norton.

Lutz, William. 1989. *Doublespeak.* New York: Harper and Row.

Morello, John T. 1988. "Argument and Visual Structuring in the 1984 Mondale-Reagan Debates: The Media's Influence on the Perception of Clash." *Western Journal of Speech Communication* 52 (Fall): 277–90.

Paivio, Allan. 1986. *Mental Representations: A Dual Coding Approach.* New York: Oxford University Press.

Puto, Christopher, and Robert Hoyer. 1990. "Transformational Advertising: Current State of the Art." In *Emotion in Advertising: Theoretical and Practical Explorations,* edited by Stuart Agres, Tony Dubitsky, and Julie A. Edell, 69–80. New York: Quorum Books.

Sontag, Susan. 1978. *A Susan Sontag Reader.* New York: Farrar, Straus and Giroux.

Wurtzel, Allan. 1983. *Television Production.* 2d ed. New York: McGraw-Hill.

7 From War Propaganda to Sound Bites: The Poster Mentality of Politics in the Age of Television

Linda R. Robertson
Hobart and William Smith Colleges

The heavy reliance on televised political campaign advertising indicates that Americans have been conditioned to accept slogans, compelling images, and emotional appeals as useful information when making decisions about our government and our way of life. If we expected complex arguments about difficult problems, we would be dissatisfied with the "sound bite." We would demand more than a mere image, and any political consultant would know that cheap appeals to fear or patriotism would turn us against the candidate rather than enhance his or her attractiveness.

The poster propaganda of World War II offers us some insight into why Americans accept televised political ads as credible. These posters may seem irrelevant today or interesting merely because they reflect a bygone era. But like television today, they were a pervasive visual medium that conveyed messages both through emotional, colorful images and through slogans intended to reduce the war's complexities to simple, easy-to-grasp notions.

America emerged victorious, legitimizing both the messages and the means for conveying them. Those persuaders learned a great deal from the use of poster propaganda during World War II. And because the generations born since the war have been saturated with visual messages, the principles of political propaganda learned during the war have prepared us to accept them via a more sophisticated visual medium.

World War II as Right-Wing Horror Show

An American director of horror films recently stated that there are two kinds of horror plots, each reflecting a different political position: one from the right and one from the left. Imagine a primitive culture of cave dwellers. Darkness is falling, and the tribe must retire into the caves, for night is a time of fear, of worrying about threats to the tribe. A right-wing horror-film script would present the threat to this huddled band as *external* to them, as something out there in the darkness. A left-wing horror-film script would present the threat to the tribe as unresolved problems *within* the tribe itself. The right-wing resolution to the conflict would be the destruction of the enemy outside. The resolution of the leftist plot would be addressing the source of internal conflict.

World War II, not surprisingly, was and remains in the popular imagination a horror show of the right. In this chapter, I will explore the ways in which the poster propaganda of World War II differed from other ways the American government either had or could have justified war. In contrast to the fascists, American poster propagandists did not exploit internal cultural, racial, or political differences. The tendency was to ignore internal dissent. Rhodes (1976) writes:

> Although in wartime internal conflicts are most damaging, in the democracies they cannot be suppressed. All democratic propagandists can hope for is to persuade people that for the duration of the war it is best not to exercise their inalienable rights—the right to grumble, to reject conscription, to be pacifists or conscientious objectors, the right to hate blacks, Catholics, Jews. (142)

World War II propaganda messages were essentially conservative: Americans were united in defending a highly desirable way of life; internal antagonisms were denied by not mentioning them. Norman Rockwell's posters depicting the "Four Freedoms" (figure 7.1) best illustrate this consciousness. In 1941, Roosevelt described Rockwell's posters as the reasons why America needed to support England in the war. In 1943, Rockwell's posters appeared in the *Saturday Evening Post* and were reproduced by the Treasury Department to support the bond drive. "No other paintings in the world," writes Guptill (1975, 40), "have ever been reproduced and distributed in such numbers" as these four pictures, which remain in print today.

The slogans of all four paintings stress that Americans are engaged in preserving what they already have: "Save Freedom of Worship," "Ours to Fight For—Freedom from Fear," "Save Freedom of

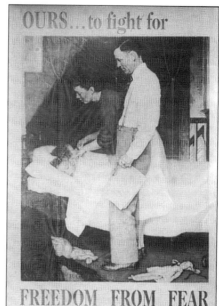

Figure 7.1. *Four Freedoms,* Norman Rockwell, 1943. Reprinted by permission of the Norman Rockwell Family Trust. © 1943 The Norman Rockwell Family Trust.

Speech," and "Ours to Fight For—Freedom from Want." Notice, too, that the essential American is white, middle class, and belongs to a stable, closely knit family. That's what "we" are like; that's what "we" want to preserve. Except for the war, all Americans would enjoy freedom of speech, freedom from fear, freedom of worship, and freedom from want.

At first blush, the essential message seems obvious. But it differs from both American justifications for World War I and Axis justifications for World War II. Japanese and German poster propaganda stressed that the purpose of the war was to establish a new world order. World War II American poster propaganda made no such promises. World War I posters, however, emphasized that the Allies were fighting to promote democracy and freedom throughout the world. Because Americans had seen World War I posters of American soldiers with such slogans as "He Is Keeping the World Safe for Democracy," similar appeals could not be made during World War II. The reason is simple. Twenty-five years earlier we were promised that World War I would be the war to end all wars. If used again, these old slogans would simply exacerbate feelings of betrayal and disillusionment with Western leadership (Rhodes 1976, 139).

This presented a special problem to those who tried to develop a propaganda message that would galvanize the nation. As Riegel (1979) notes, the function of war images is

> to make coherent and acceptable a basically incoherent and irrational ordeal of killing, suffering, and destruction that violates every accepted principle of morality and decent living. This requires . . . a predisposition of the audience to believe. (5)

Today we have difficulty recapturing the mood of isolationism that Roosevelt confronted prior to December 7, 1941. At the beginning of World War II, Americans were not predisposed to believe again the message that another war would make the world safe for democracy.

Because American propaganda appeals for World War II were limited by the propaganda precedents of World War I, propagandists instead exploited the desire for revenge upon Japan to justify the war. In the poster "Remember December 7" (figure 7.2), for instance, revenge is portrayed as a high-minded virtue. This poster evokes not only the tattered flag still waving by "the dawn's early light," but also appropriates a passage from the Gettysburg Address to justify avenging Pearl Harbor. Other posters made no attempt to gild the desire, but appealed directly to raw emotion (figure 7.3).

Figure 7.2. *Remember December 7*, Allan Saalburg, 1942. Courtesy of the National Archives.

Figure 7.3. *Avenge December 7.* Courtesy of the National Archives (44-PA-132).

As a corollary to the message that a desirable way of life was being threatened from the outside, World War II posters stressed that the material comfort of the citizen need not be diminished while the external threat was confronted (Riegel 1979, 11). This was a change from the propaganda of World War I, which called upon Americans to sacrifice on behalf of others. The World War I poster "Save Wheat" (figure 7.4) shows European peasant women pulling a plow across a field and asks the question "Will you help the Women of France?" Other posters used drawings of soldiers in the trenches to urge Americans to ration wheat in order to help feed the French (who bore the brunt of trench warfare).

Yet in his radio broadcast on December 8, 1941, President Roosevelt avoided the notion of sacrifice at home by redefining the term:

> It is not a sacrifice for the industrialist or the wage-earner, the farmer or the shopkeeper, the trainman or the doctor, to pay more taxes, to buy more bonds, to forego extra profits, to work

Figure 7.4. *Save Wheat.* Courtesy of the National Archives (RG4, 4-P-135).

longer or harder at the task for which he is best fitted. Rather, it is a privilege.

Later in the broadcast Roosevelt noted:

A review this morning leads me to the conclusion that at present we shall not have to curtail the normal articles of food.

Consonant with Roosevelt's message, World War II posters that urged conserving food showed pictures not of war-torn Europe or of soldiers on the battlefield, but of a bountiful harvest, and they offered slogans that only alluded to the war, such as "Can All You Can" and "Grow Your Own" (figure 7.5). These posters urged us to do something for ourselves—to grow our own food, to plant our own garden. Their messages reassured us that we had only to make minor changes in consumer practices. In fact, the war might even benefit the consumer left at home. One poster pictured a woman exclaiming, "I can save up to $100 every month now. Joe's in the glider troops."

The justifications of war presented in American propaganda were both reactionary—to seek revenge on an external enemy—and conservative—to preserve a nation that was superior both morally and materially. Later propaganda justified the war in even simpler terms: the purpose of the war was to end it (Fussell 1989). This message was conveyed in stark and brutal ways, as in the poster "This Is *Your* War" (figure 7.6). The image of a gigantic two-headed monster, drooling blood and grasping Lady Liberty like an ad for *King Kong,* illustrates the common war propaganda technique of depicting the enemy as terrifying and inhuman.

Norman Rockwell invoked this same theme more gently in "Hasten the Homecoming" (figure 7.7). Such images tell us that once the war is over, everything will be as it was: a contented, stable, middle-class society based on the traditional family. The soldier comes home to a happy family, his girlfriend shyly awaits him, and the neighborhood is racially integrated. Notice the amazing innocence of the returning soldier: he left a boy and returns a boy. Unscathed by battle, he looks like an Eagle Scout back from summer camp. Rockwell helps the viewer sustain the belief that such innocence can be preserved—despite the experience of war—because we are not permitted to see the face of the soldier.

This is a painful picture, a hopelessly naive fantasy. We are asked to believe that the soldier can kill and see mass dying with no ill effect. Everything will go back to normal. Our sons will return unharmed and

Figure 7.5. *Grow Your Own.* Courtesy of the National Archives (44-PA-218).

Figure 7.6. *This Is Your War,* Bert Yates, 1943. Courtesy of the National Archives.

Figure 7.7. *Hasten the Homecoming,* Norman Rockwell. Courtesy of the National Archives (44-PA-935).

unshaken by the war, our women will leave the factories and go back to the home, our society will be happy and peaceful. Nothing will have changed.

In summary, the aim of the war as conveyed in poster propaganda was neither to promote a new world order nor to sacrifice. The society is depicted as homogeneous, happy, and united in its effort to preserve a way of life against an external and monstrous enemy. Once the enemy is defeated, our previous innocence will be completely restored; social, political, economic, racial, ethnic, class, and gender-related problems do not exist. We live in Eden before the fall.

Valiant Leaders and Embodied Virtues

World War II accelerated our tendency to define political leaders as valiant—the embodiment of our heroic aspirations. Portraits of these leaders made them icons (figure 7.8). The leaders symbolized the aspirations of "the people" within a nation, with "the people" conceived as unified, as "alike," as "united." Being on the winning side, the

Figure 7.8. *Four Leaders.* Courtesy of the National Archives.

leaders gained credibility: they represented the "good" side of an absolute struggle between "good" and "evil."

Because America's aim in the war was to end it in order to restore the status quo, propaganda exaggerated the symbolic role of the presidency. In Western democracies, this symbolic role exists in some tension with the leader's role as head of government. The head of a democratic government is supposed to be the catalyst for political debate among various competing constituencies *within the state.* "Politics" is not a dirty word when a leader takes this role. But "politics" is a dirty word when an elected figure is conceived as a valiant leader embodying the people's will to defeat a common enemy, thereby symbolizing "goodness" and "strength." Under these conditions, policy debate is seen as unnecessary, because it might undermine national resolve or unity.

Similarly, national goals can be reduced to slogans because there is no need to argue about them. The leader's function is to inspire the nation and people throughout the world. Within the nation, the leader informs the citizenry of decisions that have been made that will lead to the defeat of their enemy. Thus, the role of symbolic leader in a democracy is at odds with the normal expectation that the people will decide matters essential to the nation.

Because the need for complex deliberations about policies is subordinated to this preference to inspire citizens, the leader becomes highly dependent upon mass media. And since the leader symbolizes both the people and a cluster of universal virtues, the media, in turn, become increasingly dependent upon the leader, not as the source of policy information, but for messages and images that project the leader's symbolic and inspirational qualities. Of course, these messages need not present complex reasoning about policies.

As leaders become increasingly symbolic, it also becomes easier for them to speak through a propagandist or "official spokesperson." These messages need not be the leader's own words. We now know, for instance, that some of Winston Churchill's inspirational BBC broadcasts were not spoken by him; rather, they were read by an actor who could imitate his voice. Similarly, the statement sent to the press corps "from the president" announcing the dropping of the bomb on Hiroshima was written for Truman by a reporter named William L. Laurence (Burchett 1983, 17). Leaders can thus successfully play in one domain an entirely symbolic role, one that directly opposes the role of a democratic leader.

The enhanced symbolic role of the president as leader of a unified nation naturally altered the definitions of what it meant to be a citizen. This was especially true given that it was industrial strength, natural resources, and technological advantage that determined the war's outcome. As Perrett (1985) notes, "The total wars of modern history give the decision to the side with the biggest factories" (67). Because winning the war depended on outproducing the enemy, even the most commonplace actions of the workers at home were charged with significance.

Every country involved in World War II had a propaganda campaign urging silence on its citizens. The poster "A Careless Word" (figure 7.9), which shows a dead sailor, exemplifies this campaign in America. The message here is that the homefront is intimately connected to the battlefield, that one word could kill a soldier. Note, too, that only later in the war did posters depict death and dismemberment, again emphasizing that the purpose of the war was to end it (Fussell 1989, 7–8).

Riegel (1979) notes that "the beauty of the 'careless talk' campaign was that people could feel involved in the war, playing a part in it and combating the enemy, merely by doing nothing and keeping

Figure 7.9. *A Careless Word*, Anton Otto Fischer. Courtesy of the National Archives (RG208).

their mouths shut" (15). An overt appeal to this definition of a "good" citizen was made again when Richard Nixon praised "The Silent Majority," who, unlike noisier citizens, supported the war in Vietnam simply by doing or saying nothing. Poster propaganda of World War II tended to stress that acquiescence—not trying to change things, going to work, consuming in moderation, and listening to the inspirational messages of the leader—was the primary way to help the nation survive. Silence becomes something positive, or worthwhile, or vitally necessary, or at the least, acceptable.

The Persistence of the Messages of World War II

Even this brief consideration of World War II poster propaganda provides some insight into how our consciousness is still influenced by the way the war was constructed. We can recognize in contemporary political messages many of the same themes and strategies for conveying them. For instance, we more easily understand how a candidate can build a campaign on a few metaphors, such as "a thousand points of light" or "stay the course," and images of himself surrounded by hundreds of waving flags. Having noted these continuing influences, I do not wish to make more of them than there is to make. The effectiveness of any effort to shape public opinion depends upon the predisposition of the public to believe the message. The techniques used to shape public opinion can galvanize convictions the audience already holds, but they are unlikely to change anybody's mind.

While the effectiveness of propaganda techniques is always limited, we would be naive to assume that there is no lasting effect when the same messages are repeated through a variety of official, news, information, and entertainment media over a period of decades. Over time, layers of repetition and reinforcement can construct a social reality. Such messages, repeated often enough, can limit our capacities to conceive of alternatives. Over time, such messages take on the attributes of a coherent, seminal political narrative, one which crowds out other ways of perceiving our culture (Hart 1990, 136–38).

The seminal narrative about how America engages in conflict, reduced to its easiest terms, is highly dualistic. Because it is so familiar, it can be easily told: Americans have been conditioned to understand that the most significant threat to the American way of life is external to us. When we are drawn into conflict, the public policy narrative assures us that it is not because we are an aggressor nation; rather, we are victims who respond defensively to the unjustified aggression of others. We respond with military force because we were taught by World War II that war settles problems and places America in a highly influential position in the world (Coles 1987).

This "logic" of war has consequences. One is the assumption that we can maintain an expensive military without calling upon Americans to sacrifice their standard of living. The canker in the rose is the assumption that because military preparedness is a boon to the economy, it is difficult to reduce the military budget, even when old enemies collapse.

A second consequence is that when we face the common enemy, political leaders and the media ignore social issues such as the economy and racism—issues that make us question whether we want to maintain the status quo. More than one commentator noticed that when the Persian Gulf War dominated the news, the savings and loan scandal investigations were no longer covered by the dominant media.

A third consequence is that the public policy rhetoric defines "national security" in a way that ultimately assures national insecurity. We pursue a policy of "deterrence" with revenge as its ultimate, logical outcome. Should deterrence fail, we will retaliate, even if it means our own destruction. This consequence is seldom discussed because nuclear holocaust is unimaginable. But more important, this consequence is seldom discussed because the policy itself has evolved so naturally from the narrative generated by World War II propaganda: that revenge is virtuous. Both the policy and mindset render absurd our usual assumptions about the value of human life.

These dualistic assumptions about conflict seep into political discourse in general, affecting not only the messages themselves, but also how they are conveyed. Political leaders construe both domestic and international conflicts in absolute terms of "good" and "evil." Our "enemies" are often depicted as so evil that they are inhuman: the "pineapple face" of Noriega, the "Hitlerite" Hussein, and the "Evil Empire." In such negative campaigns, the opponents are also often characterized as morally unqualified to participate in political life. They may be portrayed as "liberals," drug users, philanderers, or "soft" on crime. Rather than fostering political debate about opposing policies, these strategies try to disqualify the candidate altogether. Recall Johnson's attempt to suggest that Goldwater was the kind of fiend who would lead America to nuclear holocaust—a televised ad showing a little girl picking the petals off a daisy while a voice counts down from ten. The ad concluded with a scene of a nuclear bomb exploding.

Television appeals to the emotions through images and slogans, avoiding prolonged or complex debate; hence, the "issueless" campaign. And like the "Careless Talk" campaign of World War II, televised campaign ads, debates, and photo opportunities provide a sense of both immediacy and participation to citizens who need not leave their living rooms in order to feel that they are responsibly informed and engaged in the political process.

In addition to these continuing influences and the use of a visual medium, the definition of the president as symbolizing our aspirations during World War II continues to shape the way presidents establish their credibility (Geis 1987, 26–27). In his role as a valiant leader against the common enemy, and as the embodiment of universal virtues and aspirations for freedom, the president tends to portray the American way of life as highly desirable and available to all. Maintaining these opportunities requires little intervention, support, or official policies, except when the president tells the nation that it is confronted with some external threat. In that event, the president informs the people of decisions already made—such as the invasions of Grenada and Panama and the intervention in the Middle East—and seeks to inspire the nation to pursue the common goal of vanquishing the enemy. Disagreements or debates over policy are characterized as "politics" or "partisan politics," as if a two-party political system were somehow distasteful. In the invasion of Panama, dissent by elected officials was strongly condemned by the White House with the standard implication that it bordered on treason because it endangered the lives of our soldiers. In the Persian Gulf War, the president mobilized the military while Congress was on vacation.

But even when we are not engaged in military action, the president's role continues to carry much of the symbolic potency derived from the way the presidency was defined during World War II. The president is expected to assume symbolic roles and to develop them through images. So significant is this symbolic role that no one expects the president to author the words he says. Nor is the president expected to say much, because policies are presented visually as slogans or sound bites.

Arousing Desires of What We "Ought" To Be

This chapter does not address those who believe that the issues confronting America really do reflect a right-wing horror show that we should recognize. Nor does it address those who assume that Americans need to recognize that the issues confronting us are those of a left-wing horror script. Instead, the concerns raised here are addressed to those who recognize that the issue is larger than the question of whether the conservatives or the liberals are currently enjoying political control. A larger concern should be our desire to clarify our current condition in horror-film scripts, a genre that is formulaic, visual, and appeals to our visceral emotions, to our desire to feel fear, anxiety, and relief. Our readiness to accept simplistic explanations of reality is bad enough. What's worse is that we can imagine only two such archetypal scripts and are satisfied in our own minds that one of them pretty much explains our values.

Any culture constructs what its members ought to desire, what they ought to seek, what they ought to imitate. When a culture succeeds, symbolic identification becomes the primary object of desire (Veblen 1934). In other times and places, this drive was aroused by the mysteries of religion or by the pomp and circumstance of the state or by the poet. Americans, however, now regard visual representation not only as a highly credible source of information, but also as *the* means for arousing mimetic desires. During World War II, Americans watched newsreel footage that told them what was "really" happening at the front and were confronted in their daily lives with vivid—often larger than life—posters that shaped their understanding of the nature and purpose of the war and their role in waging it. Now Americans watch the network news and political advertisements.

The visual media's credibility during World War II contributed to television's effectiveness in constructing political consciousness. Why? Because we emerged from the war not only victorious, but also as a nation of unprecedented power, wealth, and influence. This fact authenticated the ways in which the war was constructed for the American people. This in turn validated the heavy reliance on visual media to convey simplified messages and certified the subtext of those messages, which was to justify the mentality of a nation at war. The propaganda techniques of World War II have continued to influence American political rhetoric: we have sustained the mentality of a nation at war for half a century.

We have constructed a culture that arouses in us a desire for images that make the world seem simpler than it is, a culture that leaves us regretting that we are not as innocent, as influential, or as safe as we wish to be. It is no surprise that we perpetuate these simplistic, dualistic fantasies—presented in vivid color with simple messages—fantasies the victory of World War II seemed to affirm.

Works Cited

Burchett, Wilfred. 1983. *Shadows of Hiroshima*. London: Verso Editions.

Coles, William E., Jr. 1987. *Seeing through Writing*. New York: Harper and Row.

Fussell, Paul. 1989. *Wartime: Understanding and Behavior in the Second World War*. New York: Oxford University Press.

Geis, Michael L. 1987. *The Language of Politics*. New York: Springer-Verlag.

Guptill, Arthur L. 1975. *Norman Rockwell: Illustrator*. New York: Watson-Guptill Publications.

Hart, Roderick P. 1990. *Modern Rhetorical Criticism*. Glenview, IL: Scott, Foresman/Little, Brown Higher Education.

Perrett, Geoffrey. 1985. *Days of Sadness, Years of Triumph: The American People, 1939–1945*. Madison: University of Wisconsin Press.

Rhodes, Anthony. 1976. *Propaganda: The Art of Persuasion, World War II*. New York: Chelsea House.

Riegel, O. W. 1979. *Posters of World War I and World War II in the George C. Marshall Research Foundation.* Edited by Anthony R. Crawford. Charlottesville: The University Press of Virginia.

Veblen, Thorstein. 1934. *The Theory of the Leisure Class: An Economic Study of Institutions.* New York: The Modern Library.

8 Reading Ollie North

William V. Costanzo
Westchester Community College

"The medium is the message," said McLuhan, later adding, "The medium is the *massage.*" Few public events in recent years have demonstrated the role of media in massaging messages as the televised testimony of Lieutenant Colonel Oliver North. It is hard to imagine such a figure becoming a national celebrity during the days before television, when most of the news was carried by radio and newsprint. His words may seem unimpressive in print, but that solemn face, the soldier's posture, and the decorated uniform—reproduced on millions of home screens—captivated a nation of viewers.

Where does the North phenomenon fit into the history of media in America? The founding documents of this country were written in an Age of Reason, a time when patterns of thought were attuned to the logic of the printed word. In 1776 or 1789, audiences valued a person's prose over his or her profile. By 1987, though, the year of the Iran-Contra hearings, 75 percent of the population received most of its news from television broadcasts. During the hearings, some senators who read carefully reasoned speeches received less popular attention, and probably less respect, than the silent Ollie North. Although the polls showed that 65 percent of the population believed him to be guilty of illegal doings (Martz 1987), 53 percent approved of how he handled the Iran-Contra dealings, and 93 percent believed he defended himself well (NBC News, 13 July 1987). There are important issues of credibility and judgment here. How does the medium affect our perceptions of people and events? What happens to perceptions of government when the image, especially the television image, replaces written language as the chief bearer of meaning? Oliver North's testimony illustrates how the image of the man can eclipse the letter of the law.

I will explore the role of television and print media by comparing the texts of Ollie North. I will begin with "live" coverage of the hearings, observing how the images and sounds are edited even as they happen. Then I will examine ABC and CBS news broadcasts to see how different networks represent the same event. I will compare television with print media. I intend to show not only how events are treated in various hands, but also how they are filtered differently through different media. I want to consider what kinds of news each medium favors, the kinds of messages best conveyed by each medium, and how the media influence the course of human events. I am aware that there are problems with using one symbol system, written language, to compare another system, images in television. Such comparisons show an analytic bias toward print. I hope that readers will be able to compensate by referring to the visual texts when this is possible and by drawing on the power of imagination when it is not.

My observations will be best understood in relation to a broad distinction between print and television made by media historians. Elizabeth Eisenstein (1979) and Walter Ong (1982) have stressed that reading is a rational activity that must hold up under careful scrutiny, since it can be subjected to close, repeated readings. Writers, unlike extemporary speakers, have the option of revising their discourse. Undistracted by contentious listeners, unrestricted by time slots or station breaks, writers can sharpen their diction and tighten their logic, riding a flow of thought to fresh forms of expression and ideas. Writing, then, promotes individual originality, coherence, and analytic thinking.

Television seems to promote a different kind of thinking. Postman (1985) points out that television teaches us to accept contradictions, incoherence, and multiple contexts. He cites the discontinuities of commercial interruptions and the predominance of context-free messages that can be generally applied to anyone, anytime, enabling viewers to find their place in any soap opera or sitcom no matter when they tune in. Goethals (1981) stresses the ritual nature of television: its reliance on repetition and imitation; its appeal to communal feelings; its enthymemic strategies, which suggest rather than state the underlying propositions. Ong (1982) calls attention to television's preference for storytelling over exposition, for rapid-fire montage over steady, linear construction, for integrative imagery over critical analysis. In sum, print tends to engage people in logical, analytical, individualistic forms of thinking, while television fosters holistic thought, suggestion, and community.

These differences of media and mind have been linked to political developments. Postman (1985) traces the origin of American democracy to the values of the printed word. Colonial America was committed to eighteenth-century rationalism, itself based firmly on the bedrock of literacy. The Enlightenment philosophies of John Locke, David Hume, and Thomas Reid would be unthinkable without the precise tools of written language, and it was in the intellectual crucible of the Enlightenment that Jeffersonian democracy was conceived. Postman estimates that the literacy rate for men in New England before 1700 was between 89 and 95 percent (31).

This estimate should not be too surprising. In the beginning, we were a nation of readers, and newspapers and pamphlets were then the chief conveyors of our news. Consider, for example, the striking popularity of Thomas Paine's *Common Sense,* which sold over 100,000 copies in the first three months of 1776. Best sellers reach larger numbers today, but not in proportion to the current population. Postman calculates that, in our own times, only the Super Bowl could match the audience of Paine's revolutionary pamphlet (35). He views this as an alarming trend, a degenerative departure from the rational foundations of the Declaration of Independence and the Constitution. I want to inquire beyond this cynical view, to consider whether television may in fact be broadening the basis of democracy, perhaps strengthening the original spirit of our founding documents, through qualities inherent in the medium. Let's turn, then, to the case of Ollie North.

Before his public appearance at the Iran-Contra hearings in July 1987, Oliver North was unknown. In the tiny village of Philmont, New York, where he grew up, people knew him as a nice kid. In the Marines, where he rose in the ranks through loyalty, discipline, a talent for leadership, and two Purple Hearts in Vietnam, he was known as "The Wizard" and "Blood and Guts." After his transfer to the National Security Council, working long days in a small office near the White House on secret anti-terrorist activities, he was recognized by top government officials for his tireless devotion to patriotic causes.

Then the Iran-Contra scandal broke, implicating North in shady dealings. For seven months, what emerged from occasional references in the press and broadcast news was the image of a liar, petty thief, and political naif. Then, for six days in July of 1987, he took the stand before the joint House-Senate committees. It was his steady, telegenic presence on the screen that made the difference. That handsome uniform, the patriotic bearing, and the moist, blue eyes—carried live and highlighted during the evening network news—were irresistible. Suddenly, the hearings became a super media event. A *Newsweek* poll showed that three-fourths of the nation watched North's testimony, increasing daytime television ratings by more than 10 percent. North was hailed as a new folk hero, "the Rambo of diplomacy," Jimmy Stewart, Gary Cooper, and John Wayne rolled into one (Martz 1987, 12). His name inspired haircuts, T-shirts, "Ollie for President" bumper stickers, songs, and special hero sandwiches made with red-blooded American beef, a little bologna, and shredded lettuce.

July 14, 1987, was the final day of North's testimony before the congressional committees. The major television networks carried the event, and transcripts were printed the next day in the *New York Times.* Comparing the transcripts to tapes of the original coverage reveals striking differences between print and television. On the page, North is a minor entity, marked by few words: "No, sir," "Yes, I would," "That is correct." In the lengthy columns representing speeches by congressional leaders, North's remarks are lost. Missing are the close-ups of his solemn face, the cut-ins to the ribbons on his uniform, the camera's steady focus on his profile—even when the senators are speaking. Studying the videotape reminds us how television privileges the image over the spoken word, especially when the word sounds like a prepared speech.

There is no better example of this than the speech by Representative Edward Boland, whose amendment had prohibited assistance to the Contras when North diverted funds from 1984 to 1986. For more than six minutes—a long time by television standards—Boland reads, rather badly, from a script detailing his role on the Intelligence Committee. The script is typical of congressional written discourse: many long sentences, embedded clauses, complex diction, and historical allusions. The camera covering this speech becomes restless before the first minute ends, cutting away from Boland to a close-up of North's face, slowly panning the audience, taking a long shot of the crowded photographers and journalists, returning to the speaker only when he departs from the script for a few impromptu comments. With the committee above and testifier below, North seems like a patient, stoic victim of bureaucracy.

Even in this live "unedited" coverage, the camera is already interpreting the event. In its restless movements and cuts to different points of view, it tells us that this speech is not important, that Boland is just going through the motions, that we—like the gallery of spectators and North himself—must endure another long-winded harangue. Our sympathy for North is subtly supported by the camera work and by the nature of television itself. In most shots, North appears in a three-quarter profile, while the representatives are shown full-face. Viewers are more apt to believe a person shown in profile than a person who is photographed head on; it's as if we're eavesdropping on a conversation instead of being deliberately spoken to, perhaps with calculated effect (Fiske and Hartley 1978, 62). Ironically, it was the congressional committee that decided to place the cameras at these angles, presumably to avoid a cluttered view. Did the committee unwittingly undermine its own credibility through an ignorance of television techniques?

The custom of preparing written remarks also works against the committee. On live television, the written word is often less interesting, less credible than a spontaneous remark. So while North's words may seem casual and unimpressive when printed in the *New York Times,* they appear candid and compelling on the screen. This doesn't mean that every prepared speech on television is bound to be dull or that every profile shot guarantees personal appeal. North received more public sympathy than Boland or McFarlane for other reasons—his status as an underdog, for instance, in addition to his looks—and the camera worked to display those reasons in a favorable light.

On July 14, it was primarily one person who decided what the nation viewed. Bill Linden, monitoring the event from a separate room, was responsible for choosing video from the four feed cameras that recorded the event from different angles. His choices, in turn, were broadcast on the major networks: ABC, CBS, NBC, CNN, and PBS. Linden's practiced eye and almost innate sense of audience interest proved remarkable. The camera always seemed to show what viewers wanted to see. At one point, he cut to a close-up of North's medals seconds before Senator Inouye mentioned them in his address. Was Linden working from a copy of Inouye's speech? Was Inouye responding to Linden's video monitor? Or was this just another coincidence of word and image?

On this day of the hearings, the image seemed to outperform the word. It is not that the committee members' speeches were less cogent or articulate. A careful reading of the transcripts shows most of them to be thoughtfully, often eloquently phrased. Boland's main point was that North overstepped the boundaries of the law when he diverted funds for the Contras in the name of the National Security Council. The law set by Congress, Boland argued, applies to administrative agencies like the NSC, in keeping with George Mason's counsel two hundred years ago "that the purse and the sword should never be in the same hands" (U.S. News and World Report 1987, 111). Congressman Lee Hamilton reaffirmed this concept, criticizing North for taking secret steps to violate the policies set by Congress.

Senator Inouye reprimanded North for failing to live up to the Marine honor code: "Members of the military have an obligation to disobey unlawful orders" (112). These were carefully reasoned arguments, documented by history and the law. Boland cites the Founding Fathers and the Constitutional Convention as precedents. Inouye cites Washington, Jefferson, and the Nuremberg trials. By contrast, North invoked a baseball metaphor to picture the administration and Congress as two teams on an unequal playing field: "It's sort of like a baseball game in which you [the Congress] are both the player and the umpire. . . . In the end you determine the score and declare yourselves the winner" (77). The intricate details of American legislative history are countered with one simple image from contemporary life. The committee members' details may stand up better under scrutiny, but the images—the soldier and the baseball game—make for more engaging television.

So does dramatic conflict, the kind that North's lawyer, Brendan Sullivan, used so cannily to derail the expository lines of reasoning used by North's questioners. When Inouye began to draw a parallel to the Nuremberg trials, Sullivan abruptly cut him off:

> *Inouye:* Members of the military have an obligation to disobey unlawful orders. This principle was considered so important that we, we the Government of the United States, proposed that it be internationally applied in the Nuremberg trials. And so in the Nuremberg trials we said that the fact that the defendant—
>
> *Sullivan:* Mr. Chairman, may I please. . . . I find this offensive. I find you're engaging in a personal attack on Colonel North, and you're far removed from the issues in this case. To make a reference to the Nuremberg trials I find personally, professionally distasteful, and I can no longer sit here and listen to this.
>
> *Inouye:* You will have to sit there if you want to listen.
>
> *Sullivan:* Mr. Chairman, please don't conclude these hearings on this unfair note. I have strong objections to many things in the hearings, and you up there speak about listening to the American people. Why don't you listen to the American people, and what they've said as a result of the last week? There are 20,000 telegrams in our room outside the corridor here that came in this morning. The American people have spoken, and please stop this personal attack against Colonel North.
>
> *Inouye:* I have sat here and listened to the Colonel without interrupting. I hope you will accord me the courtesy to say my piece.

Sullivan: Sir, you may give speeches on the issue, it seems to me, you may ask questions, but you may not attack him personally. This has gone too far in my opinion—

Inouye: I am not attacking him personally.

Sullivan: That's the way I hear it, sir.

Inouye: Colonel North, I'm certain it must have been painful for you, as you stated, to testify that you lied to senior officials of our Government. . . . (*New York Times,* 15 July 1987)

Sullivan diverts attention away from his client by representing Inouye's statement as a personal attack. He shifts the grounds from an argument based on law to an *argumentum ad hominem.* Further, Sullivan raises issues of authority, contrasting the senator's references to "we the Government" to "the American people" who have spoken through their thousands of telegrams. The focus shifts from a government of law to a government of people. Further, Sullivan's awareness of his role in a public, televised performance is apparent in the videotape. When he refers to the American people, he turns briefly to the camera, the only time he does so during the whole exchange. When he addresses Inouye as "you up there" and speaks of 20,000 telegrams "in our room outside the corridor here," he is positioning himself and his client on the side of the people. The camera, which shows Sullivan and North in a two-shot from the side with rows of citizens behind them, reinforces this positioning by filming Inouye and his colleagues directly from below.

But the most important achievement of Sullivan's interruption occurs in the television news of that evening. Both "ABC World News Tonight" and the "CBS Evening News" gave prominent coverage to the Sullivan-Inouye exchange. By contrast, the *New York Times* relegated the exchange to page thirteen. Its three-column headlines and front-page story portrayed North on the defensive: "McFarlane Disputes North on Key Points of Testimony; Chairmen Rebuke Colonel" (Rosenbaum 1987). This contrast in coverage may be partly a matter of editorial policy, but it also marks a difference in the media. Dramatic confrontations like the Sullivan-Inouye exchange usually play better on the screen than on the page.

It is important to remember that the medium does not dictate the message absolutely. ABC and CBS did not present the day's events in the same sequence or give the same priority to each event. CBS's Dan Rather began his broadcast by stressing the "bitterness and conflict" of the day's hearings, illustrated by a preview montage showing former National Security Advisor Robert C. McFarlane disputing North's testimony, Representative Hamilton condemning North's "policy of lies," and a committee dispute over North's slide presentation on the Nicaraguan "freedom fighters." Then the broadcast shifted to Phil Jones on Capitol Hill. CBS used file tape to underscore discrepancies between statements by McFarlane and North. When it showed the Inouye-Sullivan exchange, a voice-over explained that Inouye had lost his right arm in World War II. CBS gave less time to the exchange than ABC (about fifty seconds as opposed to seventy-five), omitting Inouye's ironic comment ("You will have to sit there if you want to listen") and trimming Sullivan's response. Then CBS cut to the remarks by Hamilton, who actually spoke first. It followed this coverage of the hearings with shots of President Reagan making no comment, a look at the increasing public support for the Contras in response to North's appearances, and a live interview with Senator Sam Nunn.

ABC's Peter Jennings began his broadcast by citing the "very considerable impression" made by Colonel North; then the camera cut to Brit Hume's report from the Capitol. The ABC broadcast gave first place to North, not to McFarlane, then showed a long excerpt of Hamilton's "stern lecture," with the camera focusing on North's silent response. The Sullivan-Inouye exchange was given more extensive coverage, as well as more extensive editing. Sullivan's speech was sharpened by skillful pruning. A thirty-second insert of Senator Rudman defending Inouye's record and defending him from ethnic slurs was grafted from another moment in the hearings. More than a minute-and-a-half was given to the committee's "squabble" over North's slide presentation. McFarlane's testimony was placed last. Like CBS, ABC highlighted North's effect on public polls (48 percent now supported aid to the Contras) and the Reagan administration's efforts to capitalize on this toward a change in foreign policy. It now appeared that North could change policy more effectively through television than through secret means.

A telling difference in the broadcasts is in their treatment of the slides that North had used to gain support from various groups for the Contra cause. The committee debated for nearly an hour about whether to show the slides, some arguing that the room could not be darkened for security reasons. It finally decided that North could give his presentation orally, without a slide projector. Whatever the committee's motives, the effect on television was to rob North's presentation of its full impact. This fact was mentioned by CBS, which showed North holding up a few slides at the hearing and telling what was on each. ABC, however, managed to get file footage of North's presentation—complete with color slides of Soviet arms and leaders—displaying in ninety seconds of prime-time news what some committee members had tried so hard to suppress during the day.

Perhaps the most remarkable comment on the hearings came not from North or Sullivan or Dan Rather, but from that old television standby, the commercial. There was Joe Isuzu announcing yet another "truly incredible sale." Joe offers viewers a new Isuzu truck for only $3.00 ("give or take $6,399"), including a free chauffeur ("providing you pay for him"). A chorus of car salesmen affirms the punch line: "You have my word on it." Like the hearings, this advertisement is about lying. Like North explaining the morality of covert operations in order to promote American interests, Joe Isuzu exposes an unstated principle of deceptive advertising in the interest of commercial profits. Interestingly, in the Isuzu ad, the sound and image lie while the printed word—the fine print on the bottom of the screen—tells the truth. It is as if television were paying special tribute to the letter of the law while subverting it in the style of "Saturday Night Live."

While television news emphasized Sullivan's interruption and North's mute image, the *New York Times* presented a more complete and balanced coverage of the day's events. It gave more attention to McFarlane, who contradicted North's implications that he had known about or authorized North's clandestine operations. In more than thirty columns of print (the textual equivalent of about fifteen half-hour television news shows), the *Times* devoted only 239 words to the Sullivan-Inouye exchange and showed just two photographs of North. Here is *New York Times* reporter R. W. Apple's description (1987) of the exchange:

> Mr. Inouye, grave and severe, read the witness provisions of the honor code forbidding cadets at the service academies—Colonel North is a graduate of the Naval Academy—to lie, mislead or deceive. The Senator implied that because Colonel North had admitted to doing all of those things, he would be a poor role model for the young Americans who looked up to him.
>
> Then the Senator began to describe the Nuremberg war-crimes trials, at which the Allies refused to accept the defenses of Nazi leaders, arguing that there is a moral obligation to disobey unlawful orders.
>
> Mr. Inouye appeared to be about to apply that principle to Colonel North's repeated contention that he had authority from his superiors for everything he did.
>
> At that point, Brendan V. Sullivan, Jr., the colonel's counsel, exploded in wrath.

"I find this offensive," he shouted. "I find you engaging in a personal attack on Colonel North, and you're far removed from the issues of this case. To make reference to the Nuremberg trials, I find personally and professionally distasteful, and I can no longer sit here and listen to this."

Mr. Inouye cracked down the gavel, and after several more hot exchanges resumed his statement. He told Colonel North that he did not agree that "in the defense of democracy" the United States should "embrace one of the most important tenets of Communism and Marxism—that the ends justify the means."

This is a good example of the burdens and privileges of print. Without the benefit of sound or image, Apple must set the scene with verbal imagery: "exploded in wrath," "cracked down the gavel," and "hot exchanges." Apple supplies background information about North's naval training and the Nuremberg trials. He also interprets the proceedings, inserting what Inouye may have implied by his reference to the honor code and anticipating what the senator was about to say about Nuremberg. Elsewhere Apple notes "the touch of bitterness" in Inouye's voice, gives a lengthy account of his military record, and explains that both he and Representative Hamilton are "widely respected by their colleagues for their skill as legislative craftsmen and for their low-key, self-effacing styles." Unlike television, print handles these commentator functions easily; Apple's interpolations seem less obtrusive than Dan Rather's. On the other hand, while television can present the visual and emotional content of each scene in a few seconds of film, Apple is limited to a few descriptive phrases; for such purposes, the screen is worth a thousand words.

For the purpose of analysis, however, print has the leading edge. Wicker's editorial (1987) in the *New York Times* dissects the Sullivan-Inouye exchange with a well-honed scalpel. He exposes Sullivan's objection as "a last effort to divert attention from Colonel North's actual deeds to something more savory . . . the colonel's new-found public support." Examining Sullivan's complaint that Inouye implied a personal link between North and Nazi Germany, Wicker finds that Inouye was making a comparison of principles, not personalities: "It is not a sufficient legal defense for any U.S. military officer to say 'I only followed orders'" (A27). Wicker questions Sullivan's motives in the broad context of the hearings, noting that the outburst came immediately after Lee Hamilton's "withering and inexorable destruction of Colonel North's claims to have done nothing improper" and just before McFarlane's anticipated contradictions of North's testimony.

Wicker concludes that Sullivan's response was less a matter of personal outrage than of procedural strategy—a lawyer's trick. To balance the argument, Wicker summarizes Hamilton's contentions that North's secret arms sales to Iran "contradicted public policy, repudiated President Reagan's pledge not to make concessions to terrorists, involved a democratic nation in dealings with a terrorist state, deceived U.S. allies, and damaged the credibility of the nation in the Middle East and throughout the world." For three full paragraphs, he enumerates Hamilton's most salient points.

Wicker is able to do in print what commentators rarely do on television. Removed from the emotional impact of the moment, wielding the analytic instruments of written language, with ample space for factual asides and qualifying issues, Wicker can tease facts from opinions and separate arguments from personalities with an objectivity we have come to expect from the printed page. To be sure, Wicker's objectivity is itself subject to scrutiny; he has his own motives, his own scalpel to grind, but it's hard to imagine Jennings or Rather listing the points of Hamilton's speech with comparable precision or particularity. To do so would violate the accepted commercial norms of television—selling to a general audience. In print, Wicker is able to restore the reasoned arguments of Hamilton that Sullivan, using the dramatic, visual propensities of television, subverted on the screen.

A daily newspaper like the *New York Times* represents the day's events through transcripts, news articles, editorials, and photographs. Since events are already a day old when the *New York Times* appears, we read it more for depth and breadth of coverage than for the latest news. Why, then, do we read weekly news magazines, which are even less current or complete? *Newsweek*'s July 20, 1987, issue offered a special report on Oliver North. On the cover was a color photograph of Ollie and his wife Betsy. Inside were more photos, captioned close-ups of North's changing moods, an insert of his medals with explanatory notes, political cartoons, results of the latest polls, and a flagship article, "Ollie Takes the Hill." A commentary by Alter (1987), "Ollie Enters Folklore," compares North to the hero of Capra's populist film *Mr. Smith Goes to Washington,* starring Jimmy Stewart:

> North has Stewart's cracking voice and patriotic gaze down pat; the nobility of the common man shines through, particularly when set off against big-city lawyers (the Claude Rains role). The difference, for those who have trouble discerning it, is that Jimmy Stewart triumphed in the end by telling the truth. Oliver North has triumphed by defiantly admitting lies. Somehow

these two quite distinct reels of American morality have been spliced together in the public mind.

Alter goes on to note how television gives unprecedented authority to the image, honoring appearance over facts, performance above substance. Alter may be criticizing television, but his critique appears in a magazine that pays tribute to the visual media. Much of *Newsweek*'s news is about the role of television in making news. In fact, though, *Newsweek*'s format, like other weeklies, resembles the word-and-image mosaic of television itself. As with the evening news, we read it as much for entertainment as for information.

Banking on North's popular appeal, *U.S. News and World Report* rushed out a 128-page souvenir publication *The Story of Lieutenant Colonel Oliver North* (1987). Filled with "exclusive color photos," "a photographic album of North family pictures," and "glimpses into Ollie's private world," this is not so much an analysis as a celebration of Olliemania. The correspondences to television are explicit; North's story is presented as a "real-life documentary truly possible only in America" (7). Throughout, the emphasis is on North's Norman Rockwell image, reinforced by photos of a backyard barbecue, a hometown barbershop, North eating dinner with the kids at Roy Rogers after church. When he reaches the hearing room, North seems like David facing a bench of government Goliaths. Much of the commentary and the transcripts themselves show North in the best light. There are long excerpts from day one of the hearings, when North shined through preliminary questioning. There is less text from day six, when the case was summed up against him. Missing entirely is the Sullivan-Inouye exchange. Perhaps the editors could have assembled a less laudatory, if less lucrative package. The point is that this special issue blends text and image, print and television. In the case of Ollie North, the form suits his purpose well.

Such was North's image at the height of his media career. Within two years North's case came to trial in a very different climate. For his testimony at the hearings, he had been granted immunity, but now was facing criminal charges. In the courtroom, without his military uniform and the magnifying lens of television cameras, North appeared to have lost his heroic aura: "In sharp contrast to the bemedaled Marine who boasted of his exploits, lectured investigating lawmakers, and defiantly took the fall for his superiors in the scandal, North seemed defensive and sometimes petulant as he fenced with prosecutor John Keker" (Martz 1989, 38).

Finding a jury unfamiliar with his former image was not easy, but the twelve citizens finally selected for the panel said they had neither read nor watched anything about the hearings (Wines 1989). After a twelve-week trial, on May 4, 1989, the jury found North guilty of three crimes: shredding documents, accepting an illegal gift (a security system for his house), and aiding the obstruction of Congress by creating false chronologies (Johnston 1989). He was acquitted of nine other charges, some more serious. The most damaging charge, conspiracy to defraud the government, had been dropped months earlier when the Reagan administration refused to declassify secret documents. In a news analysis, Apple (1989) saw the jury's verdict as a political statement rather than a legal one. In rejecting the more serious felonies, the jurors refused to consider political lying a criminal act or to make North a scapegoat for his political superiors. Apple speculated, "They seem to be asking, 'Why should he be singled out when everybody else does it?'" (A18). But the jury drew a line where North had acted like a "loose cannon"; nobody had ordered him to accept the fence, destroy incriminating papers, or falsify chronologies.

Unlike the elected representatives who presided at the televised hearings, prosecutor Keker was able to draw damaging analogies without being diverted. Keker called North "the Joe Isuzu of government," who followed Hitler's maxim that "the victor will never be asked if he told the truth." Attacking North's heroic image, Keker said, "Government by deception is not a democratic government. Government by deception is not a government under the rule of law" (Associated Press, "Prosecutor Compares North to Hitler," 19 April 1989). While Sullivan took issue with these charges, and especially with the analogies to Hitler, his objections did not make the television news. They were recorded chiefly in newsprint, without the force of drama.

The North hearings illustrate many of the tendencies that critics of the media attribute to television. Television places the image above the word, the entertaining story above logical analysis. As John Hersey observed, North "lived out a real life version of the plots that dominate half our movies and three quarters of our television" (Alter 1988). The integrity of North's image seemed to brook the logical inconsistencies in his testimony. One moment he could say that "lying does not come easy to me," and another moment he could admit that "covert operations is itself a lie" without suffering a decline in the ratings. The camera helped North with its focus on his decorated uniform, its appetite for drama, its sensitivity to visual nuance beyond the legal facts. And it stressed the audience as much as the subject, focusing on polls and frequent views of viewers, reinforcing the idea that watching television is a ritual in which we watch ourselves. In brief, television served North through its appeal to holistic thought, suggestion, and community.

We cannot, though, simply condemn television for presenting a distorted picture of North or for misleading its viewers. As Fiske (1987) has shown in his astute studies of the medium, audiences are not dupes. The meaning of a television text is a negotiated truce between the forces of production and the many potential modes of reception (14–15). Moreover, reading television requires a working knowledge of its codes: social codes, like clothes and gestures; technical codes, like editing and camera angles; and the ideological codes of race, class, and gender. Television draws on and constructs its meanings from these codes at the same time that it develops the competence to read them. In the case of Ollie North, the television public's readings may have been more accurate than critics like Postman generally concede. They may also be closer to the spirit of democracy.

I began by citing Senator Inouye's concern about a government of laws giving way to a government of people. He worried that the piles of telegrams expressing support for North demonstrated that the public was responding more to faces than to arguments. But our legal system and our government also call for competence in reading images. Wills (1978) notes this, pointing to the influence of Thomas Reid on Jefferson's philosophy. Reid asserted that "common sense"—the shared wisdom of the community—is "a necessary guide and corrective for all thought" (188). As Jefferson understood it, common sense was the heart of our common moral sensibility, the highest faculty of human judgment (183–203). When today's juries are instructed to use their common sense in weighing evidence, they are told to include the visual evidence that guides their judgment of the witnesses' reliability. They are not expected to be experts in the law, but they are counted on for their competence in reading faces as well as facts to reach a common verdict. Imagery and community, those hallmarks of television culture, are also significant features of our legal system.

More important than Ollie North, television will continue to shape our culture and our institutions. Its appeal to community and its influence on how we read images will continue to be major factors in our national life. When the televised image of a revolving prison door can alter a presidential campaign, when the image of a Chinese student halting a column of tanks can contribute to our foreign policy, or when the image of an ex-Marine can change the course of a government inquiry, we need to consider carefully the claim that television is healthy or harmful to the future of American democracy. On this question, the jury is still out. But it is likely to be a jury schooled in television's imagery and common sense.

Works Cited

Alter, Jonathan. 1987. "Ollie Enters Folklore." *Newsweek*, 20 July, 19.

———. 1988. "How the Media Blew It." *Newsweek*, 21 November, 24, 26.

Apple, R. W., Jr. 1987. "North Is Dismissed by Iran Panel with Criticism for Policy of 'Lies.'" *New York Times*, 15 July, A1, A13.

———. 1989. "Measured Judgment." *New York Times*, 5 May, A18.

Eisenstein, Elizabeth. 1979. *The Printing Press as an Agent of Change: Communications and Cultural Transformations in Early Modern Europe.* New York: Cambridge University Press.

Fiske, John. 1987. *Television Culture.* New York: Methuen.

Fiske, John, and John Hartley. 1978. *Reading Television.* London: Methuen.

Goethals, Gregor. 1981. *The TV Ritual: Worship at the Video Altar.* Boston: Beacon Press.

Johnston, David. 1989. "North Guilty on 3 of 12 Counts." *New York Times*, 5 May, A1, A19.

Martz, Larry. 1987. "Ollie Takes the Hill." *Newsweek*, 20 July, 12–20.

———. 1989. "Ollie's Tarnished Image." *Newsweek*, 24 April, 38.

Ong, Walter. 1982. *Orality and Literacy: The Technologizing of the Word.* New York: Methuen.

Postman, Neil. 1985. *Amusing Ourselves to Death: Public Discourse in the Age of Show Business.* New York: Viking.

Rosenbaum, David. 1987. "McFarlane Disputes North on Key Points of Testimony." *New York Times*, 15 July, A1, A14.

U.S. News and World Report. 1987. *The Story of Lieutenant Colonel Oliver North.* Washington, DC: U.S. News and World Report, Inc.

Wicker, Tom. 1987. "Colonel North's Last Stand." *New York Times*, 15 July, A27.

Wills, Garry. 1978. *Inventing America: Jefferson's Declaration of Independence.* New York: Doubleday.

Wines, Michael. 1989. "Selection of Jury Begins for North." *New York Times*, 1 February, A12.

9 Instant History, Image History: Lessons from the Persian Gulf War

George Gerbner
University of Pennsylvania

The year 1991 began with the world-class spectacle of the Persian Gulf War. Midway it saw the Russian coup collapse in a global blizzard of defiant imagery. Sandwiched between these events were sensational Senate hearings, televised courtroom dramas, video images of a black man beaten by Los Angeles policemen—images that later ignited a riot—and a movie that reinvented the "real" JFK. It is evident that 1991 was the year when media imagery tipped the geopolitical scales, shook the sex-role power structure, redefined urban politics, and altered the historiographic conventions of our time.

Of course, the selective process of what is communicated to whom, when, how, and with what effects has always shaped the course of private and public affairs. Until recently, however, the process remained essentially time-bound: accounts were produced and history was usually written after the fact. News was something that had already happened. Rather than witnessing history, we read about past events.

There comes a time when the accumulation of quantitative changes produces a qualitative transformation. Add heat to a pot of water and it simmers. Add speed to an account of a crisis—until it becomes not only selective and interactive, but also global and instantaneous with the event—and it becomes time-unbound with explosive consequences. Under such circumstances, the pot reaches the boiling point. The Gulf War of 1991 was such a point. In this chapter,[1] I will sketch some characteristics of instant history making, then offer a scenario and a model. I will then focus on the Gulf War, discussing what went on behind the scenes and what we might learn from it.

Instant History Making

When asked what he thought about the French Revolution, Mao Ze-dong said that it was too soon to tell (Ash 1991). Usually, official history from the ruler's point of view is about the inevitable unfolding of the glorious present. As written by losers, history is tragedy crying for redemption. When these roles change, or when long-hidden facts come to light, it takes time to sort things out. But there are times when the sorting-out process itself changes. When Saudi financier Adnan Khassoghi was asked what he thought about the war in the Persian Gulf, he said it was "like going to a movie: we paid our money, we went to the theater, we laughed, we cried, the movie ended, and an hour later we had forgotten about it" (Masland 1991).

This observation marks a change that came about after centuries of build-up. Cheap parchment replaced rare papyrus; the printing press replaced the quill; the telegraph and telephone replaced the Pony Express. We went from oral to scribal to literate to audio-visual-digital-cybernetic, mass-produced culture. The last quantum leap occurred when satellites connected everything together, all around the world. The stage was set for centrally scripted, real-time, live global imagery, evoking instant reaction and feeding media events back to influence an ongoing crisis.

Historiography is a communicative activity that relates the past to the present and the future (Briesach 1989). When the means and modes of communication change, as McLuhan and others have observed, access to and control over communications change. The telling of stories, including history, changes too. The boiling point occurs when the power to create a crisis merges with the power to direct the movie about it. Participation—witness and confirmation hitherto limited to those on the scene—can now be a vicarious global experience and response that happens while the event is still in progress (or, as in the case of *JFK*, while the event seems to be happening again). Having achieved the desired outcome, the movie ends, but the images remain in memories and in archives.

New communicative technologies confer control, concentrate power, shrink time, and speed action—to the point where reporting, making, and writing history merge. McLuhan's "simultaneous happenings"—in which "the whole world's electronic participation is presumed"—will increasingly occur in crises, trials, hearings, disasters, uprisings, and wars. Yet these are situations in which deliberate speed and careful consideration are most needed. Instead, however, past, present, and future can now be packaged, witnessed, and frozen into the memorable, moving imagery of instantaneous history—cast, scripted, directed, and produced by the winners. By triggering the rapid breakup of the Soviet Union, for instance, instant history robbed it of the transition time it needed to develop options, such as a coalition of self-governing republics (Friedman 1992). A new and real historical force came into play and gave the deliberate sorting out of things a swift kick in the pants.

Instant History, Image History

Instant history is made when access to video-satellite-computer systems blankets the world in real-time with selected images that provoke immediate reactions, influence the outcome, and then quick-freeze it all into received history. Films of Vietnam took hours or days to reach us, after the fact. It may have been the first "living room war," but not for the first few years and not in real-time. Starting with the purported incident in the Gulf of Tonkin, it was a long, slow, duplicitous build-up. Lasting eleven years, it destroyed three countries and left behind some two million dead. "Body counts" were in headlines but did not have public witness. The tide of public reaction turned only after cameras began to record unsettling images: the casual execution of an enemy suspect, naked children fleeing napalm, thatched huts burning. When cameras turn to focus on the fallen, the war is lost, or soon will be. (Accordingly, the press was barred from Dover Air Force Base where Gulf War body bags landed. It took a freelance reporter posing as a mortician to get an estimate of the casualties.)

In contrast, chaotic perestroika, made visible by glasnost, rolled into an Eastern Europe where each successive counter-revolution took half the time of the previous one. And when the long pent-up Soviet backlash led to the attempted coup of August 1991, the plotters lost control when the magic lantern was snatched from their hands. Defiant imagery flooded their timorous stance. A tidal wave of domestic and world reaction swept them from power in seventy-two hours. Instead of victors, they became victims of instant image history.

Speed and controlled imagery give instant history its thrust—and its burden. When emphasis shifts to image, complex verbal explanations and interpretations, if any, switch into supporting and explanatory rather than alternative modes. Milburn and McGrail (1990) point out that, to reach a peaceful resolution of a conflict, we must entertain a variety of perspectives and engage in complex rather than simplistic thinking. Their experiments (and others) show that dramatic imagery tends to inhibit both complexity and divergent perspectives. Instant history preempts alternatives.

Postman (1985) argues that pictures "have no difficulty overwhelming words and short-circuiting introspection" (103), while Grimes (1990) concludes that words can influence our memory of imagery. This means that voice-over narration can be recalled as a part of the actuality witnessed on the screen, even if it never occurred there. On the other hand, if the narration conflicts with the image, it may be ignored. Todd Gitlin (1991a) recounts his four-hour interview for "The NBC Nightly News" in which he stated that his opposition to the Gulf War did not conflict with donating blood for the troops. Yet the few seconds selected for the news only showed him donating blood, with his opposition to the war briefly noted in the voice-over. Viewers who confronted him afterward recalled only the image of his apparent support for the war. Gitlin wrote, "People who wouldn't be caught dead saying out loud that the news (to use the media's own favorite metaphor) mirrors reality, saw a media image and *assumed it not to be a construction, not a version, but the truth.*"

Images of actuality, selective as they may be, appear to be spontaneous and to reveal what really happens. They do not need logic to build their case. Staging "photo opportunities" to invoke powerful "reality" with a voice-over gloss and perhaps a sound bite is the new marketing tool for presidents, candidates, and wars. Williams (1991) observes that "spontaneity and immediacy deny time for reflection and evaluation. And if audience response quickly becomes news, this could exaggerate the effects of superficial responses to important world events" (17). Phelan (1991) concludes, "The further one gets from the reality, the more processed the information gets, and the more authority it assumes."

Instant history is a magic lantern projecting images on a blank screen in a temporal void, telescoping roles, parts, and outcome into the same act, appealing to prior beliefs and predilections, and triggering familiar responses. It blends into our repertoire of imagery. It is not easily dislodged, reinterpreted, or even attributed to one particular event. Worse still, we forget the title.

The Scenario and a Model

The Persian Gulf War was an unprecedented motion picture experience, cramming into its first month alone the entire preserved visual images—and firepower—of World War II. But unlike GIs "flushing out the enemy" from their hiding places, we were shown "seeing-eye" bombs zooming in on their targets followed by computer graphics tracing the ground offensive against an invisible enemy. General Schwarzkopf forbade casualty estimates, so sortie counts replaced body counts. Photographs of combat dead were censored. Sleek aircraft "sortied" over unmentionable people in unfought battles in an unseen country. The few unauthorized shots of bombs falling on civilian targets were attacked as treasonous or rationalized as "collateral damage"—a term defined by *Time* magazine as "dead or wounded civilians who should have picked a safer neighborhood." Never before were selected glimpses of actuality strung together with sound bites from photogenic crews, omniscient voice-overs from safari-clad reporters, and a parade of military experts with maps and charts at the ready, so mesmerizing, so coherent, and so contrived.

Desert Storm was the first global crisis media orchestration that made instant history. The Soviet coup six months later was the first attempt that miscarried. Opportunities for making instant history may be few and far between, but when they come, they loosen landslides that shift the political landscape: "I came back to another country," said Gorbachev when he returned from Crimean captivity. Successful crisis management by instant history requires five strategic moves or conditions: (1) access, (2) orchestration, (3) guided witness, (4) feedback, and (5) quick-freeze. I will try to spell out these conditions and illustrate with examples from the Gulf War.

First, access to real-time global imagery provides control over what is known—and, more importantly, not known—about events leading up to and making the crisis. To keep control, it is important to isolate the event from its real history, to screen out contrasting images, to marginalize dissent, and to speed the action. But grave crises have long and involved histories. Since few people know or care about these roots, they are easily ignored. Instant history making works best if presented as a response to sudden and irrational provocation. Acting in an historical vacuum, audiences fall back on conventional response patterns cultivated by everyday news and drama, such as crime and violence. Invoking the true history of the crisis risks confounding this simple scenario.

Suppressing all dissenting voices would provoke and alienate too many and, in any case, may promote exaggerated estimates of the extent of that suppression. It is better to report opposition through sound bites and voice-overs in its most limited, trivialized, offensive, or bizarre forms. This implies that the opposition is merely the obligatory nuisance protest to almost anything in a true democracy. But imagery that shows and tells from another perspective is dangerous, because it short-circuits reasoning in the wrong direction. Most of all, opponents speaking for themselves—without sound bites or voice-overs—and, even more importantly, controlling the cameras from their own points of view are to be avoided. Yeltsin's defiant gesture on top of a tank marked the turning point of the Russian coup. No such discord marred the Persian Gulf War scenario. Widely used protest footage showed opponents waving the Iraqi flag and engaging in other provocative action. Independent documentaries from the field were censored or suppressed, even when commissioned by and delivered to television networks. To keep control, image managers must speed the action. Usually, one burst of saturation coverage is all you have before interruptive voices and audiences missing their daily television ritual blunt the momentum and diminish public support. (According to a February 1992 issue of *Broadcasting*, advertisers even defected during the Gulf War.)

Second, instant history requires orchestrating a coherent environment of actuality, images, talk shows, slogans, and other evocative exhibitions. To combine mainstream media events, signs, and symbols into a harmonious whole, it is useful to invent language, signs, and actions that fit the scenario, to channel support, and to evoke some mystery. Code names and terms that fit the scenario, demonize the "enemy," and wrap jarring realities in euphemisms leave no alternative to the "them versus us" construction of the crisis. For example, they employ "terror weapons"; we use "surgical strikes." They unplug incubators to kill babies; we fight with "high-tech hardware" to keep casualties down. And if we fail, it's just "collateral damage."

Supporting signs and symbols should be integrated into everyday life: yellow ribbons on cars and on Kent cigarettes; a pro-war Super Bowl half-time pageant with President and Mrs. Bush on tape and Peter Jennings live giving upbeat reports on the destruction in progress. Orchestration means blending images and messages into a symphony that combines a crisis mentality with the need to keep business going as usual. Glory travels well. Gore does not deliver audiences in a receptive mood—unless it can be attributed to the enemy—and so the only appearance of burned children being carried out of a Baghdad shelter—"collateral damage"—was dismissed on

"The MacNeil/Lehrer News Hour" as "heavy-handed manipulation" by Iraqi propaganda.

Appeals to the Deity and to mystery also help orchestrate instant history on behalf of "the highest values." Speaking to religious leaders, then-President Bush recounted his praying before he ordered the ground attack "as Christ ordained." Bush affirmed his belief in "the first value . . . the sanctity of life." An icon of St. Irene gained worldwide attention when congregants in a Chicago church reported that it wept "tears of grief" on the eve of the Persian Gulf War. (This "weeping icon" was finally called a hoax and a publicity stunt in the *New York Times* [McFadden 1991]).

Third, instant history requires us to "participate" in a global "simultaneous happening." Of course, being a "guided witness" to history is a compelling experience. To simplify the crisis and isolate it from distracting complexities and unwanted alternatives, the audience is offered a sense of "being there," accomplished by providing what appear to be spontaneous photo opportunities, press conferences, and briefings. Properly staged briefings are especially useful because they promise inside dope straight from the photogenic source and avoid hard questions. Reviewing "The Best of 1991 Television," *Newsweek* (6 January 1992) compared Schwarzkopf's briefing to John Wayne's farewell to the troops in *She Wore a Yellow Ribbon:* "The general embodied a nation's ideal of the perfect warrior: tough, professional, charismatic, compassionate" (80).

Fourth, translating witness into participation and supportive feedback—from polls and letters to the editor to driving with lights on and honking horns—completes the interactive cycle. Making it "like going to a movie" evokes conventionally cultivated responses. The feedback reverberates in all media, crystallizes in public (i.e., published) opinion, and hastens the desired resolution.

Finally, instant history requires quick-freeze: rapidly produced videos, CD-ROM disks, paperback books, and illustrated texts celebrate the outcome as the Happy Ending. Saturating the market—including schools—for instant nostalgia with such triumphant imagery preempts historians, fights political opposition, and resists—or at least delays—revisionists.

So much for the model scenario. Now for the main event and how it was produced and performed. We may "forget the title," but we should prepare for the sequel.

The Main Event

"As the skies cleared . . . an American officer proclaimed 'a beautiful day for bombing'" wrote R. W. Apple, Jr. (1991) in the *New York Times*. Before the day was over, 750 bombing missions were completed. "'There is more stuff up there than I'd see in twenty lifetimes,' said an Air Force pilot." What may have been happening on the ground could only be surmised from a safe distance. John Balzar (1991) of the *Los Angeles Times* reported "relentless rumbling" as "the skyline flickers hot orange." In the first month, "the tonnage of high explosive bombs already released has exceeded the combined allied air offensive of World War II." But the military terminology that permeated the reporting was more sports than slaughter: "Our team has carried out its game beautifully," praised a military expert on NBC. "We ran our first play—it worked great," said a pilot interviewed on CBS. "We scored a touchdown," applauded another reporter (Parenti 1991). CBS reporter Jim Stewart spoke of "two days of almost picture-perfect assaults" (*New York Times*, 24 May 1991). Secretary of Defense Dick Cheney told U.S. Air Force personnel they conducted "the most successful air campaign in the history of the world" (Thompson and Fiedler 1991).

This "precision bombing" spectacular dumped the equivalent of five Hiroshima A-bombs on a small country of ancient culture. Targeted were the life-sustaining elements of water, power, transportation, and health-care facilities, even though this destruction had doubtful military value. When the bombing ended, hunger and disease began. A Harvard University study team estimated that the delayed effects of the bombing left a million children malnourished and 170,000 children under five years of age dying of hunger, cholera, and typhoid. The U.S. Census Bureau later reported that in 1991, the life expectancy of Iraqi males dropped twenty years, from sixty-six to forty-six; the life expectancy of women dropped ten years, from sixty-seven to fifty-seven (Weiner 1992). Middle East Watch reported that allied decisions to drop unguided bombs in daytime over populated areas without warning civilians of imminent attacks violated generally accepted practice and international law "both in the selection of targets and the choice of means and methods of attack" (Healy 1991).

And yet, the image of brave Patriots slaying deadly Scuds was probably the most memorable scene of the Persian Gulf War movie. About 158 Patriot missiles were fired. Each missle cost $700,000. They missed eight out of ten times. When they found their targets, the resulting debris caused more destruction than the Scuds alone would have. But all that was not in the script of instant history. The most thorough analysis of the Patriot anti-missile system was made by physicist Theodore A. Postol, a Pentagon science adviser and professor of national security policy at the Massachusetts Institute of Technology. He called the system "an almost total failure," even though it faced "quite primitive attacking missiles." The displays of thunder and flame seen around the world were an illusion, he said. Patriots would rush toward speeding fragments of poorly designed Iraqi Scuds that fell apart in the atmosphere as they approached their targets. The resulting fireball was mistaken as a successful interception, while in actuality the Scud warhead streaked by unscathed (Broad 1992). Johnson (1991) concluded that the Patriots were "successful mainly as psychological weapons used to fool the public." This success is shown in a survey by Morgan, Lewis, and Jhally: 81 percent of the population knew about the Patriots, while only 42 percent could identify Colin Powell.

The mighty armies that ran over Kuwait and were supposed to march on to Saudi Arabia could not be found. Poorly equipped and demoralized troops, sitting in trenches, caves, and bunkers without air cover, were napalmed to deprive those inside of oxygen and then bulldozed, burying dead and alive alike in some seventy miles of trenches. Bodies of soldiers who "suffocated in their bunkers after U.S. tanks plowed them under" were still being discovered nine months after the war (Associated Press dispatch from Nicosia, Cyprus, 5 November 1991). Defenseless convoys fleeing in panic were bombed and strafed in what pilots called a "turkey shoot." Andrew Whitley (1991) wrote:

> Nothing prepared me for the utter devastation. . . . heat-blasted wrecks piled crazily one on top of another, the U.S. Navy . . . must have used a combination of fuel-air explosives and cluster bombs against the hopelessly snarled convoy of vehicles. . . . The trail of destruction stretches a full thirty miles. . . . Within a mile-long section of the destroyed convoy, I counted more than a dozen ambulances and other vehicles bearing Red Crescent signs. (17)

The four-week Iraq massacre was more lethal than any nuclear, chemical, or biological warfare has ever been. One may question whether there really was a war. If by war we mean a conflict in which an enemy shoots back, the Persian Gulf operation was a slaughter. Official estimates ranged from 15,000 to 100,000 in direct casualties. In one report, former Navy Secretary John Lehman gave a Pentagon estimate of 200,000 dead (Mathison 1991). Whatever the correct figure for Iraqi casualties, only 146 U.S. soldiers were killed, at least 35 of them by "friendly fire" (Hackworth 1991)—a kill ratio unprecedented in military history.

The main facts of cost, casualties, and damage were kept out of briefings and censored from reports. United States and allied reporters were rigidly controlled. Independent reporters who managed to obtain information on their own were excluded from the mainstream media. NBC first commissioned, then refused to broadcast, uncensored footage of heavy civilian casualties. Then, the night before this video was to air on the "CBS Evening News," the show's executive producer was fired and the report canceled (Bernstein and Futran 1991). The media watch group Project Censored selected this "the top censored story of 1991."

Johnson (1991) monitored CNN during the twenty-seven-hour pre-war period when Iraq proposed conditional withdrawal and Soviet and Iranian peace initiatives were advanced. His study revealed that thirty military experts, but no peace experts, were interviewed. George Bush, the most frequently shown, brushed aside peace talk. Most of the others interviewed were military advocates, including Oliver North, Robert McFarlane, Jeane Kirkpatrick, Dan Quayle, and Ronald Reagan. And CNN may have been the most open to diverse views. Fairness and Accuracy in Reporting (FAIR) found that only 1.5 percent of Gulf War news sources who appeared on the ABC, CBS, and NBC nightly news were against the war, and only one of 878 sources cited represented a national peace organization. Opposition to United States action was most frequently attributed to "the enemy" (Lee 1991, 31). (Note that major military contractors sponsor news programs and sit on the boards of directors of networks and other leading media, such as the *New York Times* and *Washington Post*. NBC in particular is owned by General Electric, a supplier for every weapons system used in the Gulf.)

Instead of providing full, accurate reports and documentaries, network "docudramas," shot in sync sound on location and in Hollywood studios, took audiences to the movies during the Persian Gulf War. Realistic shots of training, tanks maneuvering in the sand, simulated trench warfare, and scripted scenes of camp life and the "home front" alternated with promos for *Die Hard 2* and *Terminator 2*. Spectacular explosions lit distant horizons, hurled vehicles, and blasted bodies in both movies. As for the docudramas, happy endings showed jubilant faces, while voice-overs spoke of "an outpouring of joy not seen since World War II." The real documentary footage of the conflict is locked in Pentagon vaults.

What was represented as a clean, swift, surgical strike to punish aggression, get rid of Saddam, and secure cheap oil, petrodollars, peace, jobs, and democracy became, in fact, a human and ecological disaster of, in the words of the United Nations inspection team, "cataclysmic proportions," achieving few, if any, of its purported aims. Amos (1991), who covered the Gulf War for National Public Radio, scoffed at the adage that truth is the first casualty of war. "In this war," she wrote, "truth was more than a casualty. Truth was hit over the head, dragged into a closet, and held hostage to the public relations needs of the United States Military" (61).

How did this happen? The saturation, manipulation, and fabrications that make up the instant history experience provide only part of the answer. A large part comes from the orchestration that drowns out the historical context, isolating the crisis from a balanced and meaningful perspective. That absence of perspective throws the spectator-witness back upon conventional conceptions of how things work in the world. And in our culture, many of these conceptions stem from the cult of violence.

The Cult of Violence

Violence has many faces. Wholesale mass executions have become increasingly technical, scientific, and deadly.[2] But they have become no more precise, killing an ever-increasing percentage of civilians, far outnumbering military casualties. The German terror-bombing of Guernica provoked worldwide outrage and Picasso's anti-war mural. By the end of World War II, thousands of air raids, the calculated destruction of Dresden, the fire-bombing of Tokyo, and the pulverizing of Hiroshima and Nagasaki numbed our senses—all for little, if any, military advantage. This trend toward increasingly skewed kill ratios culminated in the Persian Gulf War. The political bombing of civilians is no longer thought of as barbaric. Instead, we view it as potentially embarrassing information to be sanitized by euphemisms.

Retail violence is not far behind. The United States is the undisputed homicide capital of the world. We also lead industrialized countries in jailing and executing people.[3] Our streets, our schools, and our homes have become places of fear and brutality, widely publicized and profitably dramatized. The number of killings that occurred in the workplace in the 1980s was double that of the previous decade (Bayles

1991). And yet, the cult of violence is neither simply a reflection of these trends nor just a stimulus for them. It is more like a charged environment affecting many aspects of social relations, control, and power.

The facts of violence are both celebrated and concealed in the cult of violence that surrounds us. Never was a culture so filled with full-color images of violence as ours is now. Of course, there is blood in fairy tales, gore in mythology, murder in Shakespeare, lurid crimes in tabloids, and battles and wars in textbooks. Such representations of violence are legitimate cultural expressions, even necessary to balance tragic consequences against deadly compulsions. But the historically defined, individually crafted, and selectively used symbolic violence of heroism, cruelty, or authentic tragedy has been replaced by violence with happy endings produced on the dramatic assembly line.

The violence we see on the screen and read about in our press bears little relationship either in volume or in type, especially in its consequences, to violence in real life (Surette 1992). Yet much of it looks realistic, and growing up with it helps us project it onto the real world. This sleight-of-hand robs us of the tragic sense of life necessary for compassion. "To be hip," writes Gitlin (1991b), "is to be inured, and more—to require a steadily increasing boost in the size of the dose required" (247). Our children are born into a symbolic environment of six to eight violent episodes per prime-time hour alone—four times as many in presumably humorous children's programs—and an average of at least two entertaining murders a night. These dominant images of mayhem and crime misrepresent the actual nature, demography, and patterns of victimization of real-life violence. Contrary to the hype that promoted them, most uses of cable, video, and other new technologies make the dominant patterns penetrate even more deeply into everyday life. No historical, aesthetic, or even commercial rationalization can justify drenching every home with images of expertly choreographed brutality.

Movies cash in on the cult and increase the dosage. Escalation of the cinematic body count seems to be one way to get attention from a public punch-drunk on video mayhem. *The Godfather* produced twelve corpses, *Godfather II* put away eighteen, and *Godfather III* killed no less than fifty-three. In 1988, the daredevil cop in the original *Die Hard* saved the day with a modest eighteen dead. Two years later, *Die Hard 2* achieved a body count of 264. The decade's record goes to the 1990 children's movie, tie-in marketing sensation, and glorification of martial arts *Teenage Mutant Ninja Turtles*. Released as the Gulf War build-up began, it is the most violent film that has ever been marketed to children, with 133 acts of mayhem per hour. *Turtles II: Secrets of the Ooze* followed the success of the Ninjas—and of the Gulf War—through another nonstop, kick-in-the-teeth opera.

The October 14, 1991, international edition of *Variety* featured 123 pages of ads for new movies, with pictures of shooting, killing, or corpses on every other page and a verbal appeal to violence, on the average, on every page. Leading the verbal procession were *kill, murder, death, deadly,* and *dead* (thirty-three times) and *terror, fatal, lethal,* and *dangerous* (twelve times). Bringing up the rear were *rage, frenzy, revenge, guncrazy, kickboxer, maniac, warrior, invader, hawk, battle, war, shoot, fight, slaughter,* and *blood.*

Terminator 2 was the top-grossing film in the United States in 1991. Its star, Arnold Schwarzenegger, has been named "the most violent actor" by the National Coalition on Television Violence: ten of his movies averaged 109 often graphic and gruesome violent acts per hour. He was also appointed head of President Bush's Council on Physical Fitness and Sports.

Growing up in a violence-laden culture breeds aggressiveness in some and desensitization, insecurity, mistrust, and anger in most (Gerbner 1988). These are highly exploitable sentiments. They set up a scenario of violence and victimization in which some take on the role of violent perpetrators. Most, however, assume the role and psychology of victims. And as victims, they demand protection, condoning, if not welcoming, violent solutions to domestic and world problems—the Gulf War a case in point—where punitive and vindictive action against dark forces in a mean world is made to look appealing, especially when presented as quick, decisive, and enhancing our sense of control and security.

The cult of violence is the ritual demonstration and celebration of brute power—and its projection into sex, family, job, politics, and war. An overkill of violent imagery helps to instill the military attitude toward killing and to mobilize support for it. Bombarding viewers with violent images—without illuminating the real costs of violence and war—is, in the last analysis, an act of intimidation and terror. It was indispensable to the triumph of instant history in the Persian Gulf, and it is a preview of things to come.

Within weeks of the victory, Time Warner, in record time, collected and compressed enough imagery to fill five hundred floppy disks onto a single CD-ROM history of Desert Storm, which was speedily distributed to stores and school libraries. (Such a task ordinarily takes several months.) Published soon afterward was *CNN: War in the Gulf,* advertised as the "authoritative chronicle of the world's first 'real-time television war.'" Pentagon-aided victory parades and an ABC-TV docudrama "Heroes of Desert Storm"—with a thirty-second introduction by President Bush—rounded out the triumphant quick-freeze stage of instant history. And in a fitting and perceptive tribute, *Time* magazine named CNN owner Ted Turner its Man of the Year "for influencing the dynamic of events and turning viewers in 150 countries into instant witnesses of history." (Time Warner is also a one-fifth owner of the Turner Broadcasting System.)

Anatomy of a Triumphant Image

How did this model of success play out on the home front? Once the saturation bombing started and the tide of saturation coverage rose, most respondents to a Times Mirror poll were swept up in the flow. The response itself became news and sped the rush of events. Half of the respondents, most of whom wanted more diverse views before, now said they heard too much opposition. As the operation entered its second week, instant history found its true believers. Nearly eight out of ten people believed that the censors were not hiding bad news; 57 percent wanted increased military control over reporting. In a British poll, 82 percent agreed that the sorties were "precise strikes against strategic targets with minimum civilian casualties" (Times Mirror Center for People and the Press 1991). Pan's survey (1993) of audience reactions a month after the war also found that most respondents felt satisfied with the coverage; most agreed that the media "provided realistic accounts of the war," rejected the criticism that many important stories were missed, and yet agreed with the need for military censorship.

This triumph of orchestrated imagery can be gauged from the differences between responses of light and heavy television viewers of otherwise comparable groups. The Morgan, Lewis, and Jhally survey shows that three-quarters of heavy viewers (76 percent), as compared to less than half of light viewers (47 percent), "strongly supported" President Bush's decision to use military force against Iraq. Pan's study (1993) found that

> heavy TV news viewers were more satisfied with media war coverage, appraised the quality of war coverage more highly, and were less likely to criticize the media. . . . They were also more willing to accept the practice of stringent military controls over media access to information.

Two months after the war, the public rated the media coverage, military censorship, and general information about the war even higher. The Times Mirror (1991) percentage of those rating the military as "very favorable" rose 42 points, from 18 to an unprecedented 60 percent. Desert Storm commander Norman Schwarzkopf's 51 percent was the highest "very favorable" score in over 150 Times Mirror surveys, instantly fueling speculation about his political future.

Global immediacy gave us instant history. Instant history is simultaneous, global, living, telling, showing, and reacting in brief and intensive bursts. Image-driven and violence-laden, compelling as it is contrived, instant history robs us of reflection time, critical distance, political space, and access to alternatives. The horrors of a Holocaust can now be managed with glorious efficiency. The Gulf War is fading to a few flickering images: Scuds streaking through the sky and Patriots rising to intercept them—or so we thought; bombs falling down factory smokestacks with deadly accuracy—or so, too, we thought. But that was no movie. Its consequences will linger in the real world for a long time to come. This is not an isolated problem that can be addressed by focusing on media violence or crisis coverage alone. It is an integral part of a global cultural condition that increasingly poisons our symbolic environment.

Notes

1. A different version is in press as chapter 20 in *Triumph of the Image: The Media's War in the Persian Gulf, A Global Perspective* (1992). A brief summary was presented as the first Wayne Danielson Award Lecture for Distinguished Contributions to Communication Scholarship at the University of Texas in Austin, 13 November 1991.

2. Wars in the twentieth century have killed ninety-nine million people (before the Gulf War), twelve times as many as in the nineteenth century and twenty-two times as many as in the eighteenth century. Other hostilities, not counting internal state terrorism, resulted in an estimated 1,000 or more deaths per year (World Priorities 1986).

3. According to a National Center for Health Statistics study published in the *Journal of the American Medical Association* and reported in the *New York Times* (Rosenthal 1990), the rate of killings in the United States is 21.9 per 100,000 men aged 15 through 24. To compare, the rate for Austria is 0.3, for England 1.2, and for Scotland 5.0, highest after the United States. And according to Congressional hearings reported in the *Philadelphia Inquirer* (Miller 1990), between 1985 and 1989, the number of homicides nationwide increased 22 percent. Furthermore, the rate of incarceration in the United States is 407 per 100,000 citizens. This compares to 36 in the Netherlands, 86 in West

Germany, and 100 in England. And while the prison population in the United States doubled in the 1980s, the crime rate rose only 1.8 percent, suggesting that the "need to incarcerate" is out of proportion with the actual crime rate, that it is a political response to culturally generated insecurity and demand for repression.

Works Cited

Amos, Deborah. 1991. "When Seeing Is Not Believing." *Nieman Reports* 45 (Winter): 61–62.

Apple, R. W., Jr. 1991. "Allies Step Up Gulf Air Offensive; Strike Focus on Iraqis in Kuwait." *New York Times,* 12 February, A1, A12.

Ash, Timothy Garton. 1991. "Poland after Solidarity." *New York Review of Books,* 13 June, 57.

Balzar, John. 1991. "Marines Pity Iraqis as Horror Rains from the Skies." *Philadelphia Inquirer,* 5 February, 6A.

Bayles, Fred. 1991. "Eight Other Shootings at Post Office since '83." *Philadelphia Inquirer,* 15 November, 3A.

Bernstein, Dennis, and Sasha Futran. 1991. "Sights Unseen." *San Francisco Bay Guardian,* 20 March, 23.

Briesach, Ernst. 1989. "Historiography." In *International Encyclopedia of Communications,* 2: 280–84. Oxford: Oxford University Press.

Broad, William J. 1992. "Critic of Patriot Missile Says It Was 'Almost Total Failure' in War." *New York Times,* 9 January, A10.

Friedman, Thomas L. 1992. "Baker's Trip to Nations Unready for Independence." *New York Times,* 16 February, A16.

Gerbner, George. 1988. *Violence and Terror in the Mass Media.* Paris: UNESCO.

Gitlin, Todd. 1991a. "On Being Sound-Bitten." *Boston Review* 16 (December): 15–17.

———. 1991b. "On Thrills and Kills: Sadomasochism in the Movies." *Dissent* (Spring): 245–48.

Grimes, Tom. 1990. "Encoding TV News Messages into Memory." *Journalism Quarterly* 67 (Winter): 757–66.

Hackworth, David. 1991. "Killed by Their Comrades." *Newsweek,* 18 November, 45–46.

Healy, Melissa. 1991. "Group Faults U.S. on War Deaths." *Philadelphia Inquirer,* 17 November, 9A.

Johnson, Roger N. 1991. "Cultural Evolution and War: From Science to Social Science." *Bulletin of the International Society for Research on Aggression* 13.2.

Lee, Martin A. 1991. "Arms and the Media: Business as Usual." *Index on Censorship* 20 (November-December): 29–31.

Masland, Tom. 1991. "Beyond the Caricatures of Hussein and His Society." *Philadelphia Inquirer,* 1 September, 2F.

Mathison, Dirk. 1991. "Inside the Bohemian Grove: The Story *People* Magazine Won't Let You Read." *Extra,* November-December, 1, 12–14.

McFadden, Robert D. 1991. "'Weeping Icon' Returned to New York City Church." *New York Times,* 29 December, A1, A22.

Milburn, Michael, and Ann B. McGrail. 1990. "The Dramatic Presentation of News and Its Effects on Cognitive Complexity." Paper presented at the American Political Science Convention, September, San Francisco.

Miller, Bill. 1990. "Murderpace Is Surging, Panel Told." *Philadelphia Inquirer,* 1 August, 1A.

Mowlana, Hamid, George Gerbner, and Herbert I. Schiller, eds. 1992. *Triumph of the Image: The Media's War in the Persian Gulf, A Global Perspective.* Boulder, CO: Westwood Press.

Pan, Zhongdang. 1993. "Audience Evaluations of U.S. News Media Performance during the Persian Gulf War." In *Desert Storm and the Mass Media,* edited by Bradley Greenberg and Walter Gantz. Cresskill, NJ: Hampton Press.

Parenti, Michael. 1991. "Media Watch: Now for Sports and Weather." *Z Magazine,* July/August, 104.

Phelan, John M. 1991. "Image Industry Erodes Political Space." *Media Development* 38.4.

Postman, Neil. 1985. *Amusing Ourselves to Death: Public Discourse in the Age of Show Business.* New York: Viking.

Rosenthal, Elisabeth. 1990. "U.S. Is By Far the Homicide Capital of the Industrialized Nations." *New York Times,* 27 June, A10.

Surette, Ray. 1992. *Media Crime and Criminal Justice: Images and Realities.* Pacific Grove, CA: Brooks/Cole Publishing.

Thompson, Mark, and Tom Fiedler. 1991. "U.S. Hints at Strategy in Land War." *Philadelphia Inquirer,* 9 February, 1A, 4A.

Times Mirror Center for People and the Press. 1991. "The People, the Press, and the War in the Gulf." Releases on 10 January, 31 January, and 25 March. Washington, DC: Times Mirror Center for People and the Press.

Viles, Peter. 1992. "TV Networks Tout Crisis Advertising." *Broadcasting,* 3 February, 38.

Weiner, Tim. 1992. "Studies: 70,000 Deaths in Postwar Iraq." *Philadelphia Inquirer,* 9 January, 3A.

Whitley, Andrew. 1991. "Kuwait: The Last Forty-Eight Hours." *New York Review of Books*, 30 May, 17–18.

Williams, Frederick. 1991. "The Shape of News to Come: The Gulf War as an Opportunity for TV News to Show Off, and to Raise Questions." *The Quill* 79 (September): 15–17.

World Priorities. 1986. *World Military and Social Expenditures.* Washington, DC: World Priorities.

10 Authorship of Metaphoric Imagery in "Live" Television Sportscasts

Barbra S. Morris
University of Michigan

Televised sporting events contain conflicts and resolutions that are unpredictable, yet occur under controlled conditions. Dramatic "live" action unfolds in each game within the boundaries of well-established rules. Ultimately, TV sports promotions legitimately devise and deliver game "stories" that are visually compelling, spontaneously exciting, and totally accessible. In return for this lively entertainment, sports fans remain devoted to sportscasts of football, basketball, hockey, golf, tennis, racing, gymnastics, skating, and other events.

The pressure-packed immediacy of "live" televised contests is embellished by regular, up-to-date sports reports, interviews, and analyses of games and past performances. Controversies about sporting events and those who are associated with them keep fans abreast of every aspect of the sports scene. This cultural climate is not created by television alone. All mass media contribute to this pool of sports news, thereby giving sports discourse an intense resonance, immediacy, and value throughout American society. The enthusiasm with which people from all walks of life follow sports is a significant cultural phenomenon that should not be dismissed because the relevance of any single game seems short-lived or because the subject itself seems inconsequential.

Many people argue that too much television time devoted to sports, with their emphasis on win-at-all-costs competition, psychologically damages our entire culture. Yet the effects of television sports on a culture are extraordinarily complex and, therefore, difficult to identify and evaluate. We can start, though, by examining "sportstext"—the actual broadcast received on viewers' screens. Carefully examining the text itself will help us determine what sorts of messages it actually contains and how they are presented to television audiences.

It would be absurd to claim that sports are not about competition; obviously, they emphasize the desire not to lose. Determination to win is the major plotline of the dramatic stories that constitute sports commentary. Nonetheless, history tells us that sports serve many important functions in cultures. Geertz's classic article (1973) investigating the place of cock fighting within Balinese society demonstrates that sports maintain traditions and continuity within a working community. Undeniably, sports-related stories interwoven within a "live" sportscast contain layers of cultural messages that are far more complex than simple win-or-lose plots. These multiple narratives may be thought of as subplots, many of which are created primarily through visual imagery.

This chapter looks into some shared cultural values—other than competition—that the visual imagery of sports offers to television viewers. A basketball game directed by Robert Fishman of CBS Sports will serve as our model text. To fully understand how metaphors are constructed through sportstext imagery, though, we must begin with some basic observations about "live" sports telecasts. First, sportstexts are constructions of "live" events by "authors," individuals who direct and assemble the material that viewers receive on their screens. Second, combinations of images can create visual metaphors, sometimes developed into "subplots" that viewers come to regard as integral to the main plot, or competition, of any contest. Finally, transcriptions of actual sportstexts, such as the one documented in this chapter, reveal the subplots that emphasize family and cultural values.

Television Sports Director as Author

To the television audience, watching a sportscast simply means watching an event "live" and having that event fleshed out by human, historical, and statistical information that clarifies or enlivens the contest. But for people who select and present the action—shaping it into a dramatic whole—split-second decisions are constantly made about what to include in the sportstext and when to do so (Morris and Nydahl 1985). Unquestionably, the central decision maker during a typical "live" network sports production is its director, who has two concurrent responsibilities: (1) to electronically guide the game coverage of a number of on-site camera operators and (2) from a vantage point in a remote truck, to choose, from monitors displaying all the on-site camera "feeds," those images that immediately make up the "live" transmitted text. In fulfilling these dual responsibilities, a sports director is concerned with more than game action alone. Other "stories" related to it must be tracked by cameras and, if selected, woven into a coherent, compelling telecast.

Ultimately, the director fashions all available "live" game-related stories into a sportscast. In other words, the on-site director decides instantaneously in what order and in what manner images come together. Indeed, major television sports directors have considerable latitude in determining what and how content is to be folded together into a "live" production. A top-ranked director, such as Robert Fishman, is free to draw upon all action in the environs of a game, though game action ordinarily takes precedence. Further, in assembling "live" text, a director determines what kind of visual syntax should connect images: rapid or unobtrusive cuts, very slow or regular dissolves, replays, wipes, freeze frames, and so on. In other words, a sports director selects and shapes available imagery into a visual interpretation of events and, in this sense, can be considered an "author."

Before analyzing one example of sportstext, we should consider how images communicate ideas. Fiske and Hartley (1978) note that television is a complex, visual/verbal discourse that resembles spoken language, which may explain why television text seems so "natural" to viewers. In the broadest sense, *language* means "any method of communicating ideas, as by a system of signs, symbols, gestures, or the like" (490). Therefore, a television director's selecting and joining of images is a kind of "speaking" to viewers: communicating meanings, interpreting events, and employing television's signs, symbols, and gestures.

In envisioning metaphor as a process of combining characters and creating meaning, Burke (1969) reminds us that when either similar or dissimilar images are juxtaposed in a sequence, a "new" perspective emerges. An image juxtaposition, just as a word juxtaposition, "tells us something." To put Burke's definition of metaphor into a formula, character B provides a perspective upon character A, thereby leading to a new concept, which is C. Thus, Burke's idea of how metaphor works suggests that a television director may create metaphors with images in the way a poet creates metaphors with words. Moreover, Burke points out that metaphors ought to receive close attention and analysis because they are powerful structures that often appear to reveal "truth."

One further note about images as language: In much the same way print readers ordinarily are not conscious of how letters form words and words form ideas, television viewers, as they "read" a running text, usually lose awareness of *how* images create meanings. Accordingly, as a television audience reads a text, it is not the presence or combining of separate images that viewers note. Instead, they see meanings immediately revealed through the content being disclosed. In fact, the more artfully images are composed or connected, the less likely viewers are to question how or why they are placed together: a combination simply registers as right ("true") or, perhaps, as wrong ("untrue").

Intentions of the Author and Form of the Text

This section analyzes the visual language of CBS's award-winning television sports director Robert Fishman to determine whether his creation of ideas via his selections and combinations of imagery constitute authorship of visual metaphor. A log of a broadcast strip from a nationally televised basketball game Fishman directed in March 1984 appears below.

In an interview five months after this game, Fishman explained the reasoning behind the choices he made while assembling this segment of text. Fishman gave two reasons for why this sportscast was significant. First, the outcome of this game, between DePaul and Wake Forest, would determine which team would compete for the prestigious NCAA national basketball championship. Thus, an opportunity to continue in the race for the national title was the main plot in the "story" of this particular contest. Second, and of related importance, was a subplot: the impending fate of Ray Meyer, head coach at DePaul for forty-two years. Meyer would either retire from coaching after this game or continue to coach his team into the NCAA playoffs, perhaps capping off a legendary career with a coveted national championship—an accomplishment that, thus far, had eluded him.

As the following excerpt of sportstext begins, only twelve seconds remain in the contest. The game clock is stopped with the score tied at 71-71. DePaul's Kenny Patterson stands at the foul line, waiting to take a shot. If he makes both it and the resulting second half of his one-and-one foul-shot scoring opportunity, DePaul will have a two-point lead and be almost assured of at least a tie score, which would send the game into overtime. (No three-point shot as yet existed in college basketball.)

As it turned out, DePaul's Patterson missed the foul shot, and on the last tick of the game clock, Wake Forest's Danny Young hit a jump shot to give Wake Forest the win. When Young's shot succeeded, Ray Meyer's game-coaching, professional responsibilities concluded. But this scoring of the game-winning points by Wake Forest concluded only the game-time plot. Fishman had telecast time remaining to develop his subplot. Using primarily cuts, ordinary dissolves, slow dissolves, replays, and freeze frames as the syntax and punctuation for his interpretation, Fishman told viewers not about the game's winners, but about the meaning of Ray Meyer's career. (Of course, Meyer was a familiar figure to a large portion of the national audience that follows college basketball.)

During the final five minutes of the telecast, Fishman gave rapid directions to the camera operators on-site, who listened to his instructions through their headphones. As he spoke, Fishman was, at the same time, alerting the engineer beside him to the sorts of transitions that were to edit the action together. In this manner, Fishman called for the syntax and precise sequence of shots: "Take 4 [takes are cuts], dissolve to 3, slow dissolve to 5, 4 get in tight, tighter, take 4" and so forth. Such instructions instantly crafted an epilogue to Meyer's final game. Except for an interview with Meyer and his son (shots 42–49), little commentary was voiced over the imagery. In effect, then, Fishman alone delivered to viewers his own image-story or subplot about the sports contest.

The following is a shot-by-shot log of Fishman's choices. The log begins (shots 1–8) during the time-out period that immediately precedes Patterson's foul-shot attempt, which misses. With twelve seconds remaining on the game clock, Wake Forest takes possession of the ball (shot 9) and proceeds to shoot the winning basket. At this time (shot 10), Fishman begins his visual epilogue to the game, primarily interpreting Meyer's experience.

1. Long shot of Ray Meyer at DePaul bench during time-out
2. Cut to Wake Forest bench
3. Cut to crowd
4. Cut to DePaul bench
5. Cut to Joey Meyer, assistant coach and son of Ray Meyer, at DePaul bench
6. Cut to midcourt shot of DePaul's Patterson prepared to take his foul shot
7. Cut to close-up of Patterson shooting

8. Cut to midcourt shot of Patterson's foul attempt failing

9. Cut to ball in play; the midcourt camera continues to follow the play of the game as Wake Forest recovers Patterson's rebound and moves the ball toward the DePaul basket; Wake Forest's #21 makes the game-winning jump shot

10. Cut to Wake Forest player emotionally embracing Ray Meyer, DePaul's coach

11. Cut to Wake Forest team celebrating

12. Cut to Ray Meyer, complex reactions to the decisive moment expressed on his face

13. Camera follows Meyer as he begins to cross the basketball court

14. Dissolve to Garber, the winning coach, congratulating his team

15. Dissolve to Meyer walking slowly across the court

16. Dissolve very slowly back to Wake Forest team and Garber celebrating

17. Camera follows Garber, now walking across the court

18. Dissolve to Meyer wiping his eyes with a handkerchief

19. Camera follows Meyer, who resumes walking

20. Dissolve to Joey Meyer

21. Dissolve to Garber

22. Dissolve to #21, Wake Forest player, elated by victory

23. Camera follows #21 as he joins with teammates and they congratulate each other

24. Dissolve to Ray Meyer's wife watching from the stands

25. Dissolve to Ray Meyer standing on the basketball court

26. Dissolve to Wake Forest team celebrating

27. Camera follows Wake Forest team celebrating

28. Dissolve to long shot of the arena, with fans leaving

29. Dissolve to arena guards, observing the arena emptying

30. Camera pans across empty seats, showing the crowd exiting

31. Dissolve to Wake Forest team leaving the court

32. Camera follows Wake Forest player leaving the court

33. Dissolve to Ray Meyer waiting on the court

34. Dissolve slowly to Ray Meyer's wife, waiting in the stands, laughing with younger members of the Meyer family in the seats adjoining hers

35. Dissolve to freeze frame captured moments ago: Ray Meyer wiping his eyes with a handkerchief (prior shot 18)

36. Dissolve slowly back to the arena and to the continued confusion of players and fans milling around on the court

37. Dissolve back to replay of the winning shot by Wake Forest at the end of game (recovery of frame from prior shot 9)

38. Freeze frame of the winning shot at the end of the replay (recovery of the end of shot 9)

39. Dissolve to extreme close-up of DePaul cheerleader, "live" in the arena, looking distressed

40. Camera pulls back from close-up of DePaul cheerleader

41. Dissolve to replay of the winning shot (recovery of prior shot 38)

42. Cut to "live" on-court CBS interview with Ray Meyer

43. Camera pulls in to extreme close-up of Ray Meyer, whose face now fills the screen

44. Steve Grote, CBS sports announcer, notes that this is Meyer's last game as head coach of DePaul; Meyer's forty-two-year record as coach—724 wins, 354 losses—is superimposed

45–49. Remainder of a lengthy interview with Ray and Joey Meyer

50. Dissolve to Ray Meyer's grandchildren still in the stands

51. Camera pans to Ray Meyer's wife talking with Meyer family members

52. Dissolve to Ray Meyer on the court

53. Camera follows Meyer as he leaves the court for the team locker room

This broadcast log reveals the concerns of its director. Fishman vividly recalled experiencing the tension on the floor while he was engrossed in directing the sportscast from a bank of five monitors mounted on the wall of a production truck outside the arena: "I knew in the back of my mind that if it came down to a last shot, that Ray Meyer remained the focus of the game, no matter who won or lost. Without slighting the winners, the outcome of the competition wasn't all there was to be said about what was happening there."

Throughout the sequence of shots above, it may seem that Fishman is simply contrasting teams' and coaches' responses to winning and losing, emphasizing the importance of winning. Yet repeatedly cutting and dissolving between participants' contrasting emotions (shots 10–12, 13–19, 25–26, 31–33, and 41–43) actually produces the opposite effect: it integrates these two kinds of experience into a single consequence of competition.

Moreover, through the use of dissolves, slow dissolves, and then conspicuously slower dissolves and replays (shots 35, 37, 38, and 41), Fishman infuses the program's ending with what amounts to a compassionate perspective upon Meyer's loss. When asked about the placement of noticeably slower dissolves into the sportscast (shots 15–16, 33–36, and 51–53), Fishman explained:

> A cut would be too jarring. . . . There are moments that call for a dissolve . . . something signals to me "slow it down, start doing your dissolves" . . . it's not something that I was taught. . . . I can cut-cut-cut and then dissolve and it makes a statement. Because when you dissolve, you are slowing down the pace, and you are intent on saying, "Something's happening here; I'm seeing two images and the dissolve's really focusing them". . . . It just makes it dramatic. I can manipulate—I think a good director can manipulate—an event. . . . I am saying something about the relationships of these people.

Just what does Fishman say? The log reveals Fishman emphasizing a subtle attunement between Meyer and his family, especially between Meyer and his wife. To return to Burke's notion of metaphor, the image of one "character" provides a perspective upon the other, and, thus, as Meyer and his wife dissolve visually together, an idea about their relationship emerges. Each of them appears to be more aware of the other than they are of the pandemonium in the arena (dissolves 24–25 and slow dissolves 33–36 and 50–53). Also, Meyer's familial resources of loyalty, love, and companionship appear to sustain him despite his loss in an emotionally charged public setting. Fishman takes the pair's individual moments, in reality occurring at some considerable distance from each other, and fashions them into a single statement about reciprocal sympathy and support.

In addition to this metaphor of mutuality, Fishman spoke of four other ideas integrated into the telecast's final minutes: (1) the strength of sports traditions during transitions, (2) the force of continuity despite disappointment, (3) the importance of public respect for lifelong achievement, and (4) the dignity with which Coach Meyer left the game. Of course, no one would claim that the entire sportscast produced that day was the product of Fishman alone. For example, many camera movements, particularly during regular play of the game, are automatic for professional camera operators. Note the midcourt establishing shot followed by the tracking of players bringing the ball downcourt (shots 8 and 9). These represent a standard tracking sequence, conventional coverage of basketball game action. Also, despite the infrequency of audio elements noted in this particular log (shots 44–49), commentary and natural sound contributed a great deal to guiding viewers' impressions of the sportscast.

Nonetheless, images in a network sportscast generally must be "called for" by a director, and an incredible number of instant decisions (about such issues as composition, emphasis, timing, perspective, angle, figure/ground) have to be made. This segment illustrates Fishman consciously selecting and combining images in the text (twelve cuts, fifteen dissolves, five slow dissolves, three replays, and two freeze frames) as he intentionally authors a visually metaphoric subplot about Ray Meyer during a "live" telecast.

Although this discussion of Fishman's directorship is not an exhaustive exploration of all meaning in or responsibility for this sportstext, it does illustrate matters of author/director intentionality, within specific game-time and post-game-time constraints. In doing so, it raises further questions about viewers' engagement with images. At first glance, this strip of text seems to be merely "typical" sports imagery, perhaps sentimental, maybe uplifting. Nonetheless, one wonders, do viewers regard such televised stories that combine "characters" metaphorically as telling the "truth"? One might argue that the millions of viewers who follow sports by now know that directors frequently seek out human elements accompanying competition and then forge them into dramatic narratives. In other words, sports viewers expect to be led to think about stories aside from the game's final score.

After close analysis of the construction of this segment of text, one also wonders how often viewers consider that a received sportscast would come out differently in the hands of another director. When Fishman "authors" a sportscast, he seeks out sideline connections between those engaged in the sport and those who support them. Other kinds of subplots are certainly possible. For instance, another director, ABC's Abe Fortas, stated in a 1983 ESPN interview that he is primarily intent on game coverage that brings match-ups between players engaged in the contest to the forefront. In the same interview, NBC's John Gonzalez said that during a game it is individual players who provide the stories that create a great telecast. Directors, it seems, pursue personal preferences for subplots within sports events. Interestingly, despite Fishman's careful crafting of text, he has said that a game's stories tell themselves, that "the images speak for themselves." Obviously directors deliberately tune themselves into and "create" stories that they find important during the action.

This discussion has focused only on matters of authorship, sub-plots, and visual metaphors in televised sports images. In considering Fishman's choices during a mere five minutes, one becomes aware of how many combinations of images might be analyzed. Beyond this preliminary study, then, there is a genuine need for more text tran-scriptions and interviews to clarify how television directors use im-ages in constructing meaning within sportscasts.

Let's return to the initial idea posed for consideration: Is the idea of authorship of metaphoric imagery applicable to sportstext direc-tion? Keep in mind that there are major differences between "live" production, with shots being "called for" during broadcast transmis-sion by a single director on-site, and "studio set" production, where editing and re-editing occur long before actual broadcast. Finally, then, with the evidence of Fishman's log and his interview in hand, we can indeed conclude that he authored a dominant subplot in the telecast the audience watched that day. The imagery Fishman selected, the perspective he believed should be brought to the end of this game, and the visual syntax of cuts, regular dissolves, and very slow dissolves resulted in *his* particular creation of "truth" about the event. That Robert Fishman is a skillful storyteller, there is no doubt. Beyond that, one wonders, do viewers believe that "live" sportscasts are a construc-tion or an unmediated reality? This question remains to be thoroughly researched with "live" texts as they spontaneously unfold and with television viewers who bring differing levels of awareness to the texts they watch.

Competition Meets Compassion in Sportstext

Whenever we attend live sports events in person, we maintain our own perspectives on events from our stationary vantage points. We decide whom we will watch and what to make of what we see. When we are watching a televised sporting event, however, we receive mul-tiple perspectives, replays, dissolves, differing camera imagery, freeze frames, and so on—a carefully constructed, complex interpretation of events. In summary, sports on television, we might say, consist of a main plot—the actual play and outcome of the game—and numerous subplots—stories about those associated with the contest. The images are selected and composed by an author—the director—primarily for sports fans who are not on-site.

Television spectators probably "read" any sportscast as an actual account of what happened, a faithful report of the proceedings of a contest. As we discover from Fishman's sportstext, and in various directors' opinions about their craft, subplots within any game are often meant to yield compassionate insights into individuals' lives—a choice that contrasts starkly with the idea that only winning matters. In this case, Ray Meyer's retirement becomes symbolic of family solidarity and support. Moreover, Fishman is determined to reinforce national respect for Meyer and to represent well his lifetime of teaching young people to continue to try again, week after week, regardless of the outcome of any single contest.

Apparently, those who focus on the negative social influences of televised sports need to examine the full range of televised sports imagery to consider alternative visual metaphors as well. Perhaps research into all media coverage of sports would reveal more stories about players' and coaches' discipline and determination than about winning scores. Indisputably, athletes and their associates are a source of vigorous cultural dialogue, not only about competition, but also about other cultural values. Cawelti (1985) calls for media-wide textual inquiries into questions that now concern literary critics: the evolution of an artistic career, the resonances of cultural images and "rhetoric," and the characteristics of an author's style and language (373). Such inquiries clearly require close reading of actual text to uncover societal themes and values, ideological patterns, and multiple narratives. Obviously, television directors who introduce visual metaphors into sports broadcasts are saying much more to television viewers about their shared cultural beliefs than first meets the eye.

Works Cited

Burke, Kenneth. 1969. *A Grammar of Motives.* Berkeley: University of California Press.

Cawelti, John. 1985. "With the Benefit of Hindsight: Popular Culture Criticism." *Critical Studies in Mass Communication* 2: 363–79.

Fiske, John, and John Hartley. 1978. *Reading Television.* London: Methuen.

Geertz, Clifford. 1973. "Deep Play: Notes on a Balinese Cockfight." In *The Interpretation of Cultures,* 412–53. New York: Basic Books.

Morris, Barbra S., and Joel Nydahl. 1985. "Sports Spectacle as Drama: Image, Language, and Technology." *The Journal of Popular Culture* 18 (Spring): 101–10.

11 Ad Images and the Stunting of Sexuality

Carol Moog
Creative Focus, Inc.

For decades our culture has been receiving an extraordinarily effective, highly engaging, creative, mesmerizing, tireless, and endlessly stimulating sex education. Our teacher is fluent in images as well as in words. Our teacher is advertising.

Advertising uses the language of images to "talk" people into buying products. To achieve this goal, advertisers teach us, especially young people, who to be. Madison Avenue's imagery persuades its students that they will be like advertising models if they *buy* like them.

The power of advertising imagery to shape, define, and direct the sexual identities and behavior of young people far outweighs the impact of any high school sex education class. When it comes to sexuality, advertising's core curriculum is the language of pictures, hungrily, but uncritically, absorbed by students every single day.

Madison Avenue's information on sexual identities and behaviors needs to be included and critiqued as part of any sex education, whether at home or in school. Young people should be taught how to critically interpret advertising's powerful symbol system of images if they are to make realistic, objective decisions about intimacy and identity. Therefore, it is essential that teachers and parents become fluent in the language of advertising.

If sex seems rampant in advertising, it is. No other type of psychological imagery hits people closer to where they really live. Advertisers did not create the need for men and women to feel sexually viable, and advertisers did not create the insecurities people have about being able to love. These are basic issues in human development that cut right through to the core of self-esteem, where we are most vulnerable. Yet advertisers, because they are in the business of making

---

This chapter was modified from one entitled "Sex, Sin, and Suggestion" in Carol Moog's *Are They Selling Her Lips?* (William Morrow, 1990).

money, have long dangled the lure of enhanced sexuality to motivate consumers to buy.

For instance, one Seagram's Extra Dry Gin ad (figure 11.1), created by Ogilvy and Mather, employs imagery to link directly to the male unconscious. Dominating the center of the page is a huge Spanish olive, its nearly neon-red pimento pushing out at the viewer as it is engulfed by a clear, viscous liquid. Presumably, the fluid is Seagram's Extra Dry Gin, an elixir that, the headline claims, can "Arouse an Olive." Metaphorically speaking, this is a very sexy imperative and a very sexy product benefit. The olive's round shape signifies the female; in this case, with its bulging scarlet center, it is suggestive of a tumescent clitoris or nipple—essentially, an aroused woman. The invitation to "Arouse an Olive," written in classic masculine typeface, is directed at men: its message promises, and then visually delivers, a sexual seduction, complete with a climactic outpouring of liquid.

The sexual message Seagram's Extra Dry Gin symbolizes in its "olive" ad is sent even more overtly in a different ad for the same product (figure 11.2). In the upper left is a picture of an upright bottle (male) overlapping the rounded edge of an orange (female), a graphic

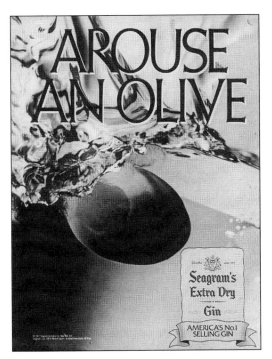

Figure 11.1. "Arouse an Olive."

Figure 11.2. "It could turn a 'maybe' into . . . 'again.' "

echo of the lower-right image of a couple in a heated embrace. As if there could be any doubt about the advertiser's imbuing this liquor with aphrodisiac powers, the copy reads like a litany of praises for the product's capabilities, ending with the line, positioned as being spoken by the lovers, "They also say it could turn a 'maybe' into . . . 'again.'" The ad's message about the link between the product and sexuality would appear to be "Get her drunk and get her in bed."

It is difficult enough that advertisers define what "sexy" is, their bombardment of images often obscuring the definitions students may cultivate on their own. But it is even worse when, once this commercial sexuality is defined, advertisers continue to exert pressure on young people to become sexy, stay sexy, and get sexier. We are a driven culture, and the fuel firing the more-is-always-better machine is internal as well as external. Madison Avenue's *pressure* to measure up is matched in intensity only by the *need* to measure up that people bring to relationships. And that need boils down to this: the need to love and be loved.

People who are secure enough to develop an enduring, mutual, and affectionate relationship with another person have accomplished an extraordinarily difficult psychological task. Too often, people get stuck in their insecurities. In their desperate determination not to expose these insecurities, they frantically try to fill up a sense of emptiness with cultural facsimiles of love. And our culture—dominated by advertising, our sergeant-at-arms of imagery—holds up an endless array of tempting surrogates in designer packaging: popularity, prestige, glamour, sexiness.

What's vicious about this particular cycle is that the more we try to prop up our outside, the more terrified we become about exposing who we really are on the inside. The discrepancy becomes too great, and the investment in the decoy self becomes too high to risk losing whatever security it provides. Probably the single biggest barrier to love is the fear of psychological exposure, of being found out and found lacking. When advertisers link products with sexuality, they lock in with people's deepest fears of being unlovable; they offer their images and products as tickets to love, when what they are really providing are more masks for people to hide behind.

For example, Young and Rubicam's ad for R. J. Reynolds Tobacco Company's More cigarettes (figure 11.3) actually uses the device

Figure 11.3. "Wanted: Tall, dark stranger."

of a personal ad to position the product as being capable of fulfilling a relationship. And the nature of that relationship, as defined by the advertiser's imagery, has nothing to do with real intimacy. The emphasis is strictly superficial, strictly sexual, and strictly uncommitted.

In the More ad, the circled classified ad reads, "WANTED: Tall, dark stranger for long-lasting relationship. Good looks, great taste a must. Signed, Eagerly Seeking Smoking Satisfaction." A brown More cigarette, the "tall, dark stranger" himself, lies across a corner of the clipping. Headlined in red at the bottom is "Find More Pleasure." Yes, the quest is on, and this cigarette promises a fast track to heightened sexual experiences. Yes, the woman placing the ad knows what she wants, and she wants more of it, and what "it" looks like, from the advertising message, is to be able to use a man to satisfy her sexual demands, and nothing else. It's cigarette as stud, stud as dildo. The ad symbolizes a sexual encounter that carries no threat of exposure, no threat of anything getting too close for comfort. The "long-lasting relationship" is with a "stranger," and it appears to be a consistent feature of More's image to put the woman in charge of keeping it that way.

In another More ad (figure 11.4), the symbolic tryst between strangers is realized, and the sexual innuendoes of the personal ad become a seductive dialogue about foreplay. In this ad, the models are African American, with the photos cropped so that only the lower halves of their faces are visible. Eye contact, with its associated potential for emotional intimacy, has been eliminated as part of the communication. These two might as well be wearing masks.

Cheesy sexual power games are recurrent themes in another long-standing cigarette campaign. Newport, a product of Lorilard, Inc., has been successfully profiting from associating cigarettes with themes of sexual dominance and submission for a decade. Targeted to a young market, the campaign's slogan is "Alive with pleasure!" What Newport's imagery suggests, in ad after ad, is that its smokers will become *sexually* alive with pleasure. The gist of the campaign is that if it feels good, do it, an insidiously shrewd strategy for a product that invites people to sell their health for a puff of momentary pleasure.

One of the campaign's ads (figure 11.5) offers an example of the sexual adventure young singles could have if they started smoking Newports. In the ad, two men carry either end of a long pole. Between them hangs, in deer-bounty fashion, their female prey. All three are having a great time as her head hangs down at exactly one man's crotch level, while her up-ended legs expose her rear to the opposite

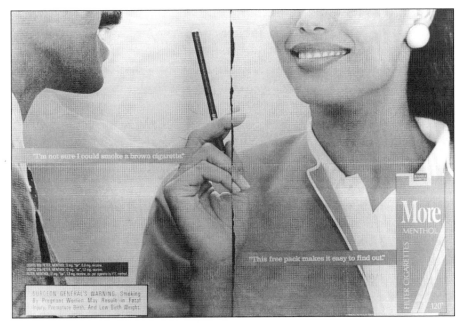

Figure 11.4. The strangers meet.

Figure 11.5. Prey.

man at just about the right level for a *ménage à trois.* Just as one of the primary justifications today's smokers give for smoking is simply that they like to smoke, sexual entanglements like the merry threesome in this ad are justified as worthy of pursuit as long as they are fun. As Newport puts it in the ad's closing line, "After all, if smoking isn't a pleasure, why bother?"

Men in this culture feel just as pressured to exude sexual prowess and proficiency as women, and advertisers provide steady, compelling reinforcement of these expectations. Ads offer men groaning boards heaped high with tasty images of available young women, all designed to whet consumer appetites. For men in this culture, trying to grow up, to move forward from sexual preoccupations into committed relationships is extremely difficult: advertisers' sexual preoccupations help keep them stuck in the quicksand of adolescent confusion—a place where it's cool and sexy to deceive women.

Young and Rubicam's ad for Cuervo Tequila (figure 11.6) illustrates these preoccupations. Here, the centerpiece is not the product, but a tall, dark, handsome, velvet-suited and bow-tied rake, wearing a slight smirk. Fixing a bedroom leer at the reader, he holds the drink he has in one hand toward a blond woman looking up at him, while he pours a bottle of Cuervo Gold into the surreptitiously held glass of *another* woman gazing admiringly at him. Women in the background smile radiantly. Cuervo Gold wants men to identify with the particular charisma of a Don Juan.

For the man who is less interested in seducing and more interested in being seduced, there's Hennessy. In Schieffolin and Somerset Company's ad for the Hennessy brand (figure 11.7), the advertiser casts the lure of a sultry, willing woman, *his* for the asking. Of course, first he would have to imbibe the cognac that, as the tag line conveys, isn't a liquor at all, but "The Spirit of the Civilized Rogue." It all looks so easy, so available. Indeed, what a fantasy of seduction: a big-as-life close-up of tousled, eyes-only-for-you, full-lipped female come-hitherness. The Hennessy ad asks men to identify with, to measure up to, the image of being the kind of man who could summon this scene, who could elicit the irresistible invitation that the woman breathes: "You don't look comfortable in that tie."

Guess Jeans is one of those advertisers with a huge stake in the attraction of some women to the sadomasochistic side of sexuality. And the women it's after are young. Until recently, its campaign featured highly provocative black-and-white photos of porcelain-skinned girls in seemingly endless encounters with salacious older men, la-

Figure 11.6. Don Juan.

Figure 11.7. Seduction.

beled only by the scribbled red-lipsticked script "George Marciano" or "Guess Jeans." Some of the more notorious scenes in Guess ads along the way included an aging Mafioso-type wearing sunglasses in postures of sexual dominance toward young, semi-buttoned women with apathetic expressions.

Another Guess ad (figure 11.8) has us facing the rear of a kneeling woman looking up at the crotch of a man standing above her, his arms folded expectantly. Although she *is* wearing a Guess jeans jacket, what is actually being advertised here? In most of the Guess ads, the advertiser's product is simply a prop for the center-stage interplay between the fragile, loosened-clothing, exposed vulnerability of a nubile female and a possessive, unsavory, daddy-like male.

The car scene in another Guess ad (figure 11.9) is especially representative of this interplay. Evocative of Louis Malle's 1978 film *Pretty Baby,* or the earlier *Baby Doll* (1956), Guess is associating an edge of danger with its brand name, a strategy that plays directly on the urgency and ambivalence of adolescents' sexual impulses. Much of the time, the Guess girls look like runaways photographed in distasteful situations that their parents would get sick over.

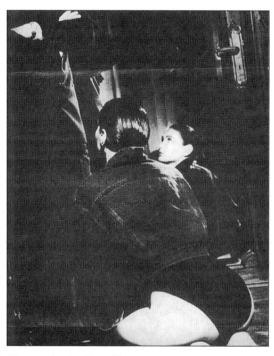

Figure 11.8. Kneeling woman.

Figure 11.9. Unsavory male.

The psychological messages sent by Guess's imagery strongly imply that girls can use their sexuality to free themselves from parental constraints. The ads create the illusion that being possessed by a powerful, older man can be a glamorous identity for a confused, angry adolescent. Being used sexually, or running away, isn't portrayed as being either self-destructive or hostile; it's presented as a daring walk on the sultry, rebel side of the tracks—the perfect counter to the ruling party of adults. In the latest from Guess, the young women in the ads are still often portrayed as sexually submissive and dominated, but now the men, like the one strong-arming a young woman from behind while she straddles him and his motorcycle (figure 11.10), are as young as the women.

In Revlon's internally produced ads for its Trouble fragrance, the psychological message is not one of female submission, but rather, one of equality between the sexes: both are equally ignorant. In one ad (figure 11.11), a woman in plunging black décolletage smiles dreamily, conspiratorially, at her audience. The object of her designs leans on a bar in the shadows, wearing black, a fashionably decadent stubble, and slightly narrowed eyes. The headline titles this scene "He's

Figure 11.10. Straddling his motorcycle.

Figure 11.11. "He's Trouble, But He's Finally Met His Match."

Trouble, But He's Finally Met His Match." What qualities does she bring to this sexual showdown? If she has sufficiently drenched herself with Trouble, she has unhinged whatever mental apparatus might have stopped her from stepping into a shallow relationship designed to come to a ruinous end. With Revlon's help, she'll match him in destructiveness. Trouble, the imagery tells consumers, can loosen those bothersome intellectual controls that so often interfere with romantic meetings in bars. As the copy explains, Trouble is "the fragrance for those times when your better judgment is better off ignored. After all, a little Trouble keeps life interesting."

Even in a time when casual sex can cause death, images of sin and suggestion continue, incredibly, to be a source of merriment for all kinds of advertisers. Johns + Gorman Films is not too proud to play. This film production company solicits business from advertising agencies the old-fashioned way: they pimp for it. Their promotional ad (figure 11.12) is tongue-in-cheek, but it is difficult to put much stock in the possibility of real change in advertisers' sexual imagery when one of their image makers introduces itself by placing the announcement "Johns + Gorman Films Is Now Open for Business in New York City"

Figure 11.12. "Open for Business."

under a black-and-white photo of a prototypical pair of prostitutes, ripped stockings and all, standing on a littered street corner looking for work.

Calvin Klein's ad for fragrance for men (figure 11.13) is a contemporary rendition of the classical myth of Narcissus. Shot in black-and-white, sleekly oblong, the product has the form of a brick of gold bullion, the same kind of gold that gilds the frame of the mirror in the photo, a mirror into which the transfixed, mesmerized face of a man enraptured by his own image is staring. He looks as if he could stay there forever. Clearly, this is the face of a man in love, and he only has eyes for himself.

Psychologically, this is a dead-end street. At the root of this kind of narcissism are feelings of worthlessness, the inability to live up to unattainable expectations coupled with an insatiable need to extract admiration from others. Advertising imagery that is intended to be sexually provocative in reality sets up a self-perpetuating cycle of narcissistic needs.

People in desperate need of validation from others are caught in a media avalanche of narcissistic images of people who feel empty and

Figure 11.13. Narcissus.

unlovable beneath their grandiose postures. The sole purpose of these images is to persuade people that the way to achieve the sexual and personal power reflected by a commercial model is to buy the associated product. Consumers buy the product often unconsciously hoping that they will win the admiration they covet. But since they are trying to measure up to somebody else's expectations, they feel just as empty as ever on the inside. The process continues to fuel the quest for approval, which, in turn, fuels the sales of products selling a promise of narcissistic gratification.

Harper's Bazaar uses narcissistic self-absorption to interest female consumers in buying the magazine. The campaign, using no copy at all, focuses on pictures of women so locked into reading a copy of *Bazaar* that they are completely oblivious to the activities of the man, however unusual, in the same room. In one ad (figure 11.14), a nude man is shown in the shower, vainly kissing the glass door, trying to get the attention of a young woman in pearls and cocktail dress engrossed in reading the magazine. The campaign, created by Margeotes-Fertitta and Weiss, Inc., is intended to be startling, slick, alienated, and ironic.

Figure 11.14. Oblivious.

But what is most arresting is the level of narcissism and distance displayed by the woman.

A similarly aloof dynamic between men and women is used to sell a very different product, Procter and Gamble's Secret Dry roll-on deodorant. In a campaign created by Leo Burnett U.S.A. to communicate the brand's long-standing position—"Strong enough for a man but pH-balanced for a woman"—a series of fashionably dressed female models, shot in color, are juxtaposed on larger-than-life, black-and-white photos of muscular, sweaty male bodies. In one of these ads (figure 11.15), the ultra-feminine, pink-suited, white-stockinged woman beams with self-satisfaction as she appears to lean against the dripping, massive back of a hard-hatted construction worker. Fearlessly, she looks out at her audience, secure in the certainty that no matter how big or how wet or how strong this man is, she will remain utterly untouched, utterly composed. Pink-gloved hands outstretched as if drying her nails, one knee bent demurely, the ultimate lady is thoroughly protected from being sullied by the slightest contact with primal man. Secret's marketing message: regardless of the intensity of a woman's perspiration, the product will keep her dry. The psycho-

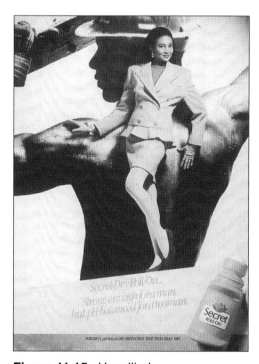

Figure 11.15. Unsullied.

logical message: it is best to stay in control, to turn away from strong sexual feelings, to focus only on yourself.

Perfume advertising abounds with images of pure self-indulgence and smug egocentricity rather than relationships. Elizabeth Arden is the sublicenser of Fendi perfume. Its advertising (figure 11.16) is dominated by a luminous photograph of a beautiful woman, eyes closed in the passion of the moment, kissing the marble lips of a sculptured male bust. The message is clear on the subject of emotional closeness: don't do it. Stick with statues and cozy up to a healthy hunk of alabaster and you won't get hurt. Fendi romanticizes emotional distance, selling a lot of perfume on the basis of an image that elevates lack of commitment and the psychological avoidance of real intimacy to an art form.

In one Calvin Klein ad for Obsession (figure 11.17), a bunch of naked people studiously avoid all contact with each other. Four muscular men and two well-toned women organize their oiled, nude bodies into approximate pairs, not all of which include one member of the opposite sex. They are arranged on or near a tall, aggressively angled white obelisk. Any sign of emotion, let alone sexual passion, has been

Figure 11.16. Sticking with statues.

Figure 11.17. Grand boredom.

eradicated. The people are turned stiffly away from each other, posturing states of grand boredom, noses hoisted in the air as if listening to a private muse. These people have no more feelings or thoughts going on than the phallic prop they surround. What's being sold here is an elaborate image of self-control through psychological detachment.

Advertisers are not the cause of people's problems with true intimacy, but neither are they the passive, neutral reflectors of how our society views relationships. In their frenzied bids for attention, advertisers frequently wave sexual imagery at consumers, hoping to be remembered. Some are; many are not. But what does set in our collective memory are portraits of stunted sexual development, portraits of sexual status displays, narcissistic glorification, and crude innuendo, portraits that are sold along with products pledging to help consumers put themselves in the power positions promoted by the advertiser as enviable.

Unless students understand how to read and analyze the language of the symbols and images bombarding them, their identities will be shaped unconsciously. And because advertising's portraits reflect essentially insecure identities, the images promoted point the way toward more, rather than less, emotional emptiness. Advertising's images of human relationships and sexuality make playing the game of measuring up to Madison Avenue downright crippling.

Ideally, relationships are strongest when both partners play with a full deck, with a sense of security and solid identity. If that doesn't happen, though, it's safer to play with fewer cards than to borrow the images of advertisers in an attempt to build a winning hand from them.

12 "Don't Hate Me Because I'm Beautiful": A Commercial in Context

Gerald O. Grow
Florida A&M University

A gorgeous model appears on the screen, looking directly at you with those compelling, magazine-cover eyes. Her voice is friendly, direct, and in complete control. By the time you become aware of her, you have heard her say, "Don't hate me because I'm beautiful." The line is carefully delivered. Its emphasis falls, lightly, on "beautiful," almost as if, discarding "beautiful" as a reason, we might find other causes to hate her. But like most television, the line—which takes about two seconds to deliver—melts into the commercial and then flows into the ongoing dramas of power, passion, and perfection that haunt the television landscape.

"Don't hate me because I'm beautiful." The line challenges us to find a context in which these words, spoken by a gorgeous model in a television commercial, make sense. This is a familiar kind of challenge, because we are, by nature, interpreters, creators, combiners, and shifters of context. On a perceptual level, we see "intelligently" by providing context, filling gaps, and extrapolating from cues. We interpret every situation in terms of the contexts that make sense of it—for meaning is not given to us whole but is made through a rich conspiracy of communication and creativity. The most ordinary elements of daily life—such as advertisements—often yield surprising results when you try to interpret them. Commentators such as Goffman (1979), Leymore (1975), and Ewen (1976) have taught us to take ads seriously, to look in them for reflections of society and for structures of meaning. In this chapter, I will present a way to map the larger mental space in which a fashion model speaking the line "Don't hate me because I'm beautiful" has meaning.

Advertising and Values

Visual images of all kinds express values, even when the style encourages us to look upon them as realistic or even objective. The beauty of the fashion model is more than a matter of looks; it represents a choice of values; it embodies, expresses, and advocates those values; it urges us to "model" ourselves on the values underlying this image of beauty. We see values of all sorts in media imagery. A commercial typical of the mid-1990s shows idealized scenes of family togetherness, with parents, children, and grandparents choreographed together in miniature dramas of family closeness. Their eyes meet, they smile, they move close, they interact in a lovely series of intimate vignettes. For thirty seconds, they offer us a world of ideal relationships. As their happy lives unfold, M&Ms candy plays a subtly increasing role in this togetherness, until it seems to be the cause, the motivating force behind this mythical moment of unity. Many commercials follow a similar strategy, associating images of desirable states of being with products.

When environmental awareness grew in the seventies, tobacco companies presented glorious images of backpackers communing with nature—and with their cigarettes. As our divorce-torn culture groped for the meaning of family in the early eighties, images of family togetherness, family reunions, and traditional extended families appeared in many commercials, associated with candy, diet cola, fast food, and other products. Billboards announce "Alive with Pleasure!" and imply that the product responsible for this happy state is Newport cigarettes. Many advertisements convey ideal images of ways to be: images of liveliness, fun, family, sex appeal, power, sophistication, patriotism, youth, adventure, and beauty. These commercials set out to convince us that products can bridge the gap between our reality and these idealized images.

Human beings are not the only creatures that respond to idealized images. In his classic study of the herring gull, Tinbergen (1953) found that the begging response of the newly hatched chick was triggered by a red spot on the bottom of the parent gull's bill. He then constructed a model that the chick preferred to the real thing. In other experiments, an oystercatcher abandoned its own egg for a giant, speckled, wooden model of an egg. These experiments are sobering demonstrations that normal responses—even those vital to survival—can be replaced by symbolic stimuli that are more powerful than natural stimuli. Tinbergen called these symbolic stimuli "supernormal sign stimuli" (1951, 44) and pointed out that people are susceptible to them as well.

Advertising's images of perfection may work like supernormal stimuli. Producers will go to mind-boggling lengths to achieve the fleeting images in commercials. Few moments in life can have the perfection of an AT&T commercial that took weeks to stage, shoot, and edit. We can seldom reach out and touch so vividly, so completely, so gorgeously, so ideally, as those immaculately staged images do in the ads. Technology amplifies the ads' perfection. Graphic designers routinely make magazine pictures even "more perfect" by deleting blemishes, enhancing color balances, moving component parts of the image around, even importing images from other photographs. No one can look as good as the image of a fashion model—not even the model herself.

The supernormal images of perfection presented in the media are worth some thought, because any kind of guiding image has a double nature. On the one hand, idealized images can uplift and give direction. In the pursuit of the unattainable, we can attain great things. The uplifting ideal may be to manifest the compassion of the Buddha, be the fastest runner in the race, or have a figure like Jane Fonda's. Even if we try but fail to attain such ideals, we remain pointed in the right direction and ennobled by the effort. After all, we belong to a culture guided by unattainable ideals: liberty, equality, happiness. Noble failure while pursuing great ideals is central to our striving, romantic spirit.

Idealized images are uplifting, however, only when there is some way to move from where we are toward the values implicit in an image. If nothing connects us with the image, so that the ideal seems unattainable, we can feel cut off from it. If the ideal is important and we cannot connect with it, an unbridgeable gap looms before us. Instead of inspiring us to cross that gap, the separate, unattainable ideal mocks and torments us. By using idealized images that have no connection with the products advertised, commercials may be promoting not the joining of the viewer and the ideal, but a separation. In depicting highly valued states of being yet offering no avenue to those states except through purchasing consumer products, advertising gives us a formula for despair.

"Despair" may sound like a harsh word to apply to a commercial, but it is accurate. Like Gatsby staring across the water at the dream of his idealized woman, consumers look across a similar gulf at the promise of values, of perfection, of states of being. We find that the offered means—the products we buy—cannot take us there. We do not gain titillating encounters through Doublemint Gum, a youthful dancer's vitality through Diet Pepsi, family closeness through Priazzo, or power and control through Z-cars. Despair is inherent in advertising because products cannot deliver the values implied by the images.

Beauty is a special instance of the way images can promote despair. Advertising promises that "perfection is obtained on your grocer's shelves. Perfection, cleanliness, godliness, gracious hospitality, and an adoring family are attained through the purchase of Lemon Fresh Joy and Drano" (Kinzer 1977, 199). Yet many women say the pursuit of such perfection has made them not more beautiful, but more powerless, more ashamed, and less appreciated by men, the supposed audience for this beauty. Lakoff and Scherr (1984) write, "Men are angry at women for possessing a power which, in fact, women do not possess; if anything, it possesses them" (279).

The complex relation of people to images has long been one of the central themes of Western literature. It is *the* subject of *Don Quixote* and a major theme throughout Shakespeare, Milton, Blake, Melville, Faulkner, Stevens, and most other great writers. The poems of William Butler Yeats explore the power images have both to liberate and to imprison. Yeats wrote poignantly of the social entrapment that begins when a growing girl puts on "burdensome beauty" ("Broken Dreams") and about how hard it is to see beyond the images we project upon one another—"only God, my dear, / Could love you for yourself alone / And not your yellow hair" ("For Anne Gregory"). For Yeats, the imagination can tap the deep creative power of "those images that yet / Fresh images beget" ("Byzantium"), but it can also create remote and unattainable images of the kind we are discussing here, images that break hearts—"self-born mockers of man's enterprise" ("Among School Children").

Beauty has not always seemed so complicated. From the time of the Greeks until the early twentieth century, philosophers and poets connected beauty with such glorious ideals as truth, goodness, and love. In Plato's *Symposium*, Socrates relates how the wise Diotima instructed him that seeing the beauty in people is only one step in a ladder that leads toward the vision of "beauty absolute, separate, simple, and everlasting." For Plato, Dante, and Keats, beauty illuminated existence: "Beauty is truth, truth beauty." In contrast, listen to the words used about beauty by modern commentators: *vacuum, depersonalized, power, paradox, envy, fear, spite, resentment, dependence, advan-*

tage, anger, possession, and *hate.* Our relationship to this idea is complex indeed.

Berger (1972) describes advertising and beauty in terms of envy: we covet the beauty and lifestyle of the people in the pictures. But envy has another meaning that has largely been lost to twentieth-century thought. Since medieval times, envy has been considered a major term for identifying the causes of human suffering. In some versions of the Seven Deadly Sins, envy was second only to pride. Plotting the death of Cassio, Iago explained, "If Cassio do remain, / He hath a daily beauty in his life / That makes me ugly" (*Othello* V.i.18–20). Shakespeare's audience would certainly have recognized this as envy. Modern writings on envy are rare, and it is remarkable that this ancient and powerful concept has receded from the moral landscape.

Schoeck (1969), however, argued that envy is a universal drive that ranges from a spiteful glee at another's misfortune to mutilation and murder for no other reason than the perpetrator felt belittled by the accomplishments of the victim. Like despair, envy derives from the separation of the person from the object of desire, combined with a sense that one is powerless to attain what is desired. Envy is a name for what happens when the urge to reach out becomes the urge to destroy.

Commercials provide the most important prerequisites for envy: (1) hyperreal models who have something the viewer desires, such as sex appeal; (2) an unbridgeable gap between the viewer and the images, caused by the failure of products to bridge that gap; and (3) the teasing, tantalizing reappearance, night after night, of this same scenario, epitomized by one gorgeous model who says, "Don't hate me because I'm beautiful." Bombarded by commercial images that imply that using products will cause them to become as suave and vivacious as the people in the ads, viewers may develop destructively envious feelings toward these idealized and unattainable images. If we think we are immune to envy, we need only recall how satisfying it is when the cover photo on the *National Enquirer* shows some golden celebrity caught looking like a drunken pig.

The concept of destructive envy is important for understanding "hate." Griffin (1981) explains why women may hate beautiful women who project impossible images of beauty: the image of the gorgeous model "is held up to her [the ordinary woman] both as what she must imitate and to show her how she has failed to live up to the pornographic ideal. It is always easier for a woman within pornographic culture to take out her rage over her silence and her powerlessness on another woman than on that culture itself. Ordinary women come to hate the women who are culture's sex symbols" (206–7).

This observation teaches us much about the shared experience of both men and women in relation to images that tell us who we are but prevent us from being ourselves. That men can hate beautiful women is not a new thought. In the television documentary *Quest for Beauty* (1987), Nina Blanchard, "the most famous model agent in Hollywood," discussed the hostility professional models arouse in men and women alike: "There is anger about beauty. . . . I think that beautiful women provoke anger when they walk into a room." The perfect woman—like the model in a commercial—is a perfect candidate for the hatred arising from envy. A more troubling instance was recorded in Beneke's collection of interviews *Men on Rape* (1982), in which one man said:

> If I were actually desperate enough to rape somebody, it would be from wanting the person, but it would also be a very spiteful thing. Just the fact that they can come up to me and just melt me and make me feel like a dummy makes me want revenge. They have power over me so I want power over them. (43–44)

Powerlessness. Separation from the object of desire. The feeling of destructive envy (the man just quoted calls it "spite," Griffin calls it "hate," Blanchard calls it "anger"). The sticky, entangling struggle between internal and external control over the images that guide one's life. These elements lurk in the context created by commercials. "Don't hate me because I'm beautiful" is the model's plea to be free from the destructive envy of the viewer—an envy that may range from catty remarks to the slashing of a model's face on a New York street. The commercial echoes the silent plea of every person of beauty, talent, wealth, luck, or distinction—the plea for protection against the sneaking, poisonous, levelling violence of envy.

Why would an advertisement direct our attention to such a difficult emotion? The answer may become clearer if we think about advertising in terms of mythology and religion.

Advertising as Mythology and Religion

From a variety of perspectives, writers (e.g., Leymore 1975) have concluded that advertising is the consumer culture's version of mythology. One of the central functions of myth has a direct bearing on our commercial. Gardner (1973) explains that myths serve to make life more bearable by reflecting back to us, in images and stories, the unavoidable dilemmas of our lives. Price (1978) similarly argues that myths give us a safe way to acknowledge destructive impulses without having to act them out. To see mythology of this kind at work, look at the magazine version of our television commercial as it appeared in the May 1988 issue of *Elle* magazine (figure 12.1).

On the left, a full-page, color picture of the model's gorgeous face bears the bold headline "Don't hate me because I'm beautiful." Opposite this picture is a block of text and a small black-and-white photo of the same model, this time with her hair stringy, disheveled, and dull, half her face pleading, the other half pained and shadowed. Here she does not look large and gorgeous; she looks like a wet, gray puppy. Here we do not need to consider an envious attack upon the stunning model; it has been accomplished for us in the small picture. It is a ritual, surrogate defacement. We are given the satisfaction of seeing her defaced without having to feel the full power of envy, violence, and guilt. The "defaced" picture in the print version of the commercial arouses and appeases the specific emotion of destructive envy. The commercial becomes a surrogate myth for those whose cultural mythology does not equip them to deal with this emotion.

From the perspective of envy, we can now consider more fully the relation of beauty to hate, which returns us to advertising in the context of religion. The hatred of beauty, I have argued, begins with hyperreal images. Such images are normal functions of the mind (Boulding 1956). Lakoff (1987) argues that all mental activity is organized by idealized concepts. These are among the most basic mental tools we have for bracketing experience, casting a web of metaphor over new events, roping an unruly mass of sensations into serviceable categories, and spinning a rich language out of words derived from basic bodily experiences. Advertising's hyperreal images, however, easily become traps by associating a wide range of human values with products and implying that the products can deliver those values. Once a viewer steps into this situation, that person has one foot in a web of potential entanglements that end in hate. After finding out ten thousand times that the product does not provide the psychological reward implied in the commercial, why should one not hate the teasing, unattainable image of the beautiful model who makes the promises?

If we hate her, it may not be for being beautiful in her own right, but because she is, among other things, part of a conspiracy that tells us that only by consuming products can we attain any ideal, value, or longing. She reminds us of all the other values that we—bombarded

Figure 12.1. "Don't hate me because I'm beautiful."

by yearnings and left with no instructions but to consume—are cut off from. We may hate her not for being a media sex symbol that teases men and puts down women, but for being part of a pornography of values that teases and frustrates our need for valued states of being, such as family togetherness, community, self-confidence, and beauty. And we may hate her for being one of the ways the powerful psychological sophistication of advertising entangles itself in our deepest thoughts and feelings.

The images of advertising leave us like the oystercatcher, brooding on a huge, hyperreal—but wooden—egg. Because products do not provide the kind of psychic payoff implied by advertising's imagery, we are left to doubt whether anything can. If we follow this doubt, a black hole opens in the heart of every image like a negative of its radiance—the black hole of failed promise. And into this black hole, dug by advertising's exploitation of so many ideal images, steps any "religion" that promises to cut through the cycle of idolatry and connect us with the one great ideal that transcends all others: God, immortality, cosmic consciousness, enlightenment, the spirit world, the deep self, the light, or whatever name "It" has. Advertising's failure to fulfill these promises leaves an opening for religion to fill. In using techniques that are fundamentally religious, advertising inadvertently advertises religion. Esslin (1976) writes:

> The TV commercial is essentially a religious form of drama which shows us human beings as living in a world controlled by a multitude of powerful forces that shape our lives.... The polytheism that confronts us here ... is the religion by which most of us actually live.... This is the actual religion that is being absorbed by our children almost from the day of their birth. (271)

Given the resemblance between advertising and religion, this essay's use of traditional religious terminology—such as envy and despair—will appear less arbitrary. With a religious intensity, advertising tells us to believe that the most vivid ideals of our culture can be easily attained if you just choose the right product, or by extension of the same kind of thinking, the right savior, philosophy, church, guru, cult, candidate, or drug. Commercials tell us over and over that little trivial actions—as small as washing our hair or gargling with a particular mouthwash—can solve life's most vexing problems and bring us happiness.

Hayakawa (1972) lamented how advertising has usurped poetic language: "Poetic language is used so constantly and relentlessly for the purposes of salesmanship that it has become almost impossible to say anything with enthusiasm or joy or conviction without running into the danger of sounding as if you were selling something" (223). Could we become distrustful of ideals altogether, because the most powerful presentations of those ideals occur in television commercials? Will we learn to hate the beautiful women used to manipulate and disappoint us? Will children come to hate the irresistible presence of real beauty when they encounter it in the world, so that they are crushed by the weight of a flower? After being nibbled to death by little broken promises, will they retain hope, faith, and goals? Though it uses some of the methods of a cultural mythology, advertising has surely failed a myth's responsibility to support personal identity, community, and spirituality.

Not all commercials exploit ideal images or imply that products will deliver values. But commercials driven by value-laden images that are unrelated to consumer products may be alienating us from the very values they exploit, confusing us about how to attain those values, laying the groundwork for despair, resentment, and apathy, and even prompting us to turn outside the culture to seek ideals that do not seem corrupted. Perhaps advertising will make Buddhists of us all.

Head down in the midst of this tangled web hangs hate—hatred of the product that fails to link us to the ideal, hatred of anything that reminds us of the tormentingly unattainable ideal, hatred of ourselves for still yearning for the exhaustingly unattainable ideal, hatred of commercials for exploiting our deepest yearnings, and hatred of those supernormally beautiful people who promise us values but deliver only products. And yet, at the heart of this hatred lies the remarkable depth and simplicity of human longing—a longing for life, ideals, values, vitality, and love. A longing for connection. For beauty. It is a longing that projects itself optimistically through symbols, images, and idealized concepts and then draws a world together in the spaces between what can be imagined and what is. It is in those spaces—cosmic spaces silently inhabiting our smallest thoughts—that we hear the resonance of "Don't hate me because I'm beautiful." And it is in those very spaces that we can create other relations between ourselves and the unattainable images of advertising, media, culture, and mind.

We can create a relation other than hate. Our main alternative is to create—to create a context more generous and expansive than the inevitable, controlling simplifications of the images we inherit, and even of the images we make. For, contrary to our commercial, we are not the haters of unattainable beauty; we are the creators of ideals of beauty, creators of ideals of all kinds. And in us lives the power to understand the origin of ideals, free ourselves from the tyranny of some, and translate others into reality. We are not, as the commercial seems to presume, separated from fulfillment by an unbridgeable gap and despairingly dependent on a missing messiah. We are the gap. We are the longing. And we are the bridge. The real challenge is to look knowingly—even affectionately—at media, advertising, culture, conventions, and all human forms and reclaim ourselves as participants and co-creators in the world of images that imprisons us as it sets us free.

Works Cited

Beneke, Timothy. 1982. *Men on Rape*. New York: St. Martin's Press.

Berger, John. 1972. *Ways of Seeing*. London: BBC; Penguin.

The Boston Women's Health Book Collective. 1984. *The New Our Bodies, Ourselves*. New York: Simon and Schuster.

Boulding, Kenneth E. 1956. *The Image: Knowledge in Life and Society.* Ann Arbor: University of Michigan Press.

Esslin, Martin. 1976. "Aristotle and the Advertisers: The Television Commercial Considered as a Form of Drama." In *Television: The Critical View,* edited by Horace Newcomb, 260–75. New York: Oxford University Press.

Ewen, Stuart. 1976. *Captains of Consciousness: Advertising and the Social Roots of the Consumer Culture.* New York: McGraw-Hill.

Gardner, Howard. 1973. *The Quest for Mind: Piaget, Levi-Strauss, and the Structuralist Movement.* New York: Knopf.

Goffman, Erving. 1979. *Gender Advertisements.* Cambridge: Harvard University Press.

Griffin, Susan. 1981. *Pornography and Silence: Culture's Revolt against Nature.* New York: Harper and Row.

Hayakawa, S. I. 1972. *Language in Thought and Action.* 3d ed. New York: Harcourt Brace Jovanovich.

Kinzer, Nora Scott. 1977. *Put Down and Ripped Off: The American Woman and the Beauty Cult.* New York: Crowell.

Lakoff, George. 1987. *Women, Fire, and Dangerous Things: What Categories Reveal about the Mind.* Chicago: University of Chicago Press.

Lakoff, Robin Tolmach, and Raquel L. Scherr. 1984. *Face Value: The Politics of Beauty.* London: Routledge and Kegan Paul.

Leymore, Varda Langholz. 1975. *Hidden Myth: Structure and Symbolism in Advertising.* New York: Basic Books.

Price, Jonathan. 1978. *The Best Thing on Television: Commercials.* New York: Penguin.

Quest for Beauty. 1987. Television documentary directed by Christopher Ralling. Arts and Entertainment Network, 13 September.

Schoeck, Helmut. 1969. *Envy: A Theory of Social Behaviour.* Translated by Michael Glenny and Betty Ross. New York: Harcourt, Brace and World.

Tinbergen, Niko. 1951. *The Study of Instinct.* Oxford: Oxford University Press.

———. 1953. *The Herring Gull's World: A Study of the Social Behaviour of Birds.* London: Collins.

III Images in Mind

13 Beyond "The Empty Eye": A Conversation with S. I. Hayakawa and Alan R. Hayakawa

Roy F. Fox
University of Missouri–Columbia

Samuel Ichiye Hayakawa (1907–1992) authored eight books about the role of language and other symbols in human behavior. He founded the International Society for General Semantics and the journal *Etc.: A Review of General Semantics*, which he edited for nearly thirty years. He also served as president of San Francisco State University and, from 1977 to 1983, as a United States Senator from California.

In the late 1930s, Hayakawa became deeply interested in the ideas of Alfred Korzybski, the founder of general semantics and author of *Science and Sanity* (1933). Korzybski argued for a system of thinking and language that reflected the constant change that occurs in reality, so that our internal, verbal "maps" could better match the real or external world. To make Korzybski's ideas more accessible to the general public, as well as to communicate his own concepts, Hayakawa published *Language in Action*. Ironically, Hayakawa's book was the Book-of-the-Month Club selection for December 1941.

Alan R. Hayakawa collaborated with his father on the extensively revised fifth edition of *Language in Thought and Action* (1990), contributing a new chapter, "The Empty Eye," on communication issues in television. A former Washington correspondent, Alan Hayakawa has written on politics and urban design for *The Oregonian* in Portland, where he earlier served as art and architecture critic, and is co-author of *The Blair Handbook,* a composition text. He is currently a writing coach at *The Patriot-News* in Harrisburg, Pennsylvania.

I met with Senator Hayakawa in July 1990 at his home in Mill Valley, California. The material in this chapter comes from that meeting and from several telephone conversations I had with both S. I. and Alan Hayakawa throughout the remainder of 1990. A small portion of my interview with S. I. Hayakawa was published in the February 1991 issue of *English Journal.*

RF: You once wrote that "the uncritical confidence that people place in words is a matter of constant amazement to me" (Hayakawa 1979). Is it easier for us to have an uncritical confidence in images than in words?

SIH: If you have an image on television of one individual choking another individual to death, you can't pretend it doesn't exist. You can't be totally neutral in the situation. That is the function of movies or art or any other representation. There's no point to any representation unless you had some reaction related to that which is depicted.

AH: I agree. It probably is easier for us to have an uncritical confidence in images. When I was young, teachers cautioned me not to believe everything I read in a book. They told me how readers mistakenly believe things because they are in print—the magic of print—the same thing my father has talked about. But we also believe that photographs represent reality. We know on some level, usually, that a painting or drawing has been through some process of synthesis by the artist. That may or may not make it an accurate report of the reality the artist saw; we know there is subjectivity and selectivity involved. But we do think seeing is believing, and makers of television and movies take great advantage of this fact. When you see a picture rather than read a written description, you generalize from a specific instance to a more general impression in a different way, more from images than from words. Because it's so difficult to make a picture of a general idea, people use pictures that are specific. If you want to do pictures about homelessness, you take pictures of one or two individuals. And a person seeing these will immediately generalize that all homeless people match this category, whether it's women fleeing abusive domestic situations or deinstitutionalized mental patients. So the danger in believing that pictures represent the world is that they are *not* used to represent just those things they depict.

RF: Is this problem related to an image's context?

AH: Yes. A picture has no past and no future; it's only in the present, only in the instant it's snapped. So if you see a picture of a police officer beating demonstrators or soldiers beating citizens, you should know these events don't occur in a vacuum. . . . There's a whole historical context that's not transmitted by the picture. It may be Serbs and Croats, Armenians and Azerbaijanis, or Catholics and Protestants. Each confrontation is based on a whole collection of disputes over time. The picture of the single instance, today's event in any of these long stories, often gives the mistaken impression that you know what's going on.

RF: [to SIH] This abstracting or selecting of images works much like the selecting of language—one of the pillars of general semantics that you popularized over fifty years ago. . . . Were you surprised by the success of *Language in Action?*

SIH: Yes, and the textbook edition was small and modest, so that it could be sold cheaply. But when it became a Book-of-the-Month Club selection, they increased the size of the type and the number of pages and made it much bigger.

RF: What do you say to people who are not familiar with general semantics? What should they do to better understand their world?

SIH: [laughing] I'd say that it's about time they read my book.

RF: Were any of your Senate colleagues familiar with your books or with general semantics?

SIH: I don't think so. There wasn't much reason for them to be because they were mature men and women . . . who didn't read *Language in Thought and Action* while going to school. They were old enough to have escaped that.

RF: Can you recall any colleagues in the government who tried to apply the rationality inherent in general semantics?

SIH: I don't recall a single instance of that.

RF: Let's get back to imagery and the average person—while not forgetting language, either.

SIH: Aren't all literate cultures deeply influenced by pictures and photographs on the one hand and by verbal text on the other?

AH: Yes. And I think that most people are tremendously sophisticated about images. There are isolated aboriginal groups in Australia who don't recognize photographs as likenesses of people and places. The point is that reading images is a learned skill. Through a series of unexamined, learned habits, we all know quite a bit about how to read images. We know when we open a magazine, turn on a television, watch a commercial, or look at a news photograph.

RF: And we make those distinctions?

AH: Yes, but the people who publish magazines and put out television work harder and harder toward blurring those divisions so that the advertising may be more credible. When we talk about crossing the line between news and advertising, some say that it raises the credibility of advertising. But I think it lowers the credibility of news. The more news looks like advertising or entertainment, the less believable it becomes. This pertains to the kind of specific truth you hope to get from news, as opposed to the more general truths you hope to get from entertainment. Fashion magazines are a good example, because it's real hard to tell which is an editorial piece on the spring stuff and which is a four-page ad layout designed to sell the spring stuff. It all tends to blur. This happens even more on television, where it's real hard to tell a "silver bullet" Coors commercial from a scene on "Miami Vice."

RF: Children's television is a classic case.

AH: Of course—where the same characters break away into the commercials and sell you something and then go back and continue their adventure. A little bit of conscious education about this stuff goes a long way. If we see the value in this kind of critical attitude, then we will teach children a little bit about art, imagery, and the media with which images are made.

RF: How do you do this with your own children?

AH: If we happen to turn on a movie that's too intense for my youngest child, I tell him, "Look, it's just pretend. That's a person dressed up in a monster suit; listen to the way they play the music to make it sound really spooky. Let's turn the sound off for a minute and watch how they did this." Or I ask him whether he thinks the movie action really happened or is just telling a story. He usually stops and thinks for a minute and then says, "I don't know. What is it?" or "It's just telling a story because. . . ."

The other thing I do is respond to ads with my children. My youngest might say, "That looks really neat. Can we get that when we go to the store?" And I have to say, "Yeah, we could" or "No, I don't want that." But I also try to ask him about that product he finds so appealing. Why does he like it? When he tells me that something is really neat, I say, "Well, okay, let's go and look at it and see if it really does things the way they say that it does on television." It's important to give kids the idea that television is full of people trying to sell more things than most people have money to buy, so you have to pick and choose. It's important that people be given some idea about what's being done to them, because most people have no idea how much images can be manipulated to make things look like what they are not—from toothpaste to political candidates.

RF: Two strong but opposing forces of imagery seem to be at work here. On one hand, we have to be consciously analytical—aware that we're abstracting on a high level. On the other hand, we have all these needs to relax and escape, to be absorbed and entertained.

AH: I'm as willing to suspend disbelief and get involved watching a film as the next person. I don't think you have to be constantly critical, but we do need to stop and do a little reality check about the attitudes and actions we watch.

SIH: I don't watch very much television . . . though I've enjoyed watching baseball games every now and then. . . . [But] it's hardly possible, if the acting is good, not to empathize with a filmed situation in one way or another.

AH: And that's what our whole dramatic tradition is about, going back to the Greek theater and the idea of collective catharsis. Television is a wonderful source of entertainment, but like anything else, it's better if you have a little perspective about the way you react to it or your involvement with it.

RF: How do you think the process of generalizing from images differs from the process of generalizing from language?

AH: The process does differ: perhaps it's a little more unconscious. If you're not conscious of the limitations of images—the selectivity of photography, painting, and drawing—then you tend to regard them as definitive examples of the real world. When there's rioting and looting, newspapers often run pictures of looters doing such and such during the power blackout following the earthquake, or whatever. Too often, people look at the papers, see people looting, and conclude, "Isn't it just like those so-and-so's?" Whether the picture comes from the Caribbean or Detroit, they immediately tend to generalize from the specific individuals doing the looting to a whole ethnic or racial group. I think that's very dangerous.

RF: Is it possible to doubt, contradict, or negate an image?

AH: You negate or contradict an image by comparing it with other images and by putting it in context, not only with other images but with what you know about reality. But a single compelling image is hard to erase. If you are fairly sophisticated, you can slant pictures the same way you can slant verbal description: by selecting detail. With words, you can describe somebody by saying he was unshaven and his clothes were ragged. That's selecting two details from which the reader is free to generalize. Or you could say his eyes were clear and his hands were steady. All four things may be true, but if you pick two, readers go one way, while if you pick the other two, they go the other way.

The same thing can be done with the camera by selecting a point of view, the camera angle, and the lighting, in order to present somebody, literally, in a favorable or unfavorable light. So, if you keep that in mind when you look at an image, you can often see why an image may make a positive or negative impression. It's particularly clear in cereal ads when you have the horizontal yellow light lighting up everything in the morning—the yellow filters and everything sort of glowing with that warmth you get from eating Grupo cereal.

RF: But even if we know all about how images or words are manipulated, can we be so consciously analytical all the time? *[to SIH]* When you read about news events, do you look at them from a semantics point of view?

SIH: No. I think about news events as events to remember. . . . I'm not conscious of approaching some things with a non-Aristotelian point of view.

RF: So to carry general semantics around with you all the time is not something you would advocate?

SIH: That's right. To carry it around with you all the time, you'd have to be more obsessed than I have ever been.

RF: Let me ask the same question another way: Have you ever lost faith in general semantics?

SIH: No, not that I recall. . . . But there is something that could be interpreted in that way. Korzybski [Alfred Korzybski, the founder of general semantics] was an extraordinarily dogmatic individual, and if you disagreed with him, well . . . you were placed in his dog house. At the same time, I was a very articulate and energetic advocate of Korzybski's ideas, although I didn't *always* agree with him in *all* respects. And I would get in trouble with him every now and then—fairly frequently, as a matter of fact. But damn it *[laughing]*, I did more for Korzybski's work than any other writer! I mean, there were a lot of good books on the subject by others, like Wendell Johnson's *People in Quandaries* (1946), but they haven't lasted as long. Their books have all died out. . . . They didn't have the carrying power.

RF: Why does yours have carrying power?

SIH: [laughing] Because I'm a good writer, that's all!

RF: Let's turn to political imagery. For example, early in Carter's campaign for the presidency, he wore a sweater on television and sat in front of a fireplace in Warm Springs, Georgia—all of which summoned the imagery of FDR, a president we trusted.

AH: I certainly agree. Image politics has devalued oratory. The major parties are falling all over each other trying to outdo each other's politics of image over substance. And I think the Republicans have had more success with this, though I don't think that's any great compliment. They have been very good at waving the flag behind photos of their candidates while slinging mud via negative television advertising.

RF: Bush's visit to the flag factory in 1988 was criticized so much in the press, that you'd think it would have backfired on him. But it didn't.

AH: I don't think it did, either. The main goal of people who do this for a campaign is to get the image of the candidate standing in front of the flag on television. The networks and news programs know that their time—which they give away—is very valuable to the campaign. They don't want to be seen as being used by the campaign by photographing the images and simply regurgitating them as news when they are in fact canned events.

So they've decided to criticize the *packaging* of the news, the packaging of the candidates. You get a picture of Bush standing in front of a display of flags with the reporter's voice-over saying, "Gee, here's Bush trying to ally himself with everything that's good about the American flag by visiting a flag factory. Did it work? We asked the average man on the street. . . ." But the campaign manager says, "I don't care *what* they said. We got Bush's picture in front of the flag on the evening news and that's what people are going to remember. They won't recall the words or the fact that the reporter tried to offer some critical distance from the image for the viewer." And I think he's right.

RF: So the press saves face by criticizing, and the campaign handlers still win.

AH: Exactly. The television press has a split personality on the subject. On the one hand, they try to do, and often do, a very good job of analyzing how an event like that is put together and what it's for. On the other hand, they can't resist running the pictures. If it's "good visual," it's good television. And so they've really become collaborators in this process. They become completely co-opted. The very little they try to do about it is not effective. This new style of reporting has gone a long, long way to devalue the words of public figures. We no longer listen to them speak, and we no longer hear them quoted. We see their pictures while the reporters tell us what they're trying to do. But we don't hear the candidate talk for great lengths of time, which, for most people, is a good way to learn about how somebody thinks.

Television has also trivialized politics by cutting the connection between the process of running for office and the process of governing. Because the process of governing does not translate well into television, we have changed campaigns a great deal so that they do. The person who actually runs the race and does the governing may be very different from the one you see on television or a billboard. In the 1968 Oregon primary, a billboard showed Robert Kennedy wearing a suit while walking on the beach. He had his shoes off, his necktie open, and his jacket slung over his shoulder. He was surrounded by a broad expanse of sand. This image made RFK seem like a mellow, shirt-sleeve kind of guy, in tune with the environment and the peace and beauty of the coast. RFK was probably a lot of things, but mellow and laid back at the coast is not a characteristic that comes across from reading accounts by people who really knew him. So political imagery cuts the connection of words. Because speeches are not reproduced, we don't hear and see how candidates think. We hear fifteen or twenty words at a time, and they are very carefully preselected. The dissonance between the campaign promise and the reality of governing is not transmitted by television. You can't show somebody *not* doing something on television.

RF: In the way we consume products, elect people to public office, obtain information, engage in recreation—are we too reliant upon images?

AH: I have a couple of responses to that. Television is like the car. Both tend to isolate us in small groups of people we already know. With the automobile, you stay inside your steel and glass bubble. You never get out in the street, walk around, and talk to people. If you live in the suburbs and drive downtown, park your car, and go into the office, and then leave the office and drive home, you're all the time isolated in this little steel and glass bubble. Well, television tends to keep you in this same bubble in your living room, filled with people you already know, so that now, on the Fourth of July, you can watch fireworks on television. I submit that something is going to be lost in the translation. You can subscribe to a video dating service; relieve yourself of all that messy and risky business of going out in public and meeting people. As a result, I think there are going to be people—there *are* people— who are more comfortable with television than with reality.

Another thing that television does concerns a point my father made years ago. Television tends to concentrate on consumption without talking about earning your way in the world. Television emphasizes people in their roles as spenders and consumers and pursuers of pleasure but not as earners and builders. Almost everybody in our society is both, but on television, you seldom see anyone earning a living. Most people have figured out that television doesn't offer any answers about *how* to get gratification. Television shows that it's great fun to attract the opposite sex, to drink Coors, and to drive a new BMW. But you can watch a long time without a clue as to how to obtain enough money to buy a six-pack of beer.

It's only when we start to believe that television contains the answers that we're going to get in trouble. But the rest of the world sees Western and American culture primarily on television, which explains why there is so much uneasiness expressed about what's generally referred to as "Western materialism." For example, the Chinese say they have to be very strict and keep out Western ideas because Western ideas lead to this terrible materialism. But our society is *not* exclusively materialistic; there is a productive side to it as well as a consuming side. And there is a spiritual side and a religious side, but none of these show up on the mainstream tube. So there's a distortion being transmitted. I can understand why people far away would look at "Dallas" and "Miami Vice" and say, "I'm not sure we want to go this far."

RF: I recently read that the number one television program in one underdeveloped country was "Hunter."

AH: I was visiting Dallas once, talking with a waitress. I told her that the city didn't all seem to be the way it looked on television, and she said that no, it wasn't. When I asked her whether the people she knew took the television program "Dallas" very seriously, she said that of course they didn't. Then I asked her what I could do around town that would be interesting. She said, "Well, you could go down to South Fork and see the ranch. I mean, it's really all down there." Then she told me what had happened in such and such episode and how that was the way things really were around Dallas. She completely belied what she'd said a minute before about the television show not being taken seriously.

RF: So, are we too reliant upon images?

AH: Who us? When we use a picture of a person reading a book to give directions to the library?

SIH: Television—it turns our brains into putty.

Works Cited

Fox, Roy F. 1991. "A Conversation with the Hayakawas." *English Journal* 80 (February): 36–40.

Hayakawa, S. I. 1941. *Language in Action.* New York: Harcourt, Brace.

———. 1979. *Through the Communication Barrier: On Speaking, Listening, and Understanding.* Edited by Arthur Chandler. New York: Harper and Row.

Hayakawa, S. I., and Alan R. Hayakawa. 1990. *Language in Thought and Action.* 5th ed. San Diego: Harcourt Brace Jovanovich.

Johnson, Wendell. 1946. *People in Quandaries: The Semantics of Personal Adjustment.* New York: Harper and Row.

Korzybski, Alfred. 1933. *Science and Sanity.* Lancaster, PA: Science Press.

14 The Image Is Not the Thing

Herb Karl
University of South Florida

Some people would argue that still or moving pictures evoke meanings quite differently from the way language does. If the meanings we make of visual imagery have the capacity, as does language, to affect our actions and beliefs, we need to understand how the process works. Thankfully, we can analyze and explain the mysteries of meaning making as they apply to language. By asking the right questions, we can verify what are called "facts" and distinguish between opinions and judgments. Unfortunately, this kind of inquiry does not hold up as well for visual imagery. For example, is a picture of a package of cigarettes true or false? Is it an opinion or a judgment? For that matter, is the meaning-making process as it applies to language in any way connected to visual imagery? Or are we talking about apples and oranges?

These are the kinds of questions addressed in this chapter. This task is doubly difficult because language itself is often an abstraction of material, and hence visual, objects; language is thus strewn with "visual" imagery. More than anything else, however, this chapter is part of an ongoing personal search for the effects of visual images in media—particularly television and film—on children and adults. I have been searching for some time and have made some interesting discoveries along the way.

The Image Processors and the Word Processors

One such discovery took place a little more than a decade ago when Charles Weingartner, David VanDercar, and I collaborated on an exploratory research project, "The Word Processors and the Image Processors: A Comparison of Their Emotional Responses to Violence in Film" (1980). The project was exploratory in the best sense of the word. We had a working hypothesis, but we had no commitment to a rigid system of data gathering. Using a number of paper and pencil tests, we collected all sorts of information from our subjects. Then we measured their below-the-level-of-consciousness "emotional" responses—in the form of skeletal muscle activity, temperature variation, and galvanic skin response—as they viewed a fictional film containing instances of violent visual imagery.

When we sorted out all the data, we made at least one curious discovery: a pattern of physiological responses, particularly galvanic skin response, which is generally regarded as a good indicator of emotional arousal. Our subjects' galvanic skin response (or skin conductance) correlated significantly with performance on a paper and pencil test presumed to reveal a bias on the part of the subjects toward processing either words or images.

Simply put, the subjects who preferred to process images rather than words seemed to grow more intensely responsive to the escalating sequence of violent imagery near the end of the film; the subjects who preferred to process words rather than images appeared to reach a "leveling-off" point, gradually returning to a state of relative calmness. Figure 14.1 reveals each group's pattern of response. Although VanDercar and I were tempted to venture some expansive explanations for this finding, Weingartner concluded our report with a pithy and discerning sentence: "It is not only beauty that lies in the eye of the beholder, but all other meanings as well" (82).

Weingartner suggests that every human being is blessed with a meaning-making apparatus—sensors connected to a central nervous system—and that while there may be similarities in how the apparatus operates, results can differ greatly. He had explored this issue some years earlier as he described the work of Adelbert Ames on the nature of perception (Postman and Weingartner 1969). Ames's demonstrations suggested that meaning does not come from the "things" outside us; rather, it comes from the meaning-making apparatus within us. Furthermore, Weingartner's conclusion intimates that there may be some common ground in the making of meaning—whether the meaning-making apparatus is responding to a sign and symbol system like language or to visual imagery.

In our study, one of the variables that seemed to affect how the apparatus functioned was what we termed a *meaning-making bias.* Those subjects with a bias toward "words" processed the emotionally charged visual imagery of the film in a rational, relatively detached manner. On the other hand, those with a bias toward "images" seemed to merge with the film's content, their emotions paralleling what was taking place on the screen. At the very least, the meaning-making apparatus of the "word" processors allowed them to regulate their

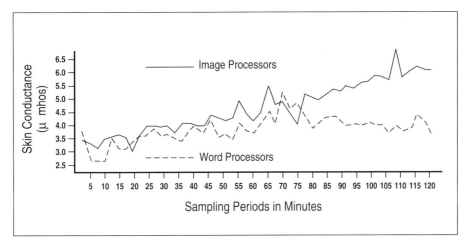

Figure 14.1. Skin conductance of "image processors" and "word processors" in response to an escalating sequence of violent imagery. Reprinted from *Etc.* (Spring 1980) with permission of the International Society for General Semantics.

emotional responses to the escalating violence, while the "image" processors appeared to surrender to it.

The Typographic Mind

In 1985, five years after the publication of our study, Neil Postman's provocative *Amusing Ourselves to Death: Public Discourse in the Age of Show Business* appeared. In it, Postman proposed what he called "the typographic mind," an idea that complements the findings of our study. Citing the sixteenth-century philosopher Erasmus and such contemporary scholars as Elizabeth Eisenstein and Walter Ong, Postman builds a case for reading and writing as mind-shaping activities:

> To engage in the written word means to follow a line of thought, which requires considerable powers of classifying, inference making, and reasoning. It means to uncover lies, confusions, and overgeneralizations, to detect abuses in logic and common sense. It also means to weigh ideas, to compare and contrast assertions, to connect one generalization to another. (51)

Postman seems to suggest that the habit of literacy contributes to the formation of a filtering mechanism through which information must pass. Those who, through educational pursuits or personal preferences, have cultivated such a filtering mechanism end up with a typographic mind. According to Postman, such folks are better able to respond to their perceptions and experiences in a rational, analytic manner. Perhaps the "word" processors in our study possessed such a filtering mechanism—one that made it possible for them to pause and reflect on what they were seeing. We might say, therefore, that an integral part of a person's meaning-making apparatus is a filtering mechanism, the formation of which may be related to such habits as reading and writing.

Incidentally, the implications of the typographic mind for education are momentous and obvious. If, as a civilization, we choose to prize the qualities Postman associates with a typographic mind— conceptual thought, deductive and sequential reasoning, a sense of order and purpose, an abhorrence of contradiction, a generous capacity for detachment and objectivity, and a tolerance for deferred gratification—then all we have to do is teach and promote from the earliest days of a child's life a value for the printed page and the act of writing. Becoming literate, therefore, is not only a prerequisite for survival in a world of print; it is the basis for a way of perceiving—of thinking about and acting upon the world.

The Filtering Mechanism

The idea of a filtering mechanism as a part of the human meaning-making apparatus is not new. Benjamin Whorf, in essays that appear in *Language, Thought, and Reality* (1956), spoke of such a mechanism many years ago. A liberal rendering of the "Whorf hypothesis" might read like this:

> A culture's experiences and perceptions shape its language; and, conversely, the language of a culture tends to shape that culture's perceptions and experiences.

Of course, "culture" here includes the individual perceptions and experiences of all the members of that culture. So the Whorf hypothesis speaks to the individual as well as the whole.

If we were to transfer this principle to the visual image, we would have:

> A culture's experiences and perceptions shape its visual imagery; and, conversely, the visual imagery of a culture tends to shape that culture's perceptions and experiences.

Turning the principle into one that subsumes both language and images requires some more editing:

> Our experiences and perceptions influence the way we make meaning; and, the way we make meaning influences our perceptions and experiences.

In this last version of the Whorf hypothesis lies a kind of theoretical framework for our study of the word and image processors, as well as an endorsement of Weingartner's notion of a common meaning-making ground shared by both language and visual imagery.

Postman, however, reminds us of an essential difference between words and images. In an interview with Bill Moyers as part of the Public Broadcasting series *The Public Mind* (1989), Postman pointed out this difference:

> Let's take a McDonald's commercial. We see a young father taking his six-year-old daughter into McDonald's. They're eating a cheeseburger, and they're ecstatic. Question: Is that true or false? Is the picture—the image—true or false? Well, the words don't seem to apply to that sort of thing. That [the images in the commercial] just *is*. I mean there is no way to access [images] the way we access statements—linguistic utterances. And so we now build up a whole world of imagery where basically we're out of the realm of logic and perhaps into the realm of aesthetics.

The "verifiability" issue so central to how language means does not appear to apply to images. Is this a fatal flaw—one that abrogates any attempt to find some common ground between the way we make meaning with and out of both language and images? Maybe not.

General Semantics: Part of the Answer?

S. I. Hayakawa transformed the legacy of Alfred Korzybski and others into some principles of general semantics that became widely accessible with the initial publication some fifty years ago of his *Language in Thought and Action,* currently in its fifth edition (1990). The principles are generalized rules detailing the pitfalls and possibilities of human language. Curiously, the Whorf hypothesis is sometimes referred to as the keystone principle of general semantics—the organizing concept that holds the principles together.

Even though Postman correctly points out an essential difference between words and images, the principles of general semantics may further define the filtering mechanism. The obvious question: Is it possible that the mechanism through which our perceptions are filtered can be structured in part by rules of meaning making that have been applied to language? Furthermore, by gutting the "truth-falsity" issue from the principles, do we dilute or eliminate their utility?

Such questions deserve a great deal more discussion than I am prepared to give them in this chapter. Nonetheless, one could begin to examine how a few of the principles of general semantics extend beyond the realm of language and into the realm of visual imagery. If, in fact, the principles apply, then we have reason to argue that a common ground—a kind of unified field theory of meaning making that holds for language and visual images—is worth considering.

I have selected three such principles from general semantics, showing in each case their applicability to visual imagery:

1. The image is not the thing.
2. You cannot know the meaning of an image unless you know its context(s).
3. An image is either relatively extensional or relatively intensional.

The Image Is Not the Thing

Just as the word is not that to which it refers, so too is the visual image not to be confused with the material object it represents. A visual image is a manifestation of a camera or an artist's brush or a computer, and each of these "tools" is in the hand of a human being with his or her own filtering mechanism. As obvious as this fact is, people often ignore it. Even Hayakawa (1990) speaks of this habit:

> In the case of drama (stage, movies, television), there appear to be people in almost every audience who never quite fully realize that a film or television show is a set of fictional, symbolic representations. (17)

To separate a visual image from the "thing" it represents requires analytic thinking—an ability to detach oneself from immediate perceptions in order to reflect on them. This simple act becomes, apparently, more complex as emotional involvement in an image intensifies. Recall, once again, the image processors in our study.

The virtues of the image-thing principle are more readily apparent in the world of commerce, where images of products, services, and ideas often are used to manipulate the consumer in ways not always in his or her best interest. In their image making, advertisers often walk a fine line between the ethical and the unethical, the moral and the immoral. Similarly, the difference between a propaganda film and a documentary frequently lies in the correspondence between the images on the screen and the reality they are presumed to represent. Without the detached reflectivity spawned by the image-thing principle, we become hostage to deep emotional reactions that inhibit reason. We become victims of our viscera.

Paradoxically, the success of a work of art—a fictional film or a novel—is often judged on the basis of its capacity to create in the mind of the viewer or reader a feeling of plausibility, if not outright believability. In other words, it is the mission of the artist to transform the image or the word into the thing. (Coleridge echoed this sentiment, suggesting that a work of art must be capable of producing a willing suspension of disbelief.) Dwight Burton (1970) has also underscored the fact that the power of an art form—especially literature—lies in its capacity to kindle an "imaginative entry," where the reader literally surrenders his or her imagination to the narrative (81–84). In each of these instances, proponents would argue that the purpose of art— whether a movie, a play, a poem, or a novel—is usually moral; the artist's intent is not to seduce, but rather to delight, to instruct, or to heal.

Nonetheless, without a semantic filter that permits a reader or a viewer to grasp the essential differences between images or words and the things to which they refer, art and reality, fiction and fact, become virtually the same. Just ask those Germans who once viewed Leni Riefenstahl's *Triumph of the Will* as they would a newsreel. Just ask many people today, especially younger viewers, who interpret Oliver Stone's *JFK* as documentary.

You Cannot Know the Meaning of an Image Unless You Know Its Context(s)

Images do not occur in isolation. They are located within contexts, and sometimes the images are themselves contexts for other images. A photograph is a representation of matter; we cannot know the matter by looking at the photograph. Yet the more we know about the matter—of which the photograph is only a representation—the more we know about the photographic image. A television "sound bite," a small chunk of film or videotape selected from a larger segment, tells us what its "editor" would like us to know. Without the larger context, we often get a distorted sense of the meaning of a sound bite's imagery— whether the imagery represents an event or a person. All of this refers to the physical context of an image.

There are other contexts in which images occur. Take, for example, the motivational context, which raises the issues of purpose and intention. Why was the image created in the first place? What was the intention of the image maker? Was the purpose to sell something? Was the intention to shape a particular attitude toward the image? By resorting to the so-called "photo opportunity," White House aides have been known to orchestrate the image of their employer for particular purposes. Terence P. Moran (1990) cites a number of examples of this, including the following:

> Images of a President [Bush] caught in a traffic jam as he sought to dramatize the budget crisis by returning to the White House from Camp David in a four-wheel drive utility vehicle instead of the Marine Corps helicopter brought echoes of President Carter in his blue sweater during the energy crisis. (6)

An Image Is Either Relatively Extensional or Relatively Intensional

Like words, images are relatively extensional or relatively intensional. Extensional words are those whose referents can actually be pointed to. The referents are concrete; hence, the words that represent them are said to have concrete or extensional meaning. The word *dog*, for instance, is extensional, especially when the dog to which we are referring is present when we make the statement "That's my dog."

Intensional words are those whose referents cannot be easily pointed to. Take, for example, the word *liberal*. Even when the person to whom we attach that word is present, our intended meaning in saying "He's a liberal" is arguable. *Liberal* has a way of evoking intensional meaning—even when it is used to label a tangible object.

The meaning-making potential of images behaves in much the same way. That is, some images, such as the one in figure 14.2, tend to evoke relatively extensional meaning. Other images, such as the one in figure 14.3, evoke relatively intensional meaning.

Conscious awareness of the extensional-intensional principle, like the image-thing and the context principles, should be regarded as more than a filtering mechanism enabling us to defend ourselves against distorted or deceptive visual imagery. Carl Jung, Joseph Campbell, and Bruno Bettelheim, among others, have ascribed considerable significance to the intensional meanings of visual imagery. To these men, images—especially those that seem to recur in the art of both primitive and modern humankind—have the power to illuminate and to instruct. The intensional meaning evoked by these images, they might argue, can do much to enlighten us and heal our troubled psyches.

Figure 14.2. Extensional image.

Figure 14.3. Intensional image. © 1994 by Lucy N. Karl.

A Final Note

I began this chapter by noting a research project that demonstrated that people markedly differ in how they process visual images. The subjects of the research were exposed to the same movie; they even viewed it at the same time. The variation in their responses was attributed to the composition of the meaning-making apparatus possessed by each subject.

I have gone so far as to suggest that a filtering mechanism is the part of our meaning-making apparatus that accounts for the differences. A mind capable of processing visual images so that a judgment can be made about their potential to corrupt or enhance, to obfuscate or illuminate, must be equipped with some sort of filtering mechanism. Whether this mechanism is a natural by-product of literacy and a bias toward language or whether it is structured by identifiable rules of general meaning making is not particularly significant. On the other hand, it is very significant that humans, one way or another, become capable of figuring out what an image is doing to them or for them.

This does not mean, however, that we shouldn't continue to probe into the nature of the meaning-making filter. For the time being, it probably wouldn't be a bad idea to promote literacy as "a way of knowing," an epistemology of print for which there is no substitute. Also, it couldn't hurt to encourage the study of general semantics and to apply its principles to a theory of meaning making that embraces images as well as language.

Works Cited

Burton, Dwight L. 1970. *Literature Study in the High Schools.* 3d ed. New York: Holt, Rinehart and Winston.

Consuming Images. 1989. Videocassette. From *The Public Mind* series with Bill Moyers. Distributed by PBS Video, New York. 58 minutes.

Hayakawa, S. I., and Alan R. Hayakawa. 1990. *Language in Thought and Action.* 5th ed. San Diego: Harcourt Brace Jovanovich.

Karl, Herb, D. H. VanDercar, and Charles Weingartner. 1980. "The Word Processors and the Image Processors: A Comparison of Their Emotional Responses to Violence in Film." *Etc.* 27 (Spring): 77–83.

Moran, Terence P. 1990. "After Satire: The Decline of Political Satire in the Age of the Photo Opportunity and the Sound Bite." Address presented at the First Annual "Dooley Days," 12 October, Irish American Heritage Center, Chicago.

Postman, Neil. 1985. *Amusing Ourselves to Death: Public Discourse in the Age of Show Business.* New York: Viking.

Postman, Neil, and Charles Weingartner. 1969. *Teaching as a Subversive Activity.* New York: Delacorte Press.

Whorf, Benjamin Lee. 1956. *Language, Thought, and Reality.* Edited by John B. Carroll. Cambridge: MIT Press.

15 Analyzing Visual Persuasion: The Art of Duck Hunting

Kay Ellen Rutledge
Georgia State University

There were moments as I sat alone in the cool, darkened theater watching the hit movie *Silence of the Lambs* that I lowered my head and closed my eyes to avoid seeing certain images. They were too violent, too vivid. I did not want to admit them to my sight or to my memory. Yet long after I had left the theater, my mind continued to play back images from the film and to re-create through imagination those scenes I had refused to watch. For a brief period, in my mind, the film maker's illusions supplanted reality. The voracious appetite of Hannibal Lecter and the delusions of the psychopathic killer, Buffalo Bill, had come to life in the images flashed upon the screen.

As our culture becomes increasingly visual and nonverbal, the intensity of images such as those in *Silence of the Lambs* is matched daily in the media. Music videos, televised bombings, glib advertisements for liquor, tobacco, cars, clothes, cosmetics, or cereals proclaim the decline of the word and the power of the image in our rhetorical environment.

In this environment, professionals—advertising experts, politicians, government propagandists, and activists—influence our behavior and alter our perceptions by creating illusions—illusions so skillfully crafted that we easily confuse them with reality. In their efforts to enhance images, these professionals sometimes distort reality. In their efforts to impress their views upon us, they may pervert truth. In their efforts to sell products, personalities, and issues ranging from life insurance to hamburgers, from nuclear energy to rock stars, they create enticing words and images that deliberately deceive.

The media have created an imbalance between professional persuaders and a public untrained in evaluating visual persuasion. We need systematic methods for training students to detect, analyze, and evaluate visual images. Visual language, when designed to alter perceptions and distort the truth, whether imprinted on paper, film, videotape, cloth, or other medium, is visual doublespeak. Borrowing from Lutz's definition (1989) of doublespeak, visual doublespeak is the use of images that pretend to communicate but really do not; images that make the bad seem good, the negative appear positive; images that shift and avoid responsibility; images used to mislead, deceive, or obfuscate the truth. Unless taught to recognize and analyze visual doublespeak, our students are in danger of becoming sitting ducks for professional persuaders, lured by attractive, convincing decoys.

To prevent this deception, students must become the hunters instead of the hunted; they must learn the difference between ducks and decoys. Because there is danger in examining visual persuasion from a single perspective, the methods suggested here may be used for analyzing both visual and verbal persuasion, as well as the interaction between words and pictures. Taught to analyze and recognize verbal and visual manipulation, students can restore the rhetorical balance between professional persuaders and the public.

The Art of Duck Hunting

The need for distinguishing true ducks from decoys, reality from illusions, stems from several factors: (1) the proliferation of visual messages by professional persuaders in an increasingly iconic culture, (2) the power of visual images to affect behavior and alter perceptions, (3) the potential for doublespeak within visual messages, and (4) the limited methods available for teaching students to analyze visual persuasion.

According to Dondis (1973), the shift from a linguistic, word-dominated culture to an iconic, image-dominated culture culminated with the common use of the camera. Photography has given ordinary people the ability to portray reality. Freed from the limitations of talent and training, as well as the bonds of language, they have been empowered to record, report, interpret, and express human experience without the mediation of artists, in much the same way Luther's Protestant followers were empowered to communicate directly with God once the Church's mediators had been removed. The progress of language toward more efficient communication through pictures, pictographs, cartoons, phonetic units, and alphabets has come full circle and ended where it began: with what Matisse described as "that state of condensations that constitutes a picture."

Our preference for visual information and experience is natural: "Sight is swift, comprehensive, simultaneously analytic and synthetic. It requires so little energy to function . . . that it permits our minds to receive and hold an infinite number of items of information in a fraction of a second" (Dondis 1973, 2). Visual representations also substitute for reality when we lack direct experience, reinforcing what we know and providing evidence that verbal language may lack. Seeing is believing, and when we cannot see for ourselves, we rely on visual representations to confirm our knowledge.

We therefore become vulnerable to the manipulation of images by others. If the images on which we rely are inaccurate or untrue, tainting our perception of reality, then our decision making is compromised. Despite the common use of the camera, visual communication—images integrated with language and sound—is practiced mainly by professionals, who saturate every medium with icons. American flags, yellow ribbons, desert camouflage fatigues, and Desert Storm T-shirts merged with images of planes, tanks, missile launchers, and smoking oil fields to convey the Persian Gulf War. Images of Madonna, Bart Simpson, and Michael Jordan appear on clothing and posters. McDonald's promotes hamburgers with miniature Barbie dolls, an image that epitomizes feminine beauty to many young girls. Adults are drawn to the graphic novels of Will Eisner, preferring stories in pictures to stories in words. And in case we do not know what the perfect CEO's wife is like, *Fortune* magazine provides images of her.

Images not only shape what we know; they affect our behavior as well. They drive us to buy, to vote, to protest, to join, to dislike, to admire, to desire. Dondis (1973) notes:

> Most of what we know and learn, what we buy and believe, what we recognize and desire, is determined by the domination of the human psyche by pictures. And it will be more so in the future. (7)

Image-conscious viewers often try to eliminate or prevent the dissemination of images that can harm their causes. Marie T. Cockran, a Georgia college professor, was responsible for having an NCAA football poster banned from distribution in 1989. She insisted that this poster, depicting two football players poised head-to-head against a background of Spanish moss and live oak trees lining the avenue to an antebellum plantation house, was offensive to African Americans. The poster, she claimed, harkened back to the oppression of slavery in the Old South, promoting racial prejudice. Ironically, the poster was approved by Alfred White, an African American who was director of promotions for the NCAA (Reese 1989). The power of an image to evoke a given response, then, is often in the eyes of the beholder.

Even more ironic, the "plantation mythology" associated with the pre–Civil War South depicts only two white social classes: wealthy planters who owned slaves and poor whites. Revisionists insist that this was not the case. Not only was the average nineteenth-century southerner a farmer with a small landholding and no slaves, but the great houses of the wealthy planters were likely to be plain log buildings with two rooms, a porch on the front, and a shed behind. The white-columned mansion of the southern plantation, it seems, is an image that has been assimilated into our collective American imagination from literature, art, and film. It has become an icon representing prosperity and success (Vlach 1991). What the professor legitimately reacted to may be described as an image representing an illusion.

Visual Persuasion: The Senders

The effect of images on our perceptions and behavior is at once a benefit and a danger. The potential for doublespeak is as great with visual communication as it is with verbal communication. Visual persuasion is the product of professionals using the best of art, psychology, sociology, marketing, advertising, and technology to zealously promote their products, programs, causes, and candidates. Their means are highly effective, and their success is greatly aided by our failure to prepare students to analyze and evaluate visual messages.

Take the character prominent in a current advertising campaign for Camel cigarettes, Old Joe (figure 15.1). An example of visual doublespeak, this character is an image crafted to make the bad seem good, the negative appear positive. It is an image used to mislead, deceive, and obfuscate the truth. Old Joe, a camel whose phallic facial features are themselves an example of visual doublespeak, enjoys the "best of the good life"—cars, boats, girls, parties, beaches, music, sports, and chilling out—while promoting the deadly habit of cigarette smoking.

This level of doublespeak is fairly obvious even to the untrained viewer. Beyond this level, however, there are other, more subtle distortions of reality, including value statements about what constitutes this "good life" and the roles of men and women. Often these distortions are targeted at today's young people, a generation nurtured on television and Nintendo.

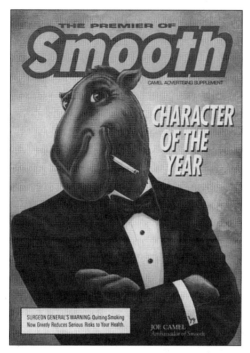

Figure 15.1. Old Joe Camel.

In fact, this is the generation to which advertisers are now pitching electronic advertisements in our schools. In 1991, DeKalb County near Atlanta installed electronic kiosks over public telephones in its junior and senior high schools in return for 15 percent of the revenues from advertisers. Students walking past the kiosks see nonstop advertising for shoes, soft drinks, and fast food. In the several brief periods students are in the hallways, high-impact commercials lasting a few seconds serve as "tailor-made entertainment" throughout the school day. The school board expects to receive more than $300,000 a year from the project. School systems in other states are also allowing advertising into their schools in similar efforts to make money (Watts 1991).

The real winners in these projects, though, are the advertisers. Hungry for access to the lucrative youth market, advertisers in the schools prey upon a captive audience. School systems, eager for supplemental funds, may also benefit. But, unable to escape the electronic messages in their schools, our children become sitting ducks. They are the losers. Speaking to reporters for the *Atlanta Journal and Constitution* on watching Channel One, one student in Georgia's Gwinett County schools commented, "I wish they had more commercials with Michael Jordan in them. I'd watch anything with him in it" (Pendered 1991).

Visual Persuasion: The Receivers

We lack curricula designed to help students understand media messages. Nonetheless, according to visual literacy proponents, students should be able to (1) read and understand visual messages and (2) plan, create, and combine visual messages for the purpose of intentional communication (Curtiss 1987, 11). To this I would add that students should be able to discern between truth and deceptive manipulation of images. Strategies for understanding and evaluating images are taken, for the most part, either from methods for analyzing language or from methods for analyzing and criticizing art. While both are helpful for understanding and making visual messages, neither is adequate to teach students about visual doublespeak.

Analyzing Visual Persuasion with Burke's Pentad and Rank's Schema

Two ways to teach students to analyze visual persuasion are Kenneth Burke's pentad (1969) and Hugh Rank's schema for propaganda analysis (1976). Used alone or together, these strategies allow viewers to get at the nature of visual messages simply, quickly, and effectively, without training in linguistic analysis, formal analysis, or art criticism. These strategies can also be made increasingly sophisticated depending on the age and experience of the student.

Kenneth Burke believes that when we communicate, we manipulate words and images to persuade others that our views of reality are correct and should be adopted. Just as we manipulate words, images, and symbols to persuade others to our views, others also manipulate these elements to impress their views upon us. Burke maintains that manipulation of verbal and nonverbal language within this context is natural, since all language, by its very nature, is persuasive or rhetorical. When one of the parties is a profit-seeking professional, however, and the other is an uncritical and often young viewer, the potential for deception and doublespeak greatly increases.

Burke developed his pentad's five elements—act, scene, agent, agency, and purpose—from drama to examine communication. Using the pentad helps to determine the view of reality being advocated by the words and images used in an act of communication and shows how verbal and nonverbal language is manipulated to achieve this effect. *Act* refers to something that is done. An act occurs when someone uses physical action or symbolic action (i.e., language) to respond to the environment or to describe a situation. Furthermore, within an act of communication, whether in words or pictures, there may be another act described or depicted.

For example, an advertisement such as the one for General Dynamics in figure 15.2 constitutes a rhetorical act. It was planned and produced by an agent, it occurs within a particular context or scene, it has a visual print medium as its agency, and its purpose is to persuade the public to accept General Dynamics products by highlighting the manufacturer's humanitarianism—the philanthropy of a corporation that produces weapons of war.

Within the advertisement, however, a different act is depicted. Two women (*co-agents*) work to repair (*act upon*) a house using the tools and skills of carpentry (*agency*) in order to meet housing needs (*purpose*). While the advertisement itself is not an act of humanitarianism, the act portrayed within it is. To truly understand the message conveyed by this image, we must use Burke's pentad to analyze both the *extrinsic* act—producing the image—and the *intrinsic* act—the image itself. We must know who produced the ad's message, the context in which it was produced, the methods used to produce it, and the reason for its production. Without this information, there is nothing to associate the act portrayed in the visual image with the advertiser. By analyzing both the extrinsic act and the intrinsic act, we are able to determine the perception of reality we are asked to accept, compare it to our own, and evaluate its credibility. If we can analyze and evaluate these things, then we are more likely to detect any efforts to distort, mislead, or deceive.

Although the act is the central element of Burke's pentad, complete analysis requires that we also examine the scene in which the act occurs, the agent or agents who performed the act, the means or agencies by which it was accomplished, and the purpose of the act. The *scene* is the setting of an act. The setting may be broad, perhaps global in scope, or it may be very limited. Visual persuasion may be considered in light of an era, a culture, a trend, or a generation, or it may be considered in the context of a very specific publication or broadcast with a limited or highly specialized audience. Burke calls the scene a container for the act and insists that the scene must fit the act it contains. Conversely, an act must fit the scene where it occurs. The act's nature is determined by the requirements of the setting. Each situation calls for certain actions, agents, and agencies.

Figure 15.2. General Dynamics ad.

Ads for the Japanese automobile Infiniti, such as the one in figure 15.3, highlight scenic elements. These ads depict tranquil scenes of ocean waves breaking on the shore, mountain streams, and rolling hillsides. The car does not appear in the scene, nor does any person. One perception of reality suggested by this visual message is that a state of harmony with nature can be achieved by owning an Infiniti. To evaluate this visual message, we must examine both the external scene—the scene in which the message was produced—and the internal or intrinsic scene—the scene depicted within the message.

An *agent* is one who performs an act. In visual persuasion, the extrinsic agent is the image maker, the artist, the photographer, the editor, the advertiser, or the publisher. The intrinsic agent is the performer portrayed within the visual image. For example, in the General Dynamics ad (figure 15.2), two women working together are depicted within the image. They are the intrinsic agents.

Agency implies the means whereby an act is accomplished. Extrinsically, the media, the technology, and the artistic elements and principles used by the image maker are the agencies by which visual persuasion is produced. Intrinsically, the agency is the means the image's agents use to accomplish their purpose. In an ad produced by the U.S. Council for Energy Awareness (figure 15.4), for instance, the

Figure 15.3. Infiniti ad.

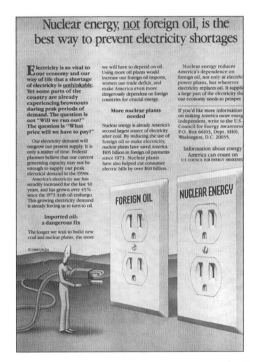

Figure 15.4. Ad produced by the U.S. Council for Energy Awareness.

agency depicted within the image is nuclear energy, the means by which the United States can avoid dependence on foreign oil. Extrinsically, the council provided the means by which the ad was created and was the vehicle used to disseminate it.

Purpose is the motive for an act, the reason an act is undertaken. Extrinsically, the purpose of a visual message may be to record, report, interpret, or express human experience. It may also be to alter perceptions and change behavior. Intrinsically, a purpose may be implied for the act within the visual image.

Communicators manipulate these elements of the pentad to achieve desired effects. By emphasizing any element within a visual message—act, scene, agent, agency, or purpose—communicators direct attention to those elements they want the viewer to accept and away from those they want the viewer to avoid. By stressing one element (or combination of elements) and downplaying others, persuaders focus viewers' attention on those that advance their own view of reality.

For instance, a series of Amiga computer ads combines the elements of agent, agency, and purpose within the image for the external purpose of selling computers. In fact, the series's main caption clearly describes this relationship among the pentadic elements. In the example here (figure 15.5), a father (*agent*) uses a computer and software (*agencies*) to help his son overcome dyslexia (*purpose*). The relationship among these three elements highlights the visual message for the ultimate purpose of presenting a reality in which severe learning problems are overcome with the proper product: Amiga's computer.

In the General Dynamics ad (figure 15.2), the image highlights co-agents engaged in positive action. The advertising image deflects attention away from General Dynamics itself and the products it manufactures—among them fighter planes—and toward humanitarian programs supported by General Dynamics. It is the humanitarian efforts whose purpose the action portrays. In any act of visual persuasion, the emphasized elements betray the persuader's intent. Using the pentad to determine the act, scene, agent, agency, and purpose of a persuasive message, we can discover the meaning and motive of the message, compare the persuader's perception of reality to our own, and judge better the message's truthfulness.

The premise behind Rank's schema for analyzing propaganda (1976) is that language manipulation is natural and neutral. According to Rank, all people *intensify* and *downplay*. They intensify their own good and downplay their own bad. Rank's schema has four postulates

Figure 15.5. Amiga ad.

about verbal and nonverbal manipulation: (1) people intensify their own good and (2) downplay the good of others; (3) people downplay their own bad and (4) intensify the bad of others. These postulates lead to Rank's guidelines for analyzing public persuasion, in our case visual messages: (1) when the persuader intensifies, the viewer should downplay; (2) when the persuader downplays, the viewer should intensify. Rank contends that the use of this schema (summarized by Rank for classroom use in the appendix to this chapter) can help equalize the imbalance between professional persuaders—advertisers, government propagandists, politicians, corporations, and religious organizations—and the public. Using this schema, students can become the hunters instead of the hunted.

To apply Rank's intensify/downplay schema to visual persuasion, we must first look for what is intensified. Such intensification can include (1) elements that are repeated within the image, (2) associations that are made between visual elements and individuals or ideas that are generally admired or hated, and (3) composition elements that emphasize the message. Next, in order to get a more balanced view of the ideas promoted in the image, we should look for what is downplayed, examining the image to determine (1) if elements have been deliberately omitted; (2) if exaggerated details, entertainment, humor, or emotion have been used to focus attention away from the rhetorical intent of the image; and (3) if elements have been combined in complex or chaotic ways to produce confusion. Finally, by downplaying what the image maker has played up and intensifying what the image maker has played down, we can better judge the message.

We can combine Burke's pentad and Rank's schema to systematically teach students to evaluate visual images. Using the intensify/downplay schema, students can decide quickly and easily which pentadic elements are highlighted in an image. Students should then intensify the pentadic elements that the persuader downplays and downplay those that are intensified in order to interpret the persuader's motives. In this manner, students can better evaluate the reality they are asked to accept.

We are bombarded by a visual propaganda blitz that is historically unequaled in its proportion and intensity. We must teach students to penetrate appearances and to evaluate the perceptions and rationality of visual persuaders. The following activities employ Burke's pentad and Rank's schema to help students distinguish ducks from decoys:

1. To emphasize intrinsic elements, give students copies of an ad from a popular magazine. Mask or delete the ad's words, if possible. Viewing only the image, have students describe the ad's content and message. By examining the ad's intensification and downplay techniques, students should point out repetition, association, composition, omission, diversion, or confusion found in the ad's visual elements.

2. Using the same ad, examine extrinsic elements. Ask students to identify the image maker (agent), the context for the image (scene), the image carrier (agency), and the purpose of the image. Students can explore the possibilities of co-agents: the artist, the editor, the publisher, the advertiser, or the advertising agent. Encourage students to broaden or narrow the scene, to consider the image in both its global context (its place in the broadest worldview) and immediate context (its placement within the publication).

3. Ask students to research the possible motives for downplaying any pentadic elements they find and to evaluate the rationality, accuracy, or acceptability of the image suggested by the ad.

4. Have students develop a position on whether the image effectively attracts potential buyers by deceiving viewers or distorting the truth. Even elementary children can construct short responses describing the ad's appeal or lack of appeal to them.

5. Ask students to relate the advertising image to its copy and to decide whether the image and copy complement or contradict one another in their portrayal of the product or service. Have them examine the language for evidence of doublespeak.

In addition to magazine ads, T-shirts, billboards, album covers, television commercials and programs, films, and videos provide an unlimited source of visual images for study. Students can undertake their own projects to apply the pentad or intensify/downplay schema to detect visual doublespeak. They might look at images in ads for specific products, such as liquor or tobacco, or across multiple media to see if those advertisements systematically intensify or downplay any particular pentadic element. They might examine ad images for the same product in different magazines or on different television programs to determine if different elements are emphasized relative to where the advertisements appear. Students can also look at how men and women or young people are portrayed by the images in various ads and determine if these images change according to where they appear.

Two analogies frame this chapter. First, the public in general and our students in particular are like sitting ducks—vulnerable to professional persuaders, hunters who entice them with the decoys of visual persuasion. Second, both the general public and our students should learn to be like hunters themselves, able to distinguish decoys from true ducks. The contrasting images of these analogies clearly show that I have manipulated language and images in somewhat the same way that advertisers and other professional persuaders do—and for the same purpose: to persuade others that my perception of visual persuasion is the correct one.

Works Cited

Burke, Kenneth. 1969. *A Grammar of Motives.* Berkeley: University of California Press.

Curtiss, Deborah. 1987. *Introduction to Visual Literacy: A Guide to the Visual Arts and Communication.* Englewood Cliffs, NJ: Prentice-Hall.

Dondis, Donis A. 1973. *A Primer of Visual Literacy.* Cambridge: MIT Press.

Lutz, William. 1989. *Doublespeak.* New York: Harper and Row.

Pendered, David. 1991. "Channel One, CNN at War in Classroom." *Atlanta Journal and Constitution,* 19 October, D3.

Rank, Hugh. 1976. "Teaching about Public Persuasion: Rationale and a Schema." In *Teaching about Doublespeak,* edited by Daniel Dietrich, 3–19. Urbana, IL: National Council of Teachers of English.

Reese, Ernest. 1989. "I-AA Game's 'Dixie' Poster Driven Down." *Atlanta Journal and Constitution,* 10 November, F3.

Vlach, John Michael. 1991. "The Reality and Mythology of the Southern Plantation." *Chronicle of Higher Education,* 9 October, B52.

Watts, Robert Anthony. 1991. "DeKalb OKs Electronic Ads in Schools." *Atlanta Journal and Constitution,* 13 August, C1.

Appendix. Hugh Rank's intensify/downplay schema. © 1976 by Hugh Rank.

INTENSIFY

Repetition

Intensifying by repetition is an easy, simple, and effective way to persuade. People are comfortable with the *known*, the *familiar*. As children, we love to hear the same stories repeated; later, we have "favorite" songs, TV programs, etc. All cultures have chants, prayers, rituals, dances based on repetition. Advertising slogans, brand names, logos, and signs are common. Much education, training, indoctrination is based on repetition to imprint on *memory* of the receiver to identify, recognize, and respond.

Association

Intensifying by linking (1) the idea or product with (2) something *already loved/desired by – or hated/feared by* (3) the intended audience. Thus, the need for **audience analysis**: surveys, polls, "market research," "consumer behavior," psychological and sociological studies. Associate by *direct* assertions or *indirect* ways; (metaphoric language, allusions, backgrounds, contexts, etc.) Some "good things" often linked with products are those common human needs/wants/desires for "basics," "certitude," "intimacy," "space," and "growth."

Composition

Intensifying by pattern and arrangement uses *design, variations in sequence and in proportion* to add to the force of words, images, movements, etc. How we put together, or compose, is important: e.g. in **verbal** communication: the choice of words, their level of abstraction, their patterns within sentences, the strategy of longer messages. Logic, inductive and deductive, puts ideas together systematically. **Non-verbal** compositions involve *visuals* (color, shape, size); *aural* (music); *mathematics* (quantities, relationships), *time* and *space* patterns.

DOWNPLAY

Omission

Downplaying by omission is common since the basic selection/omission process *necessarily omits* more than can be presented. All communication is limited, is edited, is slanted or biased to include and exclude items. But omission can also be used as a *deliberate* way of concealing, hiding. Half-truths, quotes out of context, etc. are very hard to detect or find. Political examples include *cover-ups, censorship, book-burning, managed news, secret police activities.* Receivers, too, can omit: can "filter out" or be closed minded, prejudiced.

Diversion

Downplaying by distracting focus, diverting attention away from key issues or important things; usually by intensifying the side-issues, the non-related, the trivial. Common variations include: "hairsplitting," "nit-picking," "attacking a straw man," "red herring"; also, those emotional attacks and appeals (*ad hominem, ad populum*), plus things which drain the energy of others: *"busy work," "legal harassment,"* etc. Humor and entertainment (*"bread and circuses"*) are used as pleasant ways to divert attention from major issues.

Confusion

Downplaying issues by making things so complex, so chaotic, that people "give up," get weary, "overloaded." This is dangerous when people are unable to understand, comprehend, or make reasonable decisions. Chaos can be the accidental result of a disorganized mind, or the deliberate flim-flam of a *con man* or the political *demagogue* (who then offers a "simple solution" to the confused). Confusion can result from *faulty logic, equivocation, circumlocution, contradictions, multiple diversions, inconsistencies, jargon* or anything which blurs clarity or understanding.

The INTENSIFY/DOWNPLAY schema is a pattern useful to analyze communication, persuasion and propaganda. All people intensify (commonly by repetition, association, composition) and downplay (commonly by omission, diversion, confusion) as they communicate in words, gestures, numbers, etc. But, 'professional persuaders' have more training, technology, money and media access than the average citizen. Individuals can better cope with organized persuasion by recognizing the common ways how communication is intensified or downplayed, and by considering who is saying what to whom, when and where, with what intent and what result.

16 The Riddle of Visual Experience

Vito Signorile
University of Windsor

We gain a sense of what things are by experiencing the specific "thisness" of their location in time and place. This is a very peculiar phenomenon. Since our experience is so specific, how do we learn the *generic* quality of things? How do we attain a sense of "house" from this house? A sense of "person" from this person? Also, we traffic between the generic and specific in subtle ways. How does this occur? What triggers this movement? Obviously, we sometimes respond to context. But often we are urged by factors more mysterious.

The Specific and the Generic

We find the earliest expression of this problem in Plato's dialogues. Typically, Socrates is looking for Justice, or the Good, or Piety. He wants to find these things themselves, their essences, not mere instances of them—not something that happens to be good, but Goodness itself, not a pious individual, but that quality which makes us say that an individual is pious, Piety writ large. In a common Platonic way of putting the matter, actual instances of such things participate in the Good, or in Piety, but do not themselves constitute Goodness or Piety. Plato clearly perceived the problem: How do we know the generic when all our experiences are specific? His answer was that we always knew the generic, in our prior life, of which the present one is a mere shadow.

Aristotle, on the other hand, was not willing to write off the palpable world so summarily. He was ready to grant some solidity to our sense experience. For him, the mind perceives the specific in the form of the generic. That is, the mind's way of knowing is generic: it constantly converts the sense experience of looking into generic seeing.

The problem persisted through the Middle Ages, where scholastic philosophers, building on Aristotle, distinguished the quiddity of a thing—known as its "essence"—from the haecceity of a thing—its unique, here-and-now existence. Taking a position between Plato and Aristotle, these philosophers commonly suggest that there are two things going on at the same time. Everything that comes into existence must have a specific uniqueness in time and place. But in this process, things necessarily take on a form or generic quality that is not subject to these constraints.

Needless to say, since these two aspects of a thing are so integral to one another, they are easily confused. For Thomas Aquinas, whose writings represent the apogee of medieval European philosophy, the distinction between specific and generic is a pivotal conception. Yet he was no closer than Plato and Aristotle were to solving the problem of how we come to know something's generic quality. The root of his philosophy is that nothing exists in the mind that is not first acquired through the senses. Somehow, the generic was there, embedded in the blooming, buzzing, confusing details of specific experience. As the stream of experience entered the senses, the mind was presumed able to pluck out from this mess the generic quality of things.

In language and literature, the same problem crops up in the form of a trope: *synecdoche*. This trope expresses a relationship between a general class and the specific members of the class. It constitutes a device, or an intellectual move, whereby the part can be taken for the whole. One astronaut on the moon stands for humankind; one person stands for humanity. From this it is easy to see how stereotyping is the mind's facile play with synecdoche.

Aphorisms are an interesting, though puzzling, example of this process. Puzzling because we occasionally encounter people who really don't get the "point" of aphorisms like "A stitch in time saves nine" or "A bird in hand is worth two in the bush." It seems they get stuck in the specifics of the statement, like taking the name "bicycle" to be the proper name of the object. Thus, on encountering another bicycle, they would want to know what *its* name is. But the puzzle goes either way. How is it that we can identify or detect the generic sense? Indeed, what is it that needs to be explained: our capacity to generalize or our ability to see the specific?

In relation to visual experience, the problem is that much learning, a great deal of knowledge, is built on a foundation of ostensive definitions. It is well known that, often, when a purely verbal description fails to convey desired knowledge or meaning, a visual one succeeds. Showing people what a word means or how a thing functions is a technique that works surprisingly well. People rarely take the specific example to be a proper name or to otherwise exhaust the meaning. Indeed, children are far more inclined to apply new words generically than specifically. Teaching someone to drive by negotiating specific streets gets assimilated into a generic capacity to negotiate any street (except in Boston).

In writing about Wittgenstein's theory of knowledge, David Bloor (1983) points out that a large number of meanings are conveyed by pointing to specific things:

> [Wittgenstein] says that if we want to know what meanings are, we should look at how they are explained. In every language a large number of words must be explained and introduced by ostension, i.e., by pointing to an object or feature of the kind for which the word stands. (7)

But Bloor here gives only half the story. As Baker and Hacker (1980) point out, Wittgenstein then argues that "an ostensive definition is part of the system of grammatical rules" (209). And these rules, he insists, come out of social practice, which he often referred to as "forms of life." What stands for "showing"—what is "shown" and how "showing" is done—comes out of the culture. Thus, the demonstrations of a Zen master seem strange to us until we learn how to "read" them, until we learn their "grammar."

Even though defining by showing is common in social practice, we still do not know why it works. Susanne Langer (1957) accepts it as a given. She explains:

> Unless Gestalt psychologists are right, I do not know how the hiatus between perception and conception, sense-organ and mind-organ, chaotic stimulus and logical response, is ever to be closed and welded. A mind that works primarily with meanings must have organs that supply it with forms. (90)

In an essay on pattern recognition, with an eye to finding ways in which machines can respond to images in controlled ways, Douglas Hofstadter (1985) notes the human ability to recognize letters despite the enormous variety of writing and printing styles. Thus far, no simple, algorithmic, programmable method of duplicating this feat has been devised. Taking the example of one letter, Hofstadter mentions, "The essence of 'A'-ness is not geometrical" (244). He believes our ability to recognize the essence of a letter in the limitless variations of its appearance (figure 16.1) defies explicit description and thus computer emulation.

Figure 16.1. "The essence of 'A'-ness is not geometrical."

The Generic and the Specific in Visual Imagery

It is helpful to look at how visual imagery functions on the generic-specific scale. Photographer John Szarkowski (1990), referring to his medium's "uncompromising specificity," says, "If allowed to follow its natural bent, the camera described not Man but men, not Nature, but countless precise biological and geological facts." This is a general belief about photographs. As a result of United States Senator Jesse Helms's outrage at the Mapplethorpe exhibit, the National Endowment for the Arts now has an obscenity clause in its guidelines. The clause proscribes photographs that depict events considered obscene, but has nothing to say about words that might do the same thing. No doubt, this oversight will eventually be remedied. But it underlines the fact that, as a perceptual experience, photographs are thought to have a much more immediate, you-are-there impact than nonvisual forms of symbolic depiction.

Yet, contrary to Szarkowski's claim, photographs constantly invite us to read them generically. Compare the generic sense conveyed in Dorothea Lange's 1930s photograph of a migrant "Dustbowl" mother (Florence Thompson) surrounded by her children to the specific sense of a photograph of Florence Thompson taken by Bill Ganzel forty-three years later (figures 16.2 and 16.3). The older photograph has become the very emblem of the Depression; at the same time, it evokes a timeless Madonna quality. It is generic in the way the famous picture of Marilyn Monroe struggling with her billowing skirt is generic. Both no longer depict singular events. Their impact is not in giving a you-are-there impression of a specifically unfolding event. Rather, they have become icons of an historical era. By contrast, Ganzel's later photo would easily find its place in the personal specificities of the family album.

Drawings and paintings are considered more generic than photographs and, therefore, more "distant" from the subjects they depict. Note how *The Joy of Sex,* the popular guide to sexual activity, depicts its myriad positions with drawings rather than photographs, drawings that may have been based on photographs in the first place. Are line drawings of sexual positions "instructive," whereas photographs are "pornographic"? This effect is strikingly similar to the way profession-

Figure 16.2. *Migrant Mother, Nipomo, California, 1936,* Dorothea Lange. Courtesy of the Library of Congress.

Figure 16.3. *Thompson and Daughters*, Bill Ganzel. Courtesy of the
Library of Congress.

als distance themselves from the nitty-gritty of sexual activity through
the use of technical terminology borrowed from a dead language. Is
this why, in certain court proceedings, an artist's rendering is considered permissible while photographs are not? Is the presumed arch-
specificity of the camera too much of an intrusion on the dignity of the
court or the privacy rights of the participants?

Yet compare the generic, essential meaning of two visual com-
mentaries on the U.S. invasion of Panama, one a photograph and
the other a drawing (figures 16.4 and 16.5). Does the photograph convey less generality than the drawing? Herein lies the danger in our
perception of photographs. The popular misconception that photos
give us the immediacy of stark, naked events leaves us open to two
fallacies: taking a generic for a specific and taking a specific for a
generic. When is such taking mistaking? As Hofstadter might say, we
have no algorithm.

Steven Gold's discussion of ethical issues in photographic methods of social research may help illuminate such mistaking. Gold (1989)
notes that while the principle of confidentiality is a standard ethical
norm for sociological work, "sociologists using visual techniques for

Figure 16.4. *Soldier Getting Shoe Shine*, Reuters news photograph. Courtesy of Bettmann Newsphotos.

collecting and presenting data can hide neither the identity of research subjects nor the locations where the data were collected because the physical properties of visual data make the deletion of identifying characteristics almost impossible" (100).

It is not clear, however, how much this differentiates visual data from verbal data. Nearly every important community study has failed to protect identities. Scientific studies usually present generic conclusions. The specificities of data are only a means of attaining the generic facts of scientific knowledge. Thus, the specific identities of persons in sociological studies can usually be masked without throwing the studies' scientific validity into question. The identities of towns and townspeople can readily be kept confidential.

Yet the residents of Middletown, Elmtown, Sterling County, and many other targets of published social science work lost no time in identifying individuals introduced in the studies. This action raises the reverse ethical issue: people get wrongly identified in the data. In "hiding" one identity, we create the danger of "revealing" an-

Figure 16.5. *Statue of Liberty,* Toni Ungerer. Reprinted by permission of the Annenberg School of Communications.

other, resulting in community members blaming or praising the wrong people—synecdoche run rampant.

Since the accepted belief is that pictures tell the stark, naked truth, photographs are especially vulnerable to being wrongly identified. After the United States invaded Grenada, for instance, the *Toronto Globe and Mail* (6 March 1982), one of Canada's leading newspapers, ran an op-ed piece on the event, accompanied by a photograph with an inset. Readers were led to believe that they were viewing scenes from that hapless island, until several letters drew attention to the fact that the picture was really a photograph of a street in Havana, Cuba, while the inset pictured a group of Cuban schoolchildren. Hoogendoorn (1985) remarks that this was a natural "mistake," since the whole operation against Grenada was a surrogate attack on Cuba (264).

A more recent case was reported by Alexander Cockburn (1990) in *The Nation:*

> History is a movable feast, as is depressingly illustrated in the *Gannett Center Journal* that lies before me as I write. It features

one of the most famous photographs in the world, Robert Capa's "Death in Action," taken during the Spanish Civil War. In the journal it is captioned "D-Day landing, Normandy, June 6, 1944." Ronald Reagan would have understood.

I had a similar experience pursuing permission to reprint a photograph. The photo depicted an opera ensemble, advertising the New York Metropolitan Opera season. After trying to secure permission from the New York company, I discovered that the photo was not a picture of the New York Metropolitan Opera Company, but of a Canadian opera company. And why not? If you've seen one, you've seen them all!

This habit of playing fast and loose with the specificity of pictures is an old story. Gombrich (1960) reproduces woodcuts from a fifteenth-century travelogue illustrating two cities, Damascus and Mantua (figure 16.6). It does not take a close examination to see that the drawings of the two cities are identical. Gombrich explains that the drawings simply give a visual appreciation of big cities. Certainly, they contain no other information. Very likely, neither city looked like the illustration. Travelers depending on the picture to determine when they finally arrived at one of these places would be thoroughly baffled.

Reality: Generic or Specific?

Among photographs, there is a hierarchy of the generic. Some are said to "capture the essence" of the subject—like Karsh's portraits are

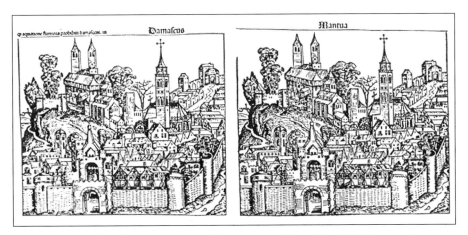

Figure 16.6. Woodcuts from the *Nuremburg Chronicle* (1493) showing Damascus and Mantua.

claimed to do. In such cases, we hear that the photograph reveals the "soul" of the person depicted. But how arbitrary can we be about this process? Some scholars say that the essential difference between Greek and Roman sculpture is that the Greeks portrayed general idealizations, whereas the Romans created personal portraits. Do these less generic personal portraits simultaneously "capture the essence" of their subjects? There is a confusion here that Plato would have appreciated. And what do they mean to us? Do we not read both genres generically, as *Greek* and *Roman* sculpture?

The same problem of reality versus ideality can be found in the perception of pictures in which we ourselves are portrayed: snapshots. Some "don't look like" us, we may say, while others, we are convinced, really capture our likeness. Does the first sort of picture tell a lie, or, better, give us the merest specific features of our appearance at an unrepresentative moment, while the second tells the truth about us? Which conveys reality? Indeed, what is the reality: generic or specific?

Consider the specificity of the photo album. Walker and Moulton (1988) analyze the phenomenon of the family album and conclude that the main problem confronting the researcher is recovering the narrative that went (or goes) with the album. Aside from their relationship to, as they say, "a life," albums have little or no coherent meaning. The photographs in them typically convey highly specific events or persons in a largely private narrative. No album aims to exhibit the generic features of, say, a society or an era. Although an album may do so, this is not what the album makers enjoy, let alone intend. Indeed, we would be annoyed at the guest who persisted in viewing our snapshots generically.

In addressing this question, it is instructive to consider children's drawings. Here we find another puzzling activity. Children produce pictures that are far more suggestive and schematic than precise and accurate. This seems to imply that children are more attuned to the *generic* quality of things. Their drawings seem to be generic in the same way that their words, when first learned, are conceived generically. There is something like this going on in the "holophrastic" utterances of children. As they first learn to speak, children tend to utter single words packed with the contents of whole sentences.

A sense of the specific, it appears, has to be learned. It is a product of maturation. Children acquire a knowledge and a language of the world initially through pointing at specific people and things. If this communication were taken in a specific way, it would seriously block their intellectual development. That this does not normally happen is evidence that we acquire knowledge through the apprehension of generic features. This is reflected in what can be called "Arnheim's Rule," which states that *our visual experience remains as general as the situation permits* (Arnheim 1969).

Children are not bothered by the discrepancy between their drawings of objects and the perception of these objects as seen directly. We find it charming and think of children as lost in imagination. Their grasp of the "real" world seems so tenuous to us. And here, "real" means the specificity of experience. Indeed, children's renditions are so generic that, although we usually have no trouble identifying their overall subject matter, we do have difficulty identifying their specificity. The simplest lines suffice to convey a picture of, for example, an elephant. But they also depict their parents, their friends, and themselves. Looking at figure 16.7, does anyone believe that the child's mother "really" looks like that? Does the child?

The gap between what one sees and what one draws raises the question of skill in producing symbolic materials. Hofstadter (1985) finds this an especially vexing question. Referring to his own experi-

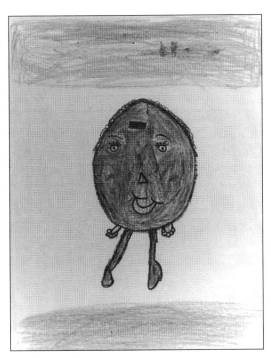

Figure 16.7. A child's drawing of her mother. (Shalinka F. Huffman, artist.)

ence learning to recognize Chinese characters sooner than he was able to write them, he asks, "How can such a fantastic recognition machine as our brain be so terrible at rendition? . . . This is a deep mystery" (35).

One answer is that the mind is trafficking in symbolic forms, the nature of which is generic. Thus, the need to learn standardized notation is a community's way of fixing denotations in a world swimming with generic meaning. An example of this comes from Gombrich (1960), who notes that artists' reproductions of things seen depend on the "schemata" of representations available to them. These are ways of rendering handed down by tradition. He recounts the story of Chinese art students who were taken by their Western-trained teacher to sketch scenes in a nearby square. The students were baffled by the project. They needed other drawings to give them an idea of how to proceed with their own renderings (74–90). In much of visual art, scenes are not so much reproduced as evoked. What counts as such an evocation is a generic quality that is culturally determined.

The situation is akin to Chomsky's distinction between linguistic performance and linguistic competence (Lyons 1978). Chomsky points out that we recognize utterances in our language that are beyond our ability to speak. With visual symbols, there is a *symbolic competence* distinctive from our *symbolic performance*. Unsurprisingly, our competence, our ability to appreciate, or read, visual symbols, is greater than our ability to reproduce them.

What is important here is that, as in language, we "fill in the gaps" in people's performances. When people speak ungrammatically, we extract the sense by virtue of our grammatical competence. Similarly, when visual materials are produced with varying degrees of aptitude, we access their meaning by using our visual competence. Thus, we are always filling in when we read visual images. Precisely how this is done has yet to be mapped out. In easy, subtle ways, we shift between the generic and specific qualities of what we see. And generic seeing, I have tried to show, is primary. What needs to be explained is how we tease out the specificity of visual images.

Works Cited

Arnheim, Rudolf. 1969. *Visual Thinking*. London: Faber and Faber.

Baker, Gordon P., and P. M. S. Hacker. 1980. *Wittgenstein: Understanding and Meaning*. Chicago: University of Chicago Press.

Bloor, David. 1983. *Wittgenstein: A Social Theory of Knowledge*. New York: Columbia University Press.

Cockburn, Alexander. 1990. "Beat the Devil." *The Nation*, 23 April, 551.

Gold, Steven J. 1989. "Ethical Issues in Visual Field Work." In *New Technology in Sociology*, edited by Grant Blank, J. L. McCartney, and Edward Brent. New Brunswick, NJ: Transaction Publishers.

Gombrich, E. H. 1960. *Art and Illusion: A Study in the Psychology of Pictorial Representation*. New York: Pantheon.

Hofstadter, Douglas R. 1985. *Metamagical Themas: Questing for the Essence of Mind and Pattern*. New York: Basic Books.

Hoogendoorn, Roberto. 1985. "The Cubanification of the Image of Grenada: The Media and the Unmaking of the Grenadian Revolution." In *Media in Latin America and the Caribbean: Domestic and International Perspectives*, edited by Walter C. Soderlund and Stuart H. Surlin, 254–68. Windsor, Ontario: Ontario Cooperative Program in Latin American and Caribbean Studies.

Langer, Susanne K. 1957. *Philosophy in a New Key: A Study in the Symbolism of Reason, Rite, and Art*. 3d ed. Cambridge: Harvard University Press.

Lyons, John. 1978. *Noam Chomsky*. Harmondsworth, England: Penguin.

Szarkowski, John. 1990. "Photography until Now: Notes to an Exhibit in New York's Museum of Art." Cited by Stuart Klawans in *The Nation*, 1 April, 446.

Walker, A. L., and R. K. Moulton. 1988. "Photo Albums: The Enigma of Amateur Vision." Unpublished manuscript.

Index

Aaker, David, 78, 84, 90
Abraham, Karl, 5, 17
Abstracting, 11
Academic prose, 22, 23, 27
Access, 127
Act, 210
Adams, Hazard, 7, 17
Advertising
    beauty, portrayal of in, 173–75
    covert messages in, 43–44
    credibility of, 186
    envy and, 174–75
    idealized images portrayed by,
        171–72
    interpretation of, 170
    longing brought about by, 179
    as mythology, 175–76
    power of, 152
    as religion, 176–79
    sexuality in, 152–69
    and values, 171–75
Agee, James, 53, 56
Agency, 211
Agent, 211
Agres, Stuart, 77, 90
Alinder, James, 56
Allen, Dr. Ivan, 32, 33
Allender, Jerome, 13, 14, 17
Alley, Joy, 34
Allness orientation, 11
Alter, Jonathan, 118–19, 120, 122
Ambiguity, 72, 77, 87, 88–89
Ames, Adelbert, 194
Amos, Deborah, 133, 138
*Amusing Ourselves to Death: Public
    Discourse in the Age of Show
    Business*, 195
Analytic thinking, 198
Aphorisms, 220
Apple, R. W., Jr., 116–17, 120, 122, 130,
    138
Archetypal images, 7
Aristotle, 11, 219
Arlington, Flossie, 51
Armitage, Shelley, 56
Arnheim, Rudolf, 4, 9, 17, 229, 230
Arnheim's Rule, 229
Ash, Timothy Garton, 124, 138
Ashton-Warner, Sylvia, xii, 29–40

Assagioli, Roberto, 13, 17
Audience, 45, 54, 121, 129

Baby Doll, 160
Baker, Gordon P., 221, 230
Balance, 10, 15
Balzar, John, 130, 138
Barrow, Thomas F., 56
Barthes, Roland, 10, 17, 56
Bayles, Fred, 133, 138
Becker, Howard S., 56
Beeby, Walter, 39
Begg, Ian, 8–9, 17, 71, 90
Beholder's share of the meaning,
    88
Bell Call, 39
Beneke, Timothy, 175, 179
Benton, Thomas Hart, 15
Bentsen, Lloyd, 72
Berger, John, 56, 174, 179
Berger, Paul, 56
Bernstein, Dennis, 132, 138
Berthoff, Ann, 12, 17
Bettelheim, Bruno, 200
Binary oppositions, 89
Blair Handbook, The, 183
Blanchard, Nina, 175
Bloor, David, 221, 230
Bohr, Niels, 3
Boland, Rep. Edward, 111, 113
Boorstin, Daniel, 15, 17
Boulding, Kenneth, 176, 180
Brand, Alice, 13, 17, 77, 90
Briesach, Ernst, 124, 138
Britton, James, 13, 17
Broad, William J., 131, 138
Bronowski, Jacob, 70, 90
Bruner, Jerome, 4, 17
Bryden, M. P., 79, 90
Bugelski, Richard, 90
Burchett, William, 101, 106
Burgess, Tony, 17
Burgin, Victor, 56
Burke, Kenneth, 143, 151, 209, 216
Burke's pentad, 209–13, 215–16
Burton, Dwight, 199, 202
Bush, George, 26, 72, 128, 129, 132, 136,
    189

Campbell, Joseph, 200
Careless talk campaign, 101–102, 104
Carey, Robert, 10, 20
Carter, Jimmy, 189
Cartier-Bresson's France, 47
Cather, Willa, 55
Cawelti, John, 151
Censorship, 131–32, 136, 137
Cheney, Dick, 130
Child talk, xi, 58–64
    building a theory of the world, 58,
        59–60
    children as meaning makers, 58, 63
    conflict between images and words,
        61–63
    creating new images from words,
        63–64
    images in, 60–61
Chomsky, Noam, 230
Churchill, Winston, 101
CNN: War in the Gulf, 136
Cockburn, Alexander, 226, 231
Cockran, Marie T., 206
Cognition, xi
Cognitive psychology, influences from,
    8–9
Coleridge, Samuel Taylor, 5, 199
Coles, William E., Jr., 103, 106
Collateral damage, 127, 128
Common sense, as a guide to thought,
    121
Common Sense (Paine), 110
Conservation experiment, 4
Constructions, 6
Constructivist view, 58
Context, xi–xii, 184–85, 199–200
Contrast, 49
Controlled imagery, 125
Conventions, 27
Cool-to-warm images, 81–88
Costanzo, William V., xii, 10, 17,
    108
Counterblast, 21
Counter-tendency to simplicity, 9
Crane, Stephen, 55
Critical thinking, 55
Cross, Donna W., 15, 17
Curtiss, Deborah, 209, 216

D'Audney, Angela, 31, 40
Darwin, Charles, 3
Davidson, Bruce, 51, 53, 56

da Vinci, Leonardo, 3, 16
de Assis, Machado, 39
Deductive argument, 25
Desktop publishing, 27
Die Hard, 134
Die Hard 2, 132, 134
Dissenting voices, suppression of, 127
Docudramas, 132–33
Dondis, Donis, 205, 206, 217
Doublespeak, 71, 205, 207, 209
Dreams, 5, 6, 32
Dual coding theory, 8
Dualism, 16
Duckworth, Eleanor, 62, 64
Dukakis, Michael, 72

Earle, Ed, 56
Eco, Umberto, 17
Edell, Julie, 77, 90
Einstein, Albert, 3, 17
Eisenstein, Elizabeth, 109, 122, 195
Eissler, K. R., 7, 17
Eliot, Alexander, 16, 17
Emig, Janet, 12, 18
Emotion, xi, 77–78
    cool-to-warm images, 81–88
    transformational messages, 78–81
    in visual messages, 76
    in writing, 13
Enlightenment, 109
Envy, 174–75
Epitaph of a Small Winner, 39
Essayist structures, 25–26
Essence, 220
Esslin, Martin, 178, 180
Etc.: A Review of General Semantics, 183
Evans, Walker, 44, 53, 56
Ewen, Stuart, 170, 180
Experience, 11
Experience experiments, 13
Expressive language, 13
Extensional images, 200–201

Fairness and Accuracy in Reporting
    (FAIR), 132
False advertising, 77
Federal Trade Commission, 77
Felt sense, 13
Fiedler, Tom, 130, 139
Filtering mechanism, 196–97, 202
First-order reality, 11

Firth, Michael, 31, 40
Fisher, M. F. K., 27
Fishman, Robert, 142, 143, 144–50
Fiske, John, 111, 121, 122, 143, 151
Flatiron, The, 48
Flower, Linda, 13, 18
Forms of life, 221
Fortas, Abe, 149
Four Freedoms posters, 93–95
Fox, Roy, 3, 69, 183, 192
Free associations, 6
Freud, Sigmund, 6
Freund, David, xii, 42
Friedman, Thomas L., 125, 138
Fry, Donald, 90
Fry, Virginia, 90
Fussell, Paul, 97, 101, 106
Futran, Sasha, 132, 138

Galton, Frederick, 4, 5, 18
Ganzel, Bill, 223
Gardner, Howard, 8, 18, 175, 180
Geertz, Clifford, 142, 151
Geis, Michael L., 104, 106
General semantics, 183, 197–201
    context, 184–85, 199–200
    extensional vs. intensional images,
        200–201
    influences from, 11, 12
    separation of image from thing,
        198–99
Generic, 219
Generic and specific
    in reality, 227
    in visual imagery, 222
Gerbner, George, xii, 123, 135, 138, 139
Gestalt psychology, influences from,
    9–10
Gitlin, Todd, 126, 134, 138
Global immediacy, 137
Godfather, The, 134
Godfather II, 134
Godfather III, 134
Goethals, Gregor, 109, 122
Goffman, Erving, 9, 18, 57, 170, 180
Gold, Steven, 224, 231
Goldwater, Barry, 104
Gombrich, E. H., 9, 18, 88, 90, 227, 230,
    231
Gonzalez, John, 149
Gowan, J. C., 4, 18
Griffin, Susan, 174, 175, 180

Grimes, Tom, 126, 138
Grow, Gerald O., xii, 170
Gruber, Howard, 3, 18
Guptill, Arthur L., 93, 106

Hacker, P. M. S., 221, 230
Hackworth, David, 132, 138
Hadamard, Jacques, 3, 18
Hagerty, M. R., 78, 84, 90
Halliday, Michael, 58, 64
Hamilton, Lee, 112
Harste, Jerome, 62
Hart, Roderick P., 103, 106
Hartley, John, 111, 122, 143, 151
Hayakawa, Alan R., x, 18, 183–92, 198,
    202
Hayakawa, S. I., x, 18, 178, 180, 183–92,
    197, 198, 202
Hayes, John, 13, 18
Healy, Melissa, 130, 138
Helms, Sen. Jesse, 222
Helsel, Sandra, 89, 90
Henderson, Elliot, 39
Henderson, Keith, 32
Here and Now II, 52
Hersey, John, 120
Hicks, Wilson, 57
Hill, Carol, 53, 56
Hilprecht, H. V., 5
Hirsch, E. D., Jr., 24
Historiography, 124
Hoffman, Stevie, xi, 58
Hofstadter, Douglas, 221, 224, 229, 231
Homicides, statistics on, 137–38
Hood, Lynley, 31, 40
Hoogendoorn, Roberto, 226, 231
Hovanec, Carol, xii, 42
How the Other Half Lives, 46, 53–54, 55
Hoyer, Robert, 79, 91
Hughes, T., 18
Hume, Brit, 115
Hume, David, 109
Huxley, Aldous, 7, 18
Hyperintertextuality, 88–89

Identities, protecting, 225
Illusions, 204
Image(s), 198
    context and, xi–xii, 184–85, 199–200
    defined, x
    effect of on behavior, 206

Image(s) *(continued)*
   importance of, x, xii–xiii
   intertextuality of, xii
   as language, 143–44
   manipulation of, xii, 11, 187, 206
   perception and emotion with, 79
   through the prism of language, xi–xii
   rhetorical nature of, xii
   as true symbols, 69
   uncritical confidence in, 184
Image-before-word group, 6–8
Imaged selves, 33–35
Image juxtaposition, 143
Imageless language, 71
Image managers, 128
Imagen, 8
Image processors, vs. word processors, 193
Imagery
   generic and specific in, 222–27
   and language, 29
   in politics, 189–91
   sensory nature of, 29–30
   teaching of, 13–14
Image studies, xii
   influences from the arts and humanities, 15–16
   influences from the sciences and engineering, 3–6
   influences from social sciences, 6–15
   loss of control in, 14–15
Imagination, xii
Imaginative entry, 199
Imaging, defined, 30
In Search of Semiotics, 10
Incense to Idols, 39
Incongruity, 88–89
Inductive argument, 25
Inner speech, 13
Inouye, Sen. Daniel, 112, 113–14, 116, 121
Instant history making, 124, 125–26
   disadvantages of, 137
   requirements for, 127–29
Intensify/downplay schema, 213–16, 218
Intensional images, 200–201
Intention, 25, 200
Internal movements, 70
International Society for General Semantics, 183
Intertextuality, xii, 88–89
I Passed This Way, 31, 38, 39

Iran-Contra hearings, 108–22
Issueless political campaign, 104

Jakobson, Roman, 10, 18
James, William, 7, 15, 18
Jennings, Peter, 115, 128
JFK, 124, 199
Johnson, Lyndon, 104
Johnson, Roger N., 131, 132, 138
Johnson, Wendell, 11, 18, 189, 192
Johnston, David, 120, 122
Jones, Phil, 115
Journal writing, 13
Joy of Sex, The, 223
Jung, Carl, 6, 7, 15, 69, 90, 200

Kandinsky, Wassily, 15
Karl, Herb, x, 193, 202
Kaufmann, Geir, 71, 91
Keats, John, 16
Keker, John, 119, 120
Kennedy, Robert, 190
Kepes, Gyorgy, 8, 18
Key Vocabulary, 31, 33, 35–36, 37, 38, 40
Khassoghi, Adnan, 124
Kinzer, Nora Scott, 173, 180
Kirkpatrick, Jeane, 132
Koestler, Arthur, 7–8, 18
Koffka, Kurt, 9
Kohler, Wolfgang, 9
Korzybski, Alfred, 11, 183, 188, 192, 197
Kosslyn, Stephen, 9, 18, 71, 91

Lakoff, George, 176, 180
Lakoff, Robin Tolmach, 173, 180
Lange, Dorothea, 222
Langer, Susanne K., 13, 221, 231
Language
   defined, 143
   viewing images through, xi–xii
Language in Action, 183, 185
Language in Thought and Action, 183, 197
Language, Thought, and Reality, 196
Laurence, William L., 101
Laws of thought, 11
Lee, Irving, 11, 18
Lee, Martin, 132, 139
Lehman, John, 131
Let Us Now Praise Famous Men, 53
Lewin, Kurt, 9

Ley, R., 79, 90
Leymore, Varda Langholz, 170, 175, 180
Liberty Tree symbol, 11
Liebling, Jerome, 57
Light, 16, 43, 52
Lincoln, Abraham, 26
Linden, Bill, 112
Literacy education, influences from, 12–15
Literary criticism, 12
Locke, John, 109
Logical fallacies, 54
Logogen, 8
Logos, 75–76
Lotto, Edward, 22, 23, 26, 28
Lowes, John, 5, 18
Luria, A. R., 8, 19
Lutz, William, 71, 91, 205, 217
Lyons, John, 230, 231

Maggie: A Girl of the Streets, 55
Malle, Louis, 160
Manipulation, xii, 11, 187, 206
Mao Zedong, 124
Martin, Nancy, 17
Martz, Larry, 108, 110, 119, 122
Masland, Tom, 124, 139
Mason, George, 112
Mathison, Dirk, 132, 139
McFadden, Robert, 129, 139
McFarlane, Robert C., 114, 132
McGrail, Ann B., 125, 139
McLeod, Alex, 17
McLuhan, Marshall, 15, 19, 21, 28, 108, 124
Meaning makers, children as, 58, 63
Meaning making
    built-in apparatus for, 194
    role of images in, xi
Meaning-making bias, 194
Media. *See also* Television
    effect of on prose, 22, 26
    print and television coverage
        compared, 109, 111–12, 114, 116
Men on Rape, 175
Mental imagery, 8
Metaphor, 143, 148
*Metaphoric Mind: A Celebration of
    Creative Consciousness, The,* 13
Metz, Christian, 10, 19
Meyer, Ray, 144–50
Milburn, Michael, 125, 139

Miller, Arthur, 3, 19
Miller, Bill, 137, 139
Mind's ear, 30
Mr. Smith Goes to Washington, 118
Moir, Hughes, 64, 65
Mondale, Walter, 75
Moog, Carol, xi, 152
Moran, Terence P., 200, 202
Morello, John T., 75, 91
Morgan, Fred, 52, 56
Morris, Barbra, xi, 141, 142, 151
Moulton, R. K., 228, 231
Movies, violence in, 134–35
Mowlana, Hamid, 139
Moyers, Bill, 24, 197

National Coalition on Television
    Violence, 135
National Endowment for the Arts, 222
National security, 103
National Wetlands Coalition, 75
Native imagery, 36, 37, 40
Negative images, 188
"Neighbor Rosicky," 55
Neisser, Ulric, 9, 19
Nelms, Ben, 64, 65
Nelson, Richard, 11, 19
Newbold, William, 5, 19
New media discourse, 24
News magazines, 118–19
Newspapers, 21
Nixon, Richard, 102
North, Oliver, xii, 132
    portrayal of by media, 108–22
Nunn, Sen. Sam, 115
Nydahl, Joel, 142, 151

O'Keeffe, Georgia, 49
O'Neil, J., 4, 19
Olson, David, 25, 28
Ong, Walter, 109, 122, 195
Oral language, 22

Paglia, Camille, 15, 19
Paine, Thomas, 110
Paivio, Allan, 8, 19, 29, 40, 71, 91
Pan, Zhongdang, 136, 139
Parenti, Michael, 130, 139
Partisan politics, 105
Patten, Bernard, 3, 19

Patterson, Kenny, 144
Peirce, C. S., 10
Pendered, David, 209, 217
Pentad, 209, 215
People in Quandaries, 189
People prose, 23
Perception, xi, 4, 9–10, 77
Perkins, David N., 5, 19
Perl, Sondra, 13, 19
Perrett, Geoffrey, 101, 106
Persian Gulf War, xii, 103, 105, 123–37
    censorship in coverage of, 131–32,
        136, 137
    as instant history, 126–33
    news media coverage of, 130–33
    opposition to, 132
    public opinion, analysis of, 136–37
Perspective, absence of, 133
Persuasion, 42. *See also* Visual
        persuasion
    role of emotion in, 77
    transformational ads and, 79
Pestalozzi, Johann, 3
Phelan, John, 126, 139
Phi-phenomenon, 9
Photographs, 42–56, 205
    contrast, 49
    light, use of in, 52
    photographer's meaning,
        determining, 51
    point of view, 47–49
    social meanings inferred from, 42,
        46–47, 52
    in writing instruction, 52–54, 56
Photo opportunities, staged, 126, 200
Piaget, Jean, 4, 58, 65
Plantation mythology, 207
Plato, 173, 219
Point of view, 47–49
Polanyi, Michael, 8, 19
Postman, Neil, 8, 15, 19, 24, 109, 121,
        122, 126, 139, 194, 195, 197, 203
Postol, Theodore A., 131
Powell, Colin, 131
Powers, John, 26, 28
President's Council on Physical Fitness
        and Sports, 135
Pretty Baby, 160
Price, Jonathan, 176, 180
Print media, influence of, 21, 109
Project Censored, 132
Propaganda, xii, 11–12

arousing desires of what ought to be,
        105–106
    careless talk campaign, 101–102, 104
    consequences of, 103–104
    effectiveness of, 103
    political leaders as valiant, 99–102,
        104
    during World War I, 95, 96
    during World War II, 92–102
Psychology, influences from, 6
*Psychosynthesis: A Manual of Principles
        and Techniques,* 13
Public Mind, The, 197
Pula, Robert, 11, 19
Pure meaning, 13
Purpose, 213
Purves, Alan, xii, 21
Puto, Christopher, 79, 91

Quayle, Dan, 72, 132
Quest for Beauty, 175, 180

Rank, Hugh, 209, 213, 217
Rank's schema, 209, 213–16, 218
Rather, Dan, 114, 116
Reader response, 12
*Ready for Sabbath Eve in a Coal Cellar, A
        Cobbler on Ludlow Street,* 46
Reagan, Ronald, 71, 75, 132
Reese, Ernest, 207, 217
Reid, Thomas, 109, 121
Reinhardt, Ad, 27
Rhodes, Anthony, 93, 95, 106
Richards, I. A., 12, 19
Rico, Gabriele, 3, 19
Riefenstahl, Leni, 199
Riegel, O. W., 95, 96, 101, 107
Riis, Jacob, 46, 53, 55, 56
*Road to Xanadu: A Study in the Ways of
        the Imagination, The,* 5
Robertson, Linda, xii, 92
Rockwell, Norman, 93, 98, 119
Roget, Peter, 21
Roosevelt, Franklin, 93, 96
Rosen, Harold, 17
Rosenbaum, David, 114, 122
Rosenblatt, Louise, 12, 19
Rosenthal, Elisabeth, 137, 139
Roth, Judith, 89, 90
Rutledge, Kay Ellen, xii, 204

Sacks, Oliver, 8, 19
Salomon, Gavriel, 9, 20
Samples, Bob, 13, 20
Samuels, Mike, 13, 20
Samuels, Nancy, 13, 20
Saturday Night Live, 116
Scene, 210–11
Scherr, Raquel L., 173, 180
Schiller, Herbert I., 139
Schoeck, Helmut, 174, 180
Scholes, Robert, 10, 20
Schwarzenegger, Arnold, 135
Schwarzkopf, Gen. Norman, 126, 129,
    137
Science and Sanity, 183
Scientific visualization, 6
Scoptophilia, 5, 6
Searle, Leroy, 56
Sebeok, Thomas, 10, 20
*Seeing with the Mind's Eye: The History,
    Techniques, and Uses of Visualization,*
    13
Selective communication, 123
Self-reports, 5
Semantic reactions, 11
Semiotics, influences from, 10
Shallcrass, J., 31, 34, 40
She Wore a Yellow Ribbon, 129
Showing, 221
Siegel, Marjorie, 10, 20
Signorile, Vito, xi, 219
Signs, 10
Silence of the Lambs, 204
Silent majority, 102
Simplicity, drive toward, 9
Simultaneous happenings, 124, 129
Sless, David, 10, 20
Slogans, 100, 105
Smith, Frank, 58, 65
Sontag, Susan, 15, 20, 69, 91
Sound bite(s), 72, 92, 105, 126, 127, 199
Soviet Union, breakup of, 125, 127
Spearpoint, 31, 37–38
Specific, 219
Spinster, 31, 35–37, 39, 40
Sportscasts, 141–51
    audience awareness of imagery in,
        150–51
    author intention and text form, case
        study of, 144–50
    shared cultural values in, 142
    sports director as author, 142–44

Sportstext, xi, 141–42
    influence of on audience, 150–51
    observations concerning, 142
Stands-for relationship, 10
Stayman, D., 78, 84, 90
Steichen, Edward, 48
Stereotypes, 54
Stewart, Jim, 130
Stewart, Jimmy, 118
Stieglitz, Alfred, 49
Stone, Oliver, 199
Stream of consciousness, 7, 15
Subsistence U.S.A., 53
Suhor, Charles, 10, 20
Sullivan, Brendan, 113–14, 116, 120
Supernormal sign stimuli, 171–72
Surette, Ray, 134, 139
Sylvia!, 31
Symbolic competence, 230
Symbolic performance, 230
Symbols, 10, 11–12
Symbolspeak, xi
    defined, 69, 70
    emotion and, 71
    levels of, 70–71
    origins of, 70
    purpose of, 89
    verbal, 71
    verbal-with-visual, 72
    visual, 72, 75–89
    visual-with-verbal, 72–75
Symposium, 173
Synecdoche, 220
Szarkowski, John, 222, 231

Teacher, 31, 34, 39, 40
Technique, 52
Teenage Mutant Ninja Turtles, 134
Television
    as collaborator in image process, 190
    coverage of Iran-Contra hearings,
        analysis of, 108–22
    influence of on perception, 108,
        121–22
    as news maker, 119
    reliance on for information, 190–91
    role of in politics, 104–106
    sportscasts, imagery in, 141–51
    violence on, 134
Television sports director, as author,
    142–44

Terminator 2, 132, 135
Tesla, Nikola, 4
Thompson, Florence, 223
Thompson, Mark, 130, 139
Thompson, Nancy S., xii, 29, 38, 41
Thought experiments, 3
Three, 35
Three Mile Island, 71
Time-binding, 11
Tinbergen, Niko, 171, 180
Transformational ad, 78
Treatise on Signs, A, 10
Triumph of the Will, 199
Truman, Harry, 101
Turner, Ted, 136
Turtles II: Secrets of the Ooze, 135
Twain, Mark, 16
Tydenan, William E., 56
Typographic mind, 195–96

Values, 171–75
VanDercar, D. H., 193, 202
Van Gogh, Vincent, 15
Veblen, Thorstein, 105, 107
Verbal language, 29
Verbal reasoning, 4
Verifiability, 197
Vietnam War, television coverage of, 125
Viles, Peter, 139
Violence, cult of, 133–36
Virtual reality, 89
Visual, 29
Visual clichés, 86
Visual culture, 42
Visual experience
    reality and, 227–30
    specific/generic, defined, 219–21
    specific/generic, in visual imagery, 221–27
Visual literacy, 42
Visual messages, power of, 76–77
Visual persuasion, xii
    activities to help students analyze, 215–16
    analyzing, 204–16
    Burke's pentad to analyze, 209–13

distinguishing reality from illusions, 205–209
    Rank's schema to analyze, 209, 213–16, 218
    the receivers, 209
    the senders, 207–209
Visual structuring, 75
Vlach, John Michael, 207, 217
Voice-over narration, 126
Vygotsky, L. S., 13

Wadden, Douglas, 56
Walker, A. L., 228, 231
Ward, Fred, 6, 20
War images, function of, 95
Wasserman, Selma, 38
Watts, Robert Anthony, 208, 217
Wayne, John, 129
Weiner, Tim, 130, 139
Weingartner, Charles, 193, 194, 202, 203
Wells, Gordon, 63, 65
Wertheimer, Max, 9
Weston, Edward, 52
White, Alfred, 207
Whitley, Andrew, 131, 140
Whorf, Benjamin, 196, 203
Whorf hypothesis, 196–97
Whole language movement, 40
Whole perception, 9
Wicker, Tom, 117–18, 122
Williams, Frederick, 126, 140
Williams, William Carlos, 16
Wills, Garry, 121, 122
Wines, Michael, 120, 122
Wittgenstein, Ludwig, 221
Word-before-image group, 6, 11–12
Workplace violence, 133
World War II, xii
    poster propaganda, 92, 93–99
Writing instruction, 26–28
Wurtzel, Allan, 75, 91

Yeats, William Butler, 173
Young, Danny, 145

Zingers, 72

Editor

Roy F. Fox, formerly director of writing at Boise State University, is associate professor of English education at the University of Missouri–Columbia, where he also directs the Missouri Writing Project. He is a member of the NCTE Commission on Composition and the NCTE Committee on Public Doublespeak. In addition to publishing articles on writing, thinking, and visual literacy, he is the author of the textbook *Technical Communication: Problems and Solutions* (1994).

Contributors

William V. Costanzo, professor of English, teaches writing, literature, and film at New York's Westchester Community College. His publications include *Double Exposure: Composing through Writing and Film* (1984) and *Reading the Movies* (1992). Dr. Costanzo serves on the Advisory Board of the PBS American Cinema Project.

David Freund is associate professor of photography at Ramapo College of New Jersey, where he and English professor Carol Hovanec teach a course that integrates photography and writing into the teaching of critical thinking.

George Gerbner, professor of communication and dean emeritus of the University of Pennsylvania's Annenberg School of Communications, has directed research projects for the President's Commission on the Causes and Prevention of Violence, the Surgeon General's Committee on Television and Social Behavior, the National Institute of Mental Health, and other organizations. Past editor of the *Journal of Communication*, Dr. Gerbner is currently working on a comparative analysis of television in twelve countries. In addition to *Triumph of the Image* (1992), his recent publications include *Beyond the Cold War: Soviet and American Media Images* (1991), *The Global Media Debate* (1993), and *Violence and Terror in the Mass Media* (1988).

Gerald O. Grow attended Harvard before receiving his Ph.D. in English from Yale. Dr. Grow has taught literature, drama, composition, and communication at San Francisco State College, St. Mary's College, and Florida State University. He now teaches magazine journalism at Florida A&M University in Tallahassee, where he writes for magazines and research journals.

Alan R. Hayakawa collaborated with S. I. Hayakawa on *Language in Thought and Action* (1990). A former Washington correspondent, he has written on politics and urban design for *The Oregonian* in Portland, where he earlier served as art and architecture critic, and is co-author of *The Blair Handbook* (1994), a composition text. He currently coaches writers at *The Patriot-News* in Harrisburg, Pennsylvania.

S. I. Hayakawa (1907–1992) authored eight books about the role of language and other symbols in human behavior. He founded the International Society for General Semantics and the journal *Etc.: A Review of General Semantics*, which he edited for nearly thirty years. Hayakawa also served as president of San Francisco State University and, from 1977 to 1983, as a United States Senator from California.

Stevie Hoffman is professor emeritus of early childhood education at the University of Missouri–Columbia, where she chaired the Advisory

Board for Missouri's National Project Construct Center. Her research interests focus on the language/thought connections children make as they construct personal knowledge during child/adult and child/child transactions. She recently served on the Executive Board of the Association for Childhood Education International as vice president for infancy and early childhood education.

Carol P. Hovanec is professor of English at Ramapo College of New Jersey, where she and photography professor David Freund teach a course that integrates photography and writing into the teaching of critical thinking.

Herb Karl is professor of English education at the University of South Florida. He served as *English Journal*'s first multimedia editor and is a charter member of the NCTE Commission on Media. He has published widely on media-related subjects in journals such as *Media and Methods, The Creative Teacher,* and *Etc.: A Review of General Semantics.*

Carol Moog, Ph.D., is a clinical psychologist and president of Creative Focus, an advertising and marketing consulting firm. As a qualitative market researcher who has consulted with Fortune 500 companies on their communication campaigns, Dr. Moog has spoken on the psychology of advertising to the American Association of Advertising Agencies and the American Marketing Association. Her book *Are They Selling Her Lips?* (1990) is a psychological study of advertising imagery.

Barbra S. Morris teaches television text analysis and academic writing at the University of Michigan, where she serves on the faculty of the English Composition Board, the Residential College, and the Department of Communication. A film maker and television producer, Dr. Morris received a Fulbright fellowship for 1993–94 to teach and conduct research in cross-cultural television analysis at Dublin City University in Ireland.

Alan C. Purves, director of the Center for Writing and Literacy and professor of education and humanities at the University at Albany, New York, has taught at Columbia and Barnard Colleges, the University of Illinois, and Indiana University. Dr. Purves has written or edited numerous books and articles, including *Writing across Languages and Cultures* (1988) and *Educational Policy and International Assessment* (1975). His book *The Elements of Writing about a Literary Work* (1968) has been translated into seven languages. His most recent book, *The Scribal Society* (1990), explores literacy in an age of information.

Linda R. Robertson chairs the Rhetoric Department at Hobart and William Smith Colleges in Geneva, New York. A member of the NCTE Task Force on the Wyoming Resolution, Dr. Robertson has published articles on rhetoric in the *Rhetoric Society Quarterly,* the *Journal of Economic Inquiry,* and other journals. She is also author of *Discovery: Reading, Writing, and Thinking in the Academic Disciplines* (1988).

Kay Ellen Rutledge is associate director of the Georgia Assessment Project of Georgia State University. Dr. Rutledge serves on NCTE's Committee on Public Doublespeak and on the Editorial Board for Scholastic Magazine's *Voices*. Her current research interests include language and perception, the analysis of public persuasion, and the assessment of teaching.

Vito Signorile teaches sociology at the University of Windsor in Ontario, Canada. His chapter is based on a paper presented at the 1990 Annual Meetings of the International Visual Sociology Association.

Nancy S. Thompson received her Ph.D. from Arizona State University. She has taught in the English Department at the University of South Carolina since 1977, working with colleagues there to build the graduate composition and rhetoric program. Her current research interests include thinking and language learning theory. Her work on Sylvia Ashton-Warner and imaging was partially funded by a grant from the University of South Carolina.

About the Cover

The painting on the front cover of *Images in Language, Media, and Mind* is based on Margaret Sutton's 1944 drawing of a man with a pipe (shown here). In the painting, the man, seated with his hands on his knees, can still be recognized, but the surroundings have been "spun into fancy." The original painting is full color, with varying shades of purple, red, yellow, and green. On the cover of this book, only one color is used to highlight a black-and-white photograph of the painting.

Commenting about her art, Sutton wrote, "These pictures are the richer imagery of an inner life, which have grown out of my workaday activities as a textile designer, a draftsman for an aeroplane, and a technical illustrator for a Linotype machine. As an assistant professor of art . . . I probed and studied and looked into the histories of art, its criticism, and philosophies, which gave me my confidence to express and draw visual form not as imitation of nature but as new constructions having their own rightness of being."

During the 1920s and 1930s, Sutton taught art in public schools and colleges in the South and studied drawing and painting in Europe and New York. She moved to New York permanently in 1939, where she worked as a technical illustrator during and after the war. Most of her work was never exhibited. More than 2,000 of Sutton's paintings and drawings were donated in 1993 to Mary Washington College in Fredericksburg, Virginia.

Cover Art: *The Webs of Fancy Are Spun into the Sky* by Margaret Sutton (1905–1990), Mary Washington College Galleries, Gift of Alfred Levitt. Reproduced by permission.